The View From
Kings Point

Las Meninas of Diego Velazquez

Magnum Chaos of Giovan Francesco Capoferri

The View From Kings Point:

The Kings Point Creative Writers Club Anthology, 2020

with a portfolio of the Kings Point Writers Club
Supplementary

EDWARD R. LEVENSON, EDITOR

Library of Congress Control Number: 2020918558
ISBN: Hardcover   978-1-6641-3238-2
                 Softcover   978-1-6641-3237-5
                 eBook   978-1-6641-3236-8

Print information available on the last page.

Rev. date: 12/03/2020

To order additional copies of this book, contact:
Xlibris
844-714-8691
www.Xlibris.com
Orders@Xlibris.com
812659

Preface to Anthology

The View from Kings Point: The Kings Point Creative Writers Club Anthology, 2020 is a worthy sequel to the 2018 edition of the same name. Again, it is a "nice little anthology," as I introduced the first one. It testifies to the conscientious and dedicated work, not to speak of the imagination and crafting skill—and the immensely valuable collegial critiquing—of the writers and poets in the group. As for the latter capacity, our members one and all have truly internalized the "best practices" of excellent writing, such as revising pieces several times, eschewing the presentation of opinions as facts, and refraining from the censorship of unpopular thoughts and expressions. Writers do need encouragement; and, to this end, I proudly assert, while maintaining genuine humility, that our Kings Point Creative Writers Club (KPCWC) anthologies are putting our writing group "on the map" in Delray Beach and Palm Beach County, Florida, and even beyond.

The literary quality of the pieces in the anthology is striking, and I go so far as to describe the variety of treatments and the range of subjects as "breathtaking."

I now list writers of expositional pieces and poetry in alphabetical order, only being able to suggest the barest taste of the gifts of each. It is striking how many contributors are accomplished in both prose and poetry.

Thea Aeide graces us with her inspiring presence.

John Bell writes about his experience in a hospital, interjecting "WhiskeyTangoFoxtrot" often, as well as about *"Klaatu barada nikto,"* and "Wolf."

Joe Bruno writes with subtlety about human capacities and relationships, situations and dilemmas, joys and setbacks.

Marilyn Cruz Orr describes nostalgia about the past, pain in relationships, the passage of time, and looking ahead to Heaven.

Laurie Faber writes poignantly about lovers, freedom, Nature, and a high-school "FOPA Club" (Friends of People with AIDS).

Sol Friedman draws on his engineering, military, world-traveler, summer-camp-management, and golf-expertise background.

David Jones, with characteristic British understatement, relates his experiences climbing Mount Kilimanjaro and living in Uganda. He describes mourning for his young friend Sidney when a teen in London.

Allan Korn, representing the Kings Point Writers Club Supplementary (see below), describes a vacation turned sour, but also successes as a medical assistant, college teacher, dog owner, home builder, and believing in himself as a writer.

Ellen Korn presents moving bittersweet memoirs about her childhood, high-school, and college experiences. Her caterpillar symbolism in her first piece is quite profound.

Jeff Langer's poems on love and loss, joy and pain, integrity and lies, and hopes and struggles "tell it like it is."

Edward/Eddie Levenson offers a poem, a presentation of one of his many personae, a reflection on COVID-19, two beginning chapters of a venture in a murder mystery, and a lament at his being "a frustrated comic."

Reva Spiro Luxenberg demonstrates virtuosity in a wide range of subjects, such as a particular woman's "fragility," a pawn shop, Stonehenge, and rock painting.

Faye Menczer describes the family's shock and grief at the recent death of son Brian.

Jim Rawlinson's narrative about a bridge in Vicksburg, Michigan, involves levels of very deep meaning.

Gayle Spanier Rawlings employs motorcycle and mountain metaphors, as well as earthly garden and feminist goddess imagery, and gives a farewell to her father in hospice.

Anne Rockwerk provides here a mere few of four score accounts of her amazing life.

David Spindell has enjoyable vignettes and short accounts—with subtle ironic endings.

Sydell Stern writes about "*Zaydy* and *Bubby*" (Grandpa and Grandma), *Chanukkah*, and "*krekhtzing*" (groaning while creaking).

Helene Suzann remembers with horror the untimely death of her sister-in-law in an automobile accident. Her punctuation of her piece is noteworthy.

Stella White describes a bear in the back seat; special sister Mary; Lillian, whom she had to "Mom"-sit; her empathy with both a goat and Forrest Tucker; and her odd neighbor Mike.

Ron Ziffer relates his recovery from alcoholism with Alcoholics Anonymous.

We debated in the group two years ago about the best title for the first anthology. After stubbornly arguing for *The Kings Point Creative Writers Club, 2018*, I subsequently experienced the breakthrough that that should be the subtitle and a catchy three- or four-word phrase should be the title. For the latter, a member suggested "Making a Point," playing on the "Point" in "Kings Point." Then another member reported on having employed Google for the origin of "Kings Point" as a point (no pun originally intended) of departure. Google revealed that Kings Point is a geographical location in Great Neck, New York—but, lo and behold, that it is also a very important term in art criticism about a particular painter's omniscient perspective: the "King's point of view."

We discussed this term in the group—and "*Eureka!*" (We've got it! [literally, in Classical Greek, "I've got it!"]). Change the word order to the word play "the view from Kings Point" and we have our title, albeit with the omission of the apostrophe of "King's" in "the King's point of view." That title received unanimous approval as *The View from Kings Point*. The "King's point of view" is the revolutionary omniscient perspective featured in the 1656 painting *Las Meninas* (Ladies in Waiting) of Spanish master Diego Velazquez. See the first frontispiece for the print. The subject of the painting is Infanta Margarita, daughter of King Philip IV of Spain and his wife Queen Mariana of Austria. Infanta Margarita has the central position in the painting. She is bathed in light in the foreground and is wearing a white gown. She has stopped in the studio to visit the artist, who is seen on the left side of the painting The omniscient point of view represented by the painting is considered to be that of the King and Queen behind the entrance to the studio in the forefront of the painting and who, presumably, are reflected in the mirror in the back.

The cover design two years ago was a band of sunlight split by a prism into a rainbow which passed through a globe and then onto the spread of our names. This time a ball of the sun is in the center, and our names are on its rays around the whole circumference. This sun is ethereal, as we thus invoke Heaven's blessings on all of us. May God keep us healthy, strong, and productive!

Afterwords, April 2020. In the inset at the top left of the cover is *Magnum Chaos*, a wood-inlay of Giovan Francesco Capoferri (1487-1534) at the Basilica di Santa Maria Maggiore in Bergamo, Italy (Wikipedia). A larger image of it is in the second frontispiece. "*Chaos*," cognate with "*chasm*," means "emptiness" or "gaping hole" in Greek. In Greek mythology it was the void out of which creation emerged, as paralleled partially in the "*tehom*" of the introduction of Genesis. It symbolizes in our context that in the midst of all of our intense strivings for completeness and perfection there may always be something missing. A multi-cultural connection is that in Judaism synagogue facades are left unfinished—"*lezekher hamiqdash*" (in memory of the Sanctuary).

A convention I have adopted in my editing is that I render the numbers from one to twelve as words but represent the numbers from 13 and higher as Arabic numerals—except where the autonomy of individual contributors requires a different way.

My heartfelt appreciation goes to all contributors for their collegiality, cooperation, and support in our shared endeavors—and especially to wife Reva and friend Jeff Langer for their unfailing wise advice and encouragement during all the stages of compilation. [See a word about the assistance of Ellen Korn shortly.]

In these months of "social distancing" during the Coronavirus pandemic, I pray—ever mindful of my maternal grandmother's death during the 1918 influenza epidemic—that we will all survive the peril and resume our productive lives in good health.

Second Afterwords, August 2020. An endeavor which had been initiated in the winter of 2020 was the Kings Point Writers Club Supplementary, an "overflow group" of the Kings Point Creative Writers Club parent group, which meets at a different day and time, for the purpose of not overloading presentations in the sessions of the latter. Members are free to belong to both groups if they wish. A member of the former is Allan Korn; and his writings—and a collaboration of his with Yours Truly—appear in the anthology in the "Addenda."

The Club members have devoted much time and energy to revising and attempting to perfect our "Rules." Not to be underestimated is a new member's input about the need for a "Mission Statement." Readers in other writing groups may be interested in what we have come up with so far, and that is why we include them here. They will undoubtedly undergo further amplification in the future. These "Rules" go beyond "procedures"; they comprise "understandings" as well.

Table of Contents

ADDENDA of the
KINGS POINT WRITERS CLUB
SUPPLEMENTARY (KPWCS)

Heartfelt Thanks to Contributors

May 2020. This is both a Second Preface and yet an additional Afterwords. The anthology, after many months, has finally come to fruition. [So we thought six months ago.] It has been my largest-scale endeavor in 48-51 years—since my Ph.D. dissertation (for the introduction to that see pages 136-158 in my *Genres Synch*). Honored and humbled by the anthology, I am exceedingly grateful to contributors.

The inclusion of a particular new contributor requires explanation. For a truly weighty personal spiritual reason I have added a 20th one over and above the 19 known to the group.

[Allan Korn became an additional 20th—for good luck!—later; but I won't be an ingrate re the 20th I am now describing.] Whereas the number 18 is a very lucky Jewish number, 19 is the opposite. For example, the weekday *Amidah* (Standing) prayer—which has 18 blessings and is known popularly as "*The Shmoneh Esreh*" ("The 18")—really now has a 19th prayer, included many hundreds of years ago, for God to subdue slanderers and evildoers. But the prayer is not called "The 19" to maintain the hope for good luck by downplaying publicly, as it were, the fact of the addition.

Contributor Jeff Langer has related to me that his pious grandfather regularly refrained from driving down 19th Street in Chicago because of its unlucky association. The meanings of the numbers are not superstitions; they are deeply ingrained Jewish cultural values which deserve "suspended disbelief" and respect.

And now we are in the midst of the COVID-19 pandemic! Though the 19 here is short for 2019—the year in which both it and the anthology began, the latter being auspicious —the stark 19 in the label evokes discomfort in me as I contemplate it.

So I introduce to you my literary Muse (wife Reva is my overall general inspiration for things good), Thea Aeide. She has revealed to me her special message and, as such, appears now as an honorary *Kings Point Creative Writers Club Anthology, 2020* contributor, the 20th.

Club members know how doggedly I have striven for cover-design consensus (and in general for that matter). I did the best I could on the design—during the "social distancing" and the unrelenting pressures of completing the book—in consulting with helpful colleagues on it.

To be more culturally inclusive and show respect to Christian members, I have inserted in the cover design the *Magnum Chaos* intarsia image in a wood-inlay of Giovan Francesco Capoferri at the Basilica di Santa Maria Maggiore in Bergamo, Italy. It represents creativity emerging out of the abyss, not to preclude other levels of meaning. "*Chaos*" in ancient Greek cosmology paralleled "*Tehom*" in Genesis and "*Tiamat*" in the Babylonian *Enuma Elish* creation myth.

My very special thanks go to wife Reva God Bless Her, Jeff Langer, and Ellen Korn for moral support and for such help as wise advice on particulars and preparation of long documents. Ellen performed an especially heroic chore in retyping 40-plus manuscript pages. It was at the last minute, and that's why I didn't mention it in my first preface. I pressed Reva into the service of transcribing a smaller—but very difficult because of my hard-to-decipher edits—eleven-page piece. "Old fogey" that I am, Reva nonetheless "robbed the cradle" in redeeming me from "unmarriedhood" four years ago. What a wife! A very productive writer, she is an amanuensis also in a pinch if I preface requests with my "not wanting to burden [her]" (private humor).

Kings Point Creative Writers Club (KPCWC) Rules Of Order

MISSION STATEMENT

The KPCWC, a "Critique Group," fosters our spirit of learning, collegiality, and friendship with the common goal of sharing and improving our work, supporting the writing efforts of experienced and inexperienced writers alike, and promoting our writing success. We welcome all forms of creative writing. It should be appreciated that the critiques/reviews of individual pieces benefit the writing of all. With our writers and poets, our excellence of organization, and our carefully formulated rules, we aspire to be a model for emulation.

RULES AND REQUIREMENTS FOR MEMBERSHIP

1. We meet in the Media Room to the right of the theatre in the Main Clubhouse Wednesdays from 1 to 3.
2. All members must reside in Kings Point (The Kings Point Golf and Country Club). Becoming a member requires attending four sessions.
3. According to the rules of the condo association, a cap on membership of "recreational clubs" is not permitted. Guests and prospective new members, are, of course, welcome to observe and even present writings according to our guidelines. Only full-time Kings Point residents and members can vote in the Club's biennial elections. Elections take place in January of the even-numbered years. Voting is conducted by secret ballot, and the tally is not announced publicly.
4. A member who plans to be absent for a lengthy period of time must notify the Secretary.
5. Members not following rules will be subject to consequences.

OFFICERS' REQUIREMENTS AND DUTIES

1. Officers, who must be year-round Kings Point residents, shall serve a two-year term. An officer, upon becoming unable to serve, must resign and a successor will be chosen in a special election.
2. The five officers constitute the "Steering Committee," decisions of which will be reached by majority vote.
3. Duties of the officers:
    a. The President calls the meeting to order, makes necessary introductions, asks the Secretary to read the minutes of the previous meeting, leads discussions of old and new business, directs the numerical order of the readings and the critiquing, and adjourns the meeting. The President is responsible for advertising Club matters in the *Kings Point News*, introducing possible subjects of interest to writers, and receiving calls from prospective members.
    b. The Vice-President is responsible for decorum, assists the President, and stands in for the President if the President should be absent.
    c. The Secretary takes attendance; reads the minutes of the previous meeting; and keeps up-to-date records of the members (names, residences, email addresses, and telephone numbers); and distributes membership applications and rules to prospective members.
    d. The Treasurer does not assess dues at present, but may collect monies in the future.
    e. The Membership Chairperson telephones and emails members when necessary and contacts prospective members.

GENERAL MEETING PROCEDURES AND GUIDELINES

1. Each person receives a permanent number, and the readings are in numerical order. The number of an absent member is skipped. The respective reading occurs at the next rotation.
2. The length of pieces is two pages, double-spaced in a twelve-point font, printed on 8-by-11-inch sheets. Presenters should distribute sufficient copies for the total of anticipated members.
3. Handwritten material is not allowed. Previously published pieces are prohibited.

CRITIQUES

1. Positive statements begin the critiquing process, to be followed by suggested corrections and revisions.
2. Critiquing takes place in clockwise order.
3. Opinions are not to be presented as facts. Comments should be focused on the written piece.
4. Readers' brief adlibs and critiquers' constructive sidebars are discouraged, but not absolutely forbidden depending upon the size of the group.
5. Correction of punctuation and grammar is welcomed.
6. When the critiques are finished, it is the reader's turn to comment.
7. Papers are returned to the reader with the reviewers' names on them so that the reader will know who made the suggestions and will be able to seek clarifications.

AMENDMENTS

1. Amendments to the rules—subject to the majority vote of both the group and the "Steering Committee"—may be made.
2. Exceptions to the rules—subject to the majority vote of the group—may be made.

**Omission of Pages for Photo and Bio of
the First Contributor Explained**

In consideration of the transcendent dimensionality of the existence
and influence of Aeide Thea/Thea Aeide, any attempt to render her
image and her bio would represent blasphemous idolatry; and we,
therefore, must make do without either.

Thea Aeide (as known Down Here)

Aeide, Thea (as addressed in the Other Dimension)

Aeide Thea introduced herself to me—at a moment of great need during the Coronavirus inactivity—as the twentieth contributor to our anthology. I wanted very much to round out the number of contributors to 20, a solid number with heft. The number 19 had symbolized for me the pain of the nineteenth prayer added centuries ago to the weekday "*Amidah*" (Standing) prayer of the Jewish liturgy, which beseeches the Almighty to foil slanderers and to destroy evil. She is a Transcendent Reality for me—though in a Jabèsian (I'll be explaining that approach elsewhere, to be sure) non-supernatural sense; but she also reveals herself in human form as Thea Aeide. I am moved by the "coolness" of her first name, Thea. I do represent her transcendent self in the cloud on the top right of the cover —"*thea*," after all, means "goddess" in Greek. Readers may recall that the small-globe prototype on the cover of the 2018 anthology had been the domain of deceased member I. Irving Rosenberg. In this context I pay respects to deceased member Karen Gula as well.

"*Aeide*" and "*thea*" are the second and third words of the first line of Homer's *Iliad*; and resonating very deeply to it, I thrilled also in analogous admiration of the first lines of Vergil's *Aeneid* and of Genesis in Hebrew Scriptures—and then composed as an introduction to the anthology my own line, which alludes to ideas and features of the other three. The line of the *Iliad* does not precede the line of Genesis in historical meaning, but I list it first because the word "*aeide*" (sing), beginning as it does with an "*alpha*" (A), serves my symbolization of Aeide Thea/Thea Aeide as the first contributor to the collection in alphabetical order, based on the Greek original in which the word "*aeide*" precedes "*thea*." (Even if the other contributors would be alphabetized according to their first names, she would still precede Anne Rockwerk.) So the "*aeide*" line is the first of the four, just as Aeide Thea/Thea Aeide is the first of the twenty contributors.

Here are the four inter-allusive lines in Greek, Latin, Hebrew, and Latin, respectively. The first, second, and fourth are in a dactylic (long-short-short vowels) rhythm. Don't push that too far for the third; Hebrew metrics are different.

1. "*Menin aeide thea Peleiadeo Achilleos*"
   (Sing, O Goddess, of the resentment of Achilles, son of Peleus), *Iliad*
2. "*Arma virumque cano Troiae qui primus ab oris*" [*venit*]
   (I sing of arms and a man who first [came] from the shores of Troy), *Aeneid*
3. "*B'reshit bara Elohim et hashamayim v'et ha'arets*"
   (At the beginning of God's creating the heavens and the earth), Genesis
4. "*Anthologiam cano secundam familiae nostrae*"
   (I sing of the second anthology of our family), Yours Truly of the Kings Point Creative Writers Club and the Kings Point Writers Club Supplementary

Now for explication. The Goddess invoked by Homer is Calliope, the Muse of epic poetry. Homer's imperative verb for "sing" is the Greek "*aeide*." "*Cano*" in the Latin versions is a clear allusion to the former. Two (equally far-out) interactive anachronistic interpretations of "*aeide*"/"*cano*" are that they are prophetic anticipations of Yours Truly's wife's mother Ada, on the one hand, and the Major League Baseball star Robinson Canó, of New York Yankees, Seattle Mariners, and New York Mets fame.

The four lines taken together involve composite thematic unity. The strife in the *Iliad* dissipates when Achilles finally receives the respect he deserves. The hero Aeneas in the *Aeneid* exemplifies how great a difference a determined individual can make. God's creative power, wisdom, and love in Scripture are replicated in the endeavors of writers, singly and in groups.

A homiletical postscript. The first letter of *"aeide"*—"A"—leads us to appreciate all the other letters of the alphabet as well. The Hebrew letter *"bet,"* and the Latin letter "C"—which, on their sides, look like cups facing inward in the respective directions of leftward in Hebrew and rightward in Latin—encourage readers to delve into the material, not looking up, down, or backwards. Indeed, that is why, as it is said, the first letter of Genesis begins with a *"bet,"* not an *"aleph."* That having been said, readers, enjoy our second anthology starting anywhere you please.

I almost forgot. As my special Muse of this anthology—wife Reva is my overall Muse—Aeide Thea/Thea Aeide has inspired me to republish my Latin ode to my publisher Xlibris, which appeared on page vii in my *Genres Mélanges Deuxième* (July, 2018).

Pro Xlibris Meque! (To Xlibris and Me!)

Mi nove liber generum primus "Mélange"[1]
Inter alios meos haud sui generis[2]
De Xlibris[3] gloriam ad maximam suam
Bonum mundi summumque et felicis auctoris.

My first "Mélange"-named genres mix is here,
Among my other books not that unique,
Cheers, Xlibris, for your greater glory
And the greatest good of all and happy author.

My gratitude to Xlibris unbounded
For will to write and pride in its production.

---

[1]   This ode was written on the occasion of the publication of my *Genres Mélange* (October 2017).
[2]   It is *not "sui generis,"* because both *"Edward's Humor" and More* (February 2017) and *Genres Mélange Deuxième* (July 2018) are also multi-genres collections.
[3]   www.Xlibris.com.

Unusual a tribute to one's self-publisher,[4]
But heartfelt all the more to one and all.

"Asot sfarim harbeh eyn qets"[5]—*LO* *"sof davar."*[6]
Tomorrow and tomorrow and tomorrow, God be willing.
More books! To life! *L'hayyim!*[7] It's very thrilling![8]

---

[4]   This very sonnet, and see my "Introduction and Acknowledgments" section, page 9, in *Genres Mélange.*

[5]   "Of making many books there is no end."—Ecclesiastes 12:12. It is ironic that both the Hebrew and the English are in the iambic rhythm.

[6]   *"Sof davar"* (the end of the matter)—Ecclesiastes 12:13. In Ecclesiastes a pious ending follows: "Fear God and observe His commandments." I have added the Hebrew word *"LO"* (not), turning verses 12 and 13 on their head: "It is not the end of the matter to say that there is no end of books. We want *more* Xlibris books."

[7]   Hebrew for "To Life!"

[8]   I have added a third line to the *volta* (the turn), making a fifteen-line sonnet and lines fourteen and fifteen a rhyming couplet.

John Bell

Bio

Born Glendale, CA 1948. Grew up in Chicago. Moved to Florida, 1993.

B.A., Baylor U.

M.Ed., Florida Atlantic University, in Curriculum and Instruction for Secondary Biology and Math.

M.Ed., Florida Atlantic University, in Environmental Education.

Florida Professional Teaching Certificate.

Widowed.

The Ballad of Wolf

Well, you can kill an In'jun
and maybe a sheriff, too
But there's one thing you should
Never, ever, ever do.

Wolf is a white-eye
Since five, Comanche raised
As soon as talk to you
He'd stake you over a fire, to slowly braise.

He won't eat you, and he'll keep you turnin'
To save you for the vermin
Who will royally feast
After waiting in the shadows squirmin'.

Captured at a very young age
He wasn't a Comanche breed
But he took totally to the training

And bought into the Comanche creed.

Theirs was a total way of life
That called on the spirits to keep minds right
Always kind to one another
God help those poor souls they had to fight.

He became the very best
At their primitive mores and ways
He took things extremely seriously
And excelled throughout his days.

Hunter, trapper, trailblazer
Tracking where no one else would go
Circle wide a'flank and wait
Then lie in ambush. You didn't even know.

Though he didn't know it at the time
These skills would serve him well
Throughout his life, when needed
Especially in moments of holy hell.

Most men know him
As a Capt'n from the war
A leader of men
And loyal to the corps.

One alone had wronged him
Gone for a long amount of time
He finally caught up with him
And left no piece larger than a dime.

Such is the man known as Wolf
A hero, veteran, marshal
A legend in his own time
And definitely impartial.

If Wolf is on your trail
Your days left are a small number
He will catch up with you
Especially while you slumber.

It's better to turn yourself in
Avoid the run and hide
Save yourself the trouble
of that long, slow, deadly, return ride.

In his life he called two his Love
They helped with all his needs
He had only two friends
And they helped with all his deeds.

So few to talk to, he wondered
Again, only a couple he admired
Would go through hell for
Kill the devil, and quench the fires.

The one thing you should
Never, ever, ever do?
Don't fuck with Wolf
It will be the end of you.

Some don't take this advice to heart
And many men have tried
For one mistaken idea or another
And many, many of them have died.

So many in fact
That the legend precedes the man
As he travels widely
Throughout this great big land.

"Klaatu Barada Nikto"

(Details have been derived from
https://en.wikipedia.org/wiki/Klaatu_barada_nikto)

The 1951 science-fiction classic *The Day the Earth Stood Still*—which I first saw in 1960 when I was twelve years old—shook me to the very core of my being. The plot involves a standoff between aliens and earthlings which bodes the destruction of Earth.

At the climax of the play, the humanoid alien protagonist of the play, Klaatu, is killed by the American military; but before he dies, he says to his comrade Helen Benson about the leader of the aliens, Gort, "There's no limit to what he can do. He could destroy the Earth…. If anything should happen to me, you must go to Gort. You must say these words: '*klaatu barada nikto.*' Please repeat that." This phrase has been described as "one of the most famous commands in Science Fiction." Helen Benson does utter the phrase; and, in response, Gort relents from destroying Earth and resurrects Klaatu from death.

During the 13 days of October 16th to 28th, 1962, The Cuban Missile Crisis confronted the world when the then-Soviet Union introduced nuclear ballistic weapons into Cuba and it was feared that nuclear war was imminent. In a deep need to find meaning—not to mention encouragement and hope—in that dire period, I saw the movie twice during the days of the crisis and once afterwards. In the 58 years since, I find myself saying *"klaatu barada nikto"* to myself often, as if it were a mantra.

Gort is a robot. As such, he is a retake of previous literary creations of helpers-turned-uncontrollables, such as the Golem of Prague and the Sorcerer's Apprentice; but he is certainly just as terrifying.

So what does *"klaatu barada nikto"* mean? Sci-Fi devotees delve into the phrase with the zeal of academic philologists. Different interpretations are "Klaatu dies, repair me, do not retaliate" and "There's hope for Earth if the scientists can be reached."

Our world in 2020 is facing a new crisis, the COVID-19 pandemic, which is as dire as the 1962 Cuban Missile Crisis; for the number of casualties world-wide is actual, not just imminent. Can *"klaata barada nikto"* embrace the meaning of humans' uniting and pooling resources to overcome both natural and human evil? It is basically a positive expression conveying the yearning of "saving Earth."

The 1918 Influenza Epidemic eventually ended. In a way, the Earth is now "standing still" until COVID-19 does end as well. Let us then invoke the immortal words *"Klaatu barada nikto!"* in our keeping our spirit strong.

My Two Experiences with a Dead President—#WhiskeyTangoFoxtrot

Experience 1

May 19, 2018 began as any other old-fart Friday. It did not end that way. At 6:30 p.m. I went to the kitchen for something, a trip I had made a thousand times before. It was dusk, but the ambient light entering through the kitchen window was sufficient to navigate by. No lights needed. Had I turned on the lights, I might have noticed the wet patch on the tile.

Bad combination: wet tile, stocking feet, low light, and being half in the bag. BANG! I hit the floor without a chance to shield myself against the blow. 70 years old. I have jumped out of airplanes, wrecked motorcycles, totaled four cars, fallen hundreds of times, and run into many a stationary object—all without serious injury. Bleeding—yes, cuts—yes, contusions—yes, bruises—yes, burns—yes, lacerations—yes; and I don't know what else! Never a broken bone or had a serious injury.

I have a system after a bad spill. Lie on the ground (floor) motionless for five minutes in the position I landed. Check neck.

Check right arm including shoulder, elbow, wrist, and digits. Ditto, left arm. Check pelvis lateral movement for lower spine injuries. Check right leg, including hip, knee, ankle, and digits. Ditto, left leg. Then, and only then, do I attempt to rise to my knees and stay there for several minutes checking for dizziness. When I feel clear-headed, I rise to an erect position and start to take care of the most serious boo-boos.

So, I began. *Neck—OK. Right arm—OK. Left arm—HOLY FUCK! JESUS H. CHRIST #WhiskeyTangoFoxtrot! Throw this fucking checklist out and go to Plan B. Hmm, never having needed a Plan B, I don't have a clue. Well, think it through, dummy. Turn slooowly onto my back. Immobilize my arm into a position of least hurt.* Call for help. My daughter and her boyfriend were in the next bedroom and came running to the cry of help.

"Call me an ambulance," I said to the boyfriend. I knew it was broken.

"Fine, but let me check you out first," he replied.

"Are you a fucking doctor?"

"No. But...."

"But, shit. Do as you're told then."

The ambulance arrived about 15 minutes later, checked me out, gave me a shot, and drove me to the ER after asking me 4,000 questions and hooking me up to 50 different machines. In case you haven't figured it out by now, the dead President is JFK, as in JFK Hospital. I was admitted, questioned with the same 4,000 questions (to see if my answers changed substantially) and got hooked up to another 50 different machines. Hospitals have the best machines. At around 12:30 a.m. Saturday I was informed that my ulna was broken, they have arranged to admit me and were going to do surgery in the morning. It was by then 1:00 a.m., so, #WhiskeyTangoFoxtrot.

Saturday. October 20, 2018, 7:00 a.m. They brought around the breakfast cart and gave me my meal.

"Get the fucking nurse in here!" I shouted to the stunned food worker.

"What's your problem?" said the nurse as she entered the room ten minutes later.

"I'm having surgery this morning, and they gave me a breakfast tray," I sneered back.

"We don't have you scheduled for surgery today." she replied.

Son-of-a-bitch. #WhiskeyTangoFoxtrot. Lied to again in less than six hours.

"I want to see the surgeon. NOT the admitting doctor, NOT the floor doctor, NOT the doctor assigned to me, but the surgeon that was supposed to be operating on me this morning," I exclaimed in my best smart-ass voice. "Also, I'll give you fair warning, if he is not operating on me by tomorrow morning, I'm out of here, so do the fuckin' paperwork."

"The doctor won't be around until late this afternoon," she replied.

"I'll wait—like I have something else to do."

Lunch passed. Medication passed. Numerous readings of vital signs passed. On one such occasion I was sitting on the edge of the bed when they came in for something.

"You're not supposed to be out of bed, it's on your chart, 'Non-ambulatory,'" the second-string nurse said.

I hopped, yes hopped, off the bed and went into a tirade. #WhiskeyTangoFoxtrot. "I don't give a fuck what's on the stinkin' chart. Change it! Look, let me explain it to you. My elbow is broken. The rest of my body is fully functional. See?" First standing on one foot, then the other. Doing one-armed jumping jacks (hospitals have the best meds). Spinning around. "So. when I tell you I'm ambulatory—believe it," I stated with derision.

"OK, I'll report that," said the second-stringer. "Call us if you have to go to the washroom." #WhiskeyTangoFoxtrot. Fat chance.

At 3:30 p.m., the surgeon entered. He explained that my ulna was broken into four pieces. He would have to insert a Titanium plate into a two-inch incision, but he could not do it until Thursday. #WhiskeyTangoFoxtrot.

"OK, but I'm checking out after you leave."

"I'm not the admitting doctor, so I can't give you a release."

"Who said anything about a release, I'm just leaving."

"I can't prescribe any meds for you and the admitting doctor won't give you any." #WhiskeyTangoFoxtrot. What a fucking racket. This is the penance you pay for defying their silly rules.

"Fuck it, I'll bite down on a stick, or kiss a rattlesnake, or some silly shit like that." Little did he know I had left-over meds at home.

"OK, see you Thursday."

I signed some papers saying I'm an asshole and left.

Experience 2

Got a call the surgery was moved up to Tuesday afternoon. Fine with me. By then I'll be out of meds.

"Hello. Mr. Bell, so nice to see you again," the cashier said cheerily. *What the fuck is she so cheery about? Oh, the one-armed bandit is about to pay out, again. I wondered who the one armed-bandit was. Is it figurative, as in Humana—or literal, as in the one-armed person sitting across from her?*

The surgery and recovery were textbook. The only thing I questioned was the insertion of a nerve blocker in my left shoulder. "Is this something new?" I asked the anesthesiologist.

"Nope, about 20-years old. It works well and you won't feel a thing for 24 hours," he replied.

24 hours of recovery sounds like something I could use.

Exit the hospital and drive to Walgreen's drive-thru pharmacy. After giving the clerk my prescription for Percocet®, answering 20 questions, handing over my IDs, him checking the computer and seeing I had a boo-boo that needed meds, he finally determined I wasn't a junkie. Fuckin' junkies make life miserable for everyone else. #WhiskeyTangoFoxtrot.

"Only problem is we're closing and it will be more than an hour wait," the clerk said.

"What time do you open in the morning?"

"Nine o'clock."

After some advanced calculations, I determined I was good until 3:00 p.m. the next day, so I nodded OK and left. About 11:00 p.m. that night my fingers started tingling. Strange, but never having a broken bone I didn't know what to expect. I didn't know how many nerves were blocked with this nerve-blocker, but by 12:00 a.m., they started to come back online one at a time. Each nerve revived, brought back its own level of pain associated with it. #WhiskeyTangoFoxtrot. #WhiskeyTangoFoxtrot. #WhiskeyTangoFoxtrot. I went through any left-over pain killers I had, my daughter had, her boyfriend had, the neighbor had—and it still wasn't enough. I started looking for suitable sticks to chew on, or rattlesnakes to kiss, anything to stop this fucking pain. To channel my best Franklin Delano Roosevelt—*Yesterday, October 20th, a date which will live in agony. My body was brutally, and suddenly, attacked by the Empire of Pain....* #WhiskeyTangoFoxtrot. Enough of that shit. That was the pain talking.

Guess who was first in line at nine o'clock when Walgreen's Pharmacy opened? Mercifully, my script was ready, and I treated myself to a double dose. #WhiskeyTangoFoxtrot. Only live once. By the time I reached home, the meds kicked in. Bliss, euphoria, and relaxation leading to some much needed, and overdue, *geschlafen.*

Postscript: Finally checked out my two-inch incision. #WhiskeyTangoFoxtrot. The thing is over seven inches long and looks gnarly. #WhiskeyTangoFoxtrot. Wait till I see that surgeon. I'm not vain, so I don't care about scars, but #WhiskeyTangoFoxtrot. It gives me something to rib him about.

©2017 John W. Bell
jbell60@gmail.com

The Case of the Missing Device (Part VIII)—a Sherlock Holmes Take-Off

We were greeted at our hotel by young Gregson at 10:00 a.m. sharp. The journey to Plymouth was very comfortable, quiet, and without incident.

"Here we are, Mr. Holmes," said Gregson. "I hope you have a fruitful meeting."

"Are you not to accompany us?" I retorted.

"No, thank you, we have not enough battery for the return trip, so I will have to seek a kindly establishment to allow me to recharge. I have all the necessary cables and adapters for whatever I might encounter," replied Gregson.

Holmes slid Gregson a piece of paper.

"Here is the telephone number of Mr. Durant's office. Pray call us with an estimate of pick-up, if you would be so kind," said Holmes. We all exited the vehicle, save Gregson, and made our way into the offices of Specific Motors, where we were greeted by Mr. Durant's secretary who showed us to Mr. Durant's office.

After rapping she said, "The gentlemen you were expecting are here to see you, sir."

"Why, come in," uttered Durant. "Good of you to stop by. Need anything? Water? Soda? No? Well, please be seated. What may I do for you, gentlemen?"

"We are here, at my brother Mycroft's request, to probe any irregularities in the formations of the auto industries," replied Holmes.

"Oh, and what irregularities might there be?"

"The theory that electric vehicles are being discriminated against vis-a-vis internal combustion petrol-engine vehicles," stated Holmes.

Durant folded his fingers together, touching his chin, and appeared to be in deep thought. "Mr. Holmes, if you don't mind, I should like to share a rather recent history lesson with you."

Holmes nodded.

"The people have spoken, sir. Motorcars came into wide-spread use on British roads during the early 1880s, Petrol stations are virtually appearing overnight on every street corner. The refining of oil has of late run into a few snags due to the lack of refineries, not the lack of petroleum. Every seaport in England is working 24 hours a day to unload foreign steel for automobile production. This is becoming an increasingly scarcer commodity, as the Americans are also into this automobile craze we are experiencing. All of England's mills from Manchester to Birmingham are operating 24 hours in steel production and every machine shop and stamping mill is operating 24 hours on automobile production. We have no fewer than 10 factories for automobile assembly and have enough orders to justify another 10. It seems that every man-jack is involved in automobile production in one form or another.

"To be honest with you, sir, electric vehicles have several major advantages over petrol-powered vehicles. They are faster, more efficient, non-polluting, and odorless. Also, they are easier to fabricate and have fewer moving parts. Ergo, less to go wrong. The one factor holding them back is a lack of charging stations and the time to recharge. This is understandable as England has just started its electrification program, with service to houses and businesses being its primary goal. For a while electric-charging stations will be on an as-needed basis. But, the main problem with electric automobiles is the lack of range in the current batches of lead-acid batteries. I fear it will take many decades, if not centuries, before this problem is solved. In the meanwhile, a petrol vehicle can carry several hundreds of miles of petrol with a single ten-minute stop. No, sir, as I have said, the people have spoken in resounding favor of petrol."

At this point Mr. Durant's secretary entered the room. "Telephone message for Mr. Holmes, sir," she said, while passing a note to Holmes. Holmes scanned the message

"Nothing wrong, I hope," stated Durant.

"No, it is from our driver saying he will need several more hours to recharge the vehicle, and he will pick us up hence at the Ruskin Arms, where he bids us to have our lunch repast."

"A fine eating establishment. I recommend it heartily. Take a left out the front doors, after two streets (about 200 yards) take a right. It is in the middle of the block, you can't miss it. Mr. Holmes, you have just experienced first-hand the major problem with electric vehicles."

We took our leave of Mr. Durant and within moments were on foot heading towards the Ruskin Arms.

Joe Bruno

Bio

I was born and raised in the far northern reaches of New York in 1954. A Regents Scholarship recipient, I attended three New York colleges. Multiple periods of ill health and convalescence from childhood through the present often meant that reading was one of the few activities I could pursue. I have owned thousands of books on a variety of subjects and have read most of them and many others. All that reading led to a desire to write.

I have explored a multitude of topics within several genres, including poetry, opinion, humor, science, and fiction. My work has appeared in a local newspaper in Kernersville, North Carolina, as well as in local, state, and national union publications. A self-published book of poetry sold well, and one of my short stories appeared in a regional collection produced in Greensboro, North Carolina.

I helped establish poetry readings at the Kernersville Library in North Carolina, where a 2000 solo event was standing-room-only. I was the emcee for poetry nights at the High Point, North Carolina, Barnes and Noble; and I was a member of two North Carolina writing groups. I am now President of The Kings Point Creative Writers Club, a critique group, in Delray Beach, Florida.

Unreal Estate

J. E. Bruno, Copyright 2000

If you've got a little money, and you're tired of paying rent,
and you don't want to live in your car or in a tent.
then go see a realtor, they've got a special book.
that's filled with homes for sale, waiting for you to take a look.
All the pictures are so pretty, each house a precious stone,

its surroundings are a "setting," you search for one that stands alone.
This is when you find out that the language realtors speak
is designed to pique your interest, to hint they have just what you seek.
The words they choose, sometimes, do not quite tell it "like it is,"
but like the bubbles in the champagne, they give it pop and fizz.
They use many catch-words, like "wonderful," or "grand,"
to let us know this isn't just a house slapped on some land.
If they say a house is cozy (another word is "cute"),
there's room enough to hang your hat, but not your Sunday suit.
Gentle slopes sound quite pleasant, and rolling hills of clover.
You'll curse them hills each time you mow, and pray you don't roll over.
Rustic is a home for those who find a woodsy feel enchanting.
Who wants to spend a hundred grand, and still feel like they are camping?
Victorians are lovely homes, quaint and quite becoming,
if you like cardboard insulation, and ninety-year-old plumbing.
Of course, I know that lots of homes have had some upgrades made–
Make sure when you buy these homes there's no liens that must be paid.
And when these homes are falling apart, near the end of their lifespan,
they cheerfully say it's a "fixer-upper," a special for the handyman!
So whether you're in the market for a starter, or upgrading.
There's plenty of realtors sitting by their telephones and waiting,
for that single call that gets them all to rush with smiling faces,
to show you some great investments, and some terrific places.
But don't forget to look behind the puffery and polish.
Make sure it's ready to live in, and not ready to demolish.
And no matter if it's in the country, or part of some suburban sprawl,
You'll sign at least one page that means the bank still owns it all.

Fifteenth Summer

J. E. Bruno, Original Copy 1995, revised 11-2-18

May was almost over. Lawns were greening up. I got our lawn done and walked to every house on the street to see who might want to hire me to mow their yard. I got one taker, a half-mile away. He was a retired city man who had bought the house five months earlier. I knew I should have discussed terms first. After nearly three hours of pushing the mower I was then ordered around for another three hours. I cleaned up trash and limbs, raked, and sweated. Finally, he could find no more for me to do and he asked me how much I thought I should get.

Minimum wage was only a buck fifty-five at the time, so I calculated and gave him what I thought was a safe answer. "At least ten."

He handed me a five-dollar bill, saying, "That's about what it's worth to me."

Of all the things I thought to say I chose something slightly past the edge of politeness. I spoke calmly. "I won't mow your lawn again at that price, and I don't think you will find anyone else who will, either." He waved me off with a scowl, and I pushed the mower home.

My father asked me about it two days later. "Did you tell Jim Caleb he had to mow his own lawn?"

"I told him he wouldn't get anyone else to do it for what he was paying. He paid me five dollars. I walked a mile with the mower, mowed for three hours, worked three more hours cleaning up his yard. Add the price of gas. What kind of idiot would work for less than minimum?"

In a rare step from the stubborn nature that I inherited from him in full, my father changed his mind and agreed with me—weakly, but he did agree. "Oh, I didn't know about the other work. You're right. I'll talk with him."

About ten days after that I saw a younger kid mowing Caleb's lawn as I was walking to town. I stopped and asked him what he was getting for the job.

"Eight bucks, and it's his new mower and gas."

I was walking away when Caleb called to me. He handed me a five. "This even us up?" Before I could answer, he asked another question. "Would you do some more work for me at minimum? This other kid isn't too handy."

I was glad to tell him the county job program had come through. I had a job at the local playground—the easiest kind of work anyone could get. Caleb didn't give up. He told me to come back in the fall to help him clean up. He would let my father know when he wanted me. It sounded like a deal was made without my input. I hesitated long enough for him to take it as an agreement. I was not eager to work for anyone who would first cheat me, then hire someone else rather than give me the opportunity at a fair rate.

Every weekday I walked past the Caleb house as I went to and from my summer job. Even at minimum wage my job was work only in the slightest sense of the word. I saw the other kid mowing a few times, wondered why Caleb never did it himself. The kid planted his flower beds for him, too. Marigolds and cosmos bloomed for weeks in the mid-summer sunshine.

Labor Day weekend came at last. The days of summer were gone, and school would resume on a Tuesday. Early Monday morning my father woke me up. "Caleb wants you to come work today, says you made a deal, so you'd better get going."

What timing this guy has. I wasn't looking forward to spending the holiday, especially Labor Day, working for that old guy. There was a town celebration going on with a parade, games, and concessions. I was knocking on Caleb's door twenty minutes later, hoping that the sooner I got to work, the sooner I'd get done.

He opened the door smiling. First, I raked leaves. After two hours of that, I was led to a huge woodpile, which I drew from and ranked in his shed. Caleb came out, not to help, but to criticize, finding problems with almost every stick of wood I stacked. I knew

some of the neighbors were fussy and competitive when it came
to their firewood, building sturdy outside ranks in ornate patterns,
bark side up to keep it dry.

"What are you going to do with the wood?" I asked.

"What do you think? I'm going to burn it, of course."

"Then as long as it's stacked so it won't fall over, it won't matter
how pretty the ranks are. No one will see it in here."

He walked away, shaking his head. A while later he brought out
two slices of bread with margarine and a tinge of peanut butter
between them, along with a dingy glass of a weak tepid tea.

"Here's some lunch for you," he said, beaming as if he was
bringing me a wonderful treat. I mumbled thanks, ate it as quickly
as I could, and went back to work.

His criticism continued. He had me loading a wheelbarrow, carting
load after load of yard waste to a ditch. He found fault with how
I loaded the wheelbarrow, how I walked under the load, and how
I dumped the stuff in the ditch. I had no more argument to give
him, because no matter how I tried to keep up with his suggestions,
it seemed that he would change them to keep me always short of
what he expected.

As the day cooled, the brief northern summer was becoming a
memory, and I was thinking of things that I could learn in school
so that I wouldn't have to do manual labor the rest of my life for
people who couldn't be pleased. Old Caleb had one more job for
me before I could go home to supper.

"Last chore." he said, "pull out all these dead flowers from the two
beds by the driveway, then come to the house and we'll settle up."

Making a last attempt to be helpful. I had a question. "Do you want
me to save the seeds?"

"What for?"

"To plant next year. For more flowers."

"They won't grow," he said. "Why do you think they sell them in
stores?"

"But that's what we...."

"I've never heard of such foolishness, boy, just pull them out. Throw them away! Take them to the ditch with the other yard waste."

I could see that he was more upset than he had been all day. Here I was trying to be helpful, and this city man thought the only way to get flowers was to get them from a store.

When I finished up, Caleb let me into the house and handed me a twenty. On the counter I could see several pill bottles. He caught me as my gaze stuck on them.

"You see all that stuff? You'd think that with all these pills I could do some of my own work around here. Doctor thinks I do too much as it is. It's an awful thing to get old."

He pointed to the bill that hung limp in my hand. "Is that enough?"

"Yes, yes sir. Thank you."

He patted my shoulder as he let me out the door. I walked home, wondering how it must feel to have someone else do all your work for you. While I had been slow to embrace the value of hard work, I understood how much of it is needed in every home. Everyone shared at my house in what needed doing. That's the way I had learned.

When I got home I emptied my pocket onto a sheet of newspaper. I had taken several flower heads of marigolds and cosmos. Even though they would have gone to waste in the trash heap, I couldn't get over the small, nagging pangs of guilt I felt for taking the seeds. I let them dry for a week, then stored them in a small jar. With the warming of the following spring, I planted them in our own flower garden. When they sprouted and began to develop, I couldn't look at them without thinking of Caleb saying they wouldn't grow. Those feelings of guilt were fading.

The flowers didn't just grow—they bloomed magnificently, and my mother asked where the pretty new flowers came from. I said, simply and truthfully, that they were from seeds that someone was going to throw away. Her smile erased my last bit of guilt.

Tolerance is a pocket where we carry seeds of promise.

Neighbors

J. E. Bruno, Copyright 1997, Revised 2018

We may choose where we live, but chance determines our neighbors. With luck we will find those who live near us tolerable. Friendly and helpful neighbors do exist outside the realm of family-oriented TV programming, but like any relationship the balance can be easily upset. Children, so full of innocence, cannot foresee the adult reactions that result from children playing their games. Children see everything as a game, an adventure, or a wonder to be explored.

As a former child myself, I can attest to some of the ways children can strain neighborly relations. Before the age of four I was caught on two occasions doing things that rattled our neighbors. Led by the relatively mature seven-year-old in our little gang, we climbed in and, most of us, back out of a chicken yard. The chicken yard owner caught the one boy who remained inside and yelled angrily at the rest of us as we ran away. We were old enough to know what anger was without knowing how grown-ups got that way. Perhaps we scared a few hens out of production, and we did get a scolding. Running to our home next door was not the clean getaway we supposed it to be.

After that trespass and spanking slipped from our youthful minds, we visited the neighbors' place again. We "found" a basket of apples on their porch, and we helped ourselves. The neighbors saw us commit the petit larceny, and their threats to call the police kept me hiding from them for years afterwards, ducking behind trees and bushes whenever I saw a police car. "Finders-keepers" does not apply to anything found on your neighbors' porch. Neighborly relations had reached a low point, and coincidentally, we moved not long after that.

At age seven I was encouraged by one teenaged neighbor to call the teenaged girl next door some funny words I had never heard before. I learned another lesson by the seat of my pants. I guess I had to find out for myself that older kids enjoy getting younger kids to say things that best not be said. Soon we moved again, though I had no difficulty believing in the coincidental nature of our frequent moves.

Across from our newest house was a rental house. New neighbors were moving in and out in a regular rotation pattern. I was no more or less aggravating than any other pre-teen boy, yet for at least three neighbor boys who outsized me I was a handy target for fists, sticks, stones, and other more noxious projectiles. I survived, and that was a testament to their well-meaning efforts to assist me in the process of growing up. This I deduced by their frequent habit of combining the pelting with comments directing me to grow up. One of the rental residents had a liking for fresh produce, finding lots of it in our garden. He might have escaped some suspicion had he been less obvious. The missing tomatoes and corn could have been blamed on raccoons and squirrels. Then our largest pumpkin was taken in the night, carved into a grinning jack-o-lantern, and placed in the window facing our house by the next evening. We knew the local raccoons were not that artistic. The line between nerve and foolishness can be blurry, and this was one neighbor guy who likely had a foot on each side of that line. This was the first time that I realized that someone other than me and my friends had violated the code of neighborliness, giving me a new perspective. From that time on, I have found myself more often on that same ground, getting the negative effects of insensitive neighbors. The seed of moral and ethical behavior had sprouted and grown within me. I tried to tolerate my neighbors, no matter the depths of their inconsideration.

In one suburban setting I withstood the incessant barking of the dog next door for as long as I could. I found that whispering "Shhhh" when he barked would quiet him for a few minutes at a time. When he was no longer curious enough to respond to the shushing with silence, I imitated his bark. That worked even better. However, my own barking did not go unnoticed. My other neighbor checked with the county, found I didn't have a license for the "dog" that they heard, and got the county to send an official notice to license my non-existent pet. I silently endured as much of the real barking as I could, and then I moved.

Next, I moved way out in the country, where neighbors and their pets roamed about untethered. I replaced my imaginary dog with the real thing, and hand-lettered a warning sign for potential intruders

"BEWARE: VISCOUS DOG"

One neighbor stopped in and told me that the sign was spelled wrong. I pointed to the sluggish, snoring pile of fur on the porch. One of the dog's eyes opened halfway, his fullest recognition and alert to potential intruders.

"No," I said. "The sign is right. His name is Molasses."

Temporal Contusion

J. E. Bruno, Copyright 1999, 2019

My throat and eyes were dry. My head felt like it kissed the concrete. There was a throbbing bump between my forehead and left ear. Not my first hangover, or fight. I couldn't seem to recall drinking or fighting. At least I don't falsely swear off the stuff every time I get a headache. I tried to focus my brain before I opened my eyes. Dark—too dark to see anything. There are sounds of breathing, a ticking noise, someone yelling or singing several walls away. Please let me be home.

Couldn't be. It didn't feel like home at all. Through the strong odor of alcohol and cigarette smoke I know this can't be home. A hint of commercial disinfectant seemed to drift along, nearly lost in a scent cloud borne of pungent humanity. I could not avoid the strong odor of men—men who needed a shower more than I did. Even in my early twenties, interminable student, I was lucky to have stayed out of jail for this long. Hell, as long as just being drunk in public is a crime in my town, I have avoided a hundred visits to the tank. Mercy fell partly upon me. I guess another hour passed. The second waking was a rerun. Not much has changed, except I could detect daylight, even with my eyes closed. A faint coffee smell drifted along with the more obnoxious scents. What the hell? Forcing my eyes open, I braved the light that was increasing around me. Not jail–good. Not much better. Some kind of flop, maybe a homeless shelter. I threw off the coarse blanket. I was dressed in my normal style: boots, jeans, t-shirt, ballcap, and a denim jacket. The clothes were familiar enough, kind of new-looking.

It was automatic, reaching into my pocket to learn the extent of my binge. Usually I have a few bucks left over. No money. No wallet. No change. Somebody had to have taken my wallet. I usually kept a ten or a twenty there, if I had it. Muggers might believe that is all I've got. When my student loans came, sometimes a month after a semester was over, I carried the cash around. In my normally grubby state, who would know that I could have a thousand or more on me? Not this morning. I felt along the left side of my front pocket where I am in the habit of adding a secret place to hold a knife. There was no knife, no sheath—no special pocket at all. After a night a year ago when I was robbed of my last four dollars I had begun to carry a blade in a leather sheath I made from an old shoe. Four bucks isn't much, unless it's all you've got. I didn't plan to let anyone take my money again without a fight. Someone got me anyway, and with no secret pocket these jeans can't be mine either.

Along the right side of my waistband I felt what should be a folded twenty, wrapped around a couple of quarters. These *are* my pants. I took inventory of my other pockets: comb, matches, a tissue, and three toothpicks. This did little to improve the start of my day. Around me, four guys slept on thin mats on the floor. Snores across the hall meant more of the same scenery. The light, harsher now that it was more directly on my face, glared on the greasy-looking window. I got up slowly, moaning from a few sore places, not knowing how they got that way. The hall was painted a spring green, smeared with the accumulated grime of the hundreds of hands that had guided drunk men's bodies between the walls. I could see a large room with a desk and tables at the far end of the hall, the only possible way out. Two shabby men were putting benches in a row. I located the source of the coffee aroma, moved toward it. A man in a minister's collar and a black coat stepped between me and the urn. "Rules!" he said. "Sermon first, then breakfast."

I saw the door to the outside. "I don't need anything that badly." I said.

He didn't say any more. I was out the door. The sudden full sun was too bright. Out of place. Made my head hurt more. Along the street there were...palm trees? Last I recalled I was too far up north for anything like that. North was home, with pine trees, mountains, and winter that took up too many months of the year. How did I get here? Where was here? The more I walked the more I figured I must be in Florida. I could smell salt water; and I walked in the direction of the sun, several blocks, until the ocean appeared in the distance.

There was a sidewalk cafe with pink awnings and tables. A couple was walking from their table, and as soon as they went around a corner, I grabbed for their leavings. I drained a half-cup of too-sweet coffee, lipstick on the rim, gone in a gulp. A full glass of water disappeared as if I opened my throat and it fell straight down into my stomach. A thin waiter was moving towards me.

"Hey! Don't touch my tip, you bum!"

I hadn't noticed the two ones that he rushed to grab. Crackers and a roll were in my pocket as he snatched the two singles. I picked up a triangle of toast, giving the waiter my sharpest "Don't mess with me" look. I made a fist and growled at him. "You shouldn't call people names when they're bigger than you."

He took a step back, his mouth moving silently. I crammed the toast into my mouth. Hunger, begging, and eating discards–none of that was new to me. It was always a cycle with my scholarship leaving a couple hundred, then a carryover loan, then the big semi-annual loan. The checks were irregular, and in between were the leaner days. I signed whatever they put in front of me. Eating a stranger's leftovers wasn't so bad. Better than searching cans and dumpsters with hunger and thirst pushed back a little from my thought process. I walked away from the café quickly, thinking that they could call the cops. How in the hell did I get to Florida? Some of my drinking buddies were crazy enough to put me on a train south, in a car on a car carrier perhaps. They wouldn't spend any money on such a prank. That would cut into the drink budget. I could not remember any trip, or last night at all. I remembered a girl named Sylvia from the night before. Or was it the night before that?

Traffic was building on the streets. Some of the cars I saw were unfamiliar. Then again, most of the cars where I lived were old, ten or more years. Never really see many new ones. Never follow the ads, either. I'd rather read a book than a paper, not much use for TV.

No matter how I got here, I had to get back. My little third-floor room was the longest walk away that it's ever been. Options. Twenty bucks, no ID, no one to call that would or could help. I wouldn't steal as long as I could get work under the table. I didn't consider taking leftovers stealing. That was using food that would have gone to waste. Broom, mop, shovel, hammer—my forearms were solid from one or the other of these since I was big enough to get hired. Never any benefits. Longest time on any job? Three months. I didn't have to worry about where to sleep. Inside or out, didn't matter in Florida. Might take three or four days to get enough cash to get back to the north and my home.

I started walking north. Might as well get a little closer to my eventual destination. Two miles or two thousand, each step was in the right direction. The first construction site I came to "let" me carry three-quarter plywood for two hours. Didn't care much for bosses who used that term, like it's going to be fun. I took the ten bucks they gave me and moved on. I lucked into another building site where a foreman needed help. Used a shovel until dark, backfilling a new foundation where the bulldozer couldn't get in because they saved as many of the palm trees as possible. The foreman was good to go and get sandwiches, smart not to ask questions.

I had hope. "Got anything for me tomorrow?"

"Show up by seven. We've got two other sites working. We'll be sure to find you something if you are on time and sober."

I thanked him, pretending that I had a place to go home to. The food I was given would keep me good for the night. I walked around the block and sat on a bench, giving the other workers time to clear out. I walked back to the building site, propped up pieces of plywood to make a wooden "tent" along one of the inside walls. It was home for the night.

I was stiff and sore when my mental alarm got me up and going. It was starting to lighten up towards the horizon. I figured I had about an hour to go get a bite to eat and get back. The portable toilet on the site was adequate, but I needed to clean up.

A gas station bathroom was a welcome spot to get myself ready for another day. I was shocked at my face in the mirror. There were bumps, scrapes, and cuts on my face; blue-black bruises with yellow edges gave me a gruesome look. It would heal, but it was no wonder why some people had been backing away from me. I washed off the worst of the dirt and dried blood, smeared liquid soap under my arms, rinsed and blotted with paper towels. Inside the gas station high-priced grocery items beckoned. Damn the price. I had little time to get back to the worksite, and I had to eat in order to work. A box of six donuts and a quart of milk cost four bucks. Downed it all in five minutes, made it to the site as the foreman was arriving from the opposite direction. I imagined him leaving a comfortable bed and a pretty wife, getting a balanced meal into his stomach. I wondered what he was thinking about me.

"On time," he said, practically shouting, as if in disbelief, "very good. Let's see what you can do with a hammer. We want to get the rest of the walls up 'cause the roof trusses are on the way, should be here soon.

I did my best, made few mistakes. I didn't see how it got ordered, but a kid showed up with three pizzas. The sun was beginning to redden some wisps of cloud in the west. The foreman pulled out a six-pack from a big red cooler on the back of his truck.

"Work tomorrow?" I asked.

"Preachers and the devil the only ones who work on Sunday. If you want to work Monday, you'll find us in Emory—seventy miles south of here. I can give you the address. We won't be back here until Tuesday. Let me give you what you I owe for your two days' work."

He pulled out a mass of folded bills, counted off ten twenties. "I could use you, should you want to come to the Emory job."

I was shocked. "That's a week's pay. You barely got two day's work from me...."

"Anyone paying you two bills a week is cheatin' you. It's yours and you earned every cent. I wish all my men put in the same effort."

He offered me a ride, but I told him I had some business that needed doing. After hiding out for a while, I came back to the walls I had been putting up all day. I got my wooden tent together once again and settled in for the night. As I fell asleep, I had thoughts about staying where I was, forget going back north. The money was better than I would get, should I finally get my degree. Planning to be a teacher was the same as planning to be poor. This new situation was an open door if I would choose it. My education was leading to a bunch of doors that I hadn't as much as knocked on yet.

Sunday broke hot. Took hours to find the bus station. No one was out and about, the streets full of cars and trucks, no pedestrians to speak of. The guy at the ticket window told me a ticket to Starne's Point was $112. It was a lot of money, but what could I say? I paid and waited for the boarding announcement, ticket in my pocket.

I visited the bathroom, coming out to find the cops talking to the ticket guy. I slid by them looking over their shoulders. They had a picture of me. My growth of beard, along with the bruises and ballcap pulled down low, helped to disguise me. They walked right by me, no more than a glance my way. Damn—what did I do? I went back to the ticket window.

"Who they looking for?"

The guy slid the picture toward me. "Kinda looks like you."

"Why do they want that fella?"

"They didn't say. We're supposed to call if we see you. I mean him."

I put a twenty on top of the picture, then said, "I don't think they're going to find him around here, do you?"

"I think you're right. He's probably long gone."

Things seemed okay. I got on the bus. The driver looked at my ticket, then talked to me like I was five years old. "We'll be going for three stops, then you will change buses in Georgia. I'll let you know. From there, you will have about 22 more hours to New York."

We didn't get that far. More cops and a roadblock, not five miles out from the bus station. They were all standing there, looking up and down the bus while I sat slumped in my seat playing the part of a sleeper. Through my nearly closed eyes I saw the cops and the driver talking along the driver's side of the bus. One of the cops appeared to be pointing directly at me. I slumped down some more. Since they were all on the driver's side I took the only way out, slipped down the aisle and out the door. I ran straight for some trees, the only cover closer than a hundred yards. I made it to the little grove, looked back to see them all getting on the bus to search for me. The older cop was waving his arms around. They knew I had been on the bus, but my run for the trees had not been seen. I waited until dark, came back to the road, and started hitching.

I walked all night. I had had bad luck hitching before, never as bad as this. A thousand cars and trucks went by. Now it was looking like rain. I got off the road, feeling some hunger pains, looking for any place where I could get some shelter. There was a row of gaudy fast-food places, names I had never heard before. I picked the closest one, washing up before getting a couple of reasonably priced breakfast sandwiches. People's expressions when they were near me let me know that washing was not all I needed to do. I had to get a new shirt. The funk of wearing the same shirt for three or more days was getting to *me*, too. I saw a man who appeared to be a member of the outsiders—homeless. He gave me directions to the closest used-clothing store, and I gave him a buck for the information.

I got two T-shirts for a buck each, rolling one up tight to fit in my inside jacket pocket. I went around the building to change. Before I could get the new shirt on. I got a look at my belly. Two surgical scars. I had had only one as far as I could remember. The newer scar was red, no more than a few months old. Was I going nuts? I was shaking. Did someone drug me? Was I hallucinating? I had breathed exhaust and walked all night. But I'm sure I would remember having surgery. I tapped the newest scar, finding it slightly tender. My head suddenly felt very heavy, my eyes blurry, wouldn't clear.

I found my way to a bridge in a small park, figured I needed sleep more than anything. I found a sandy place under the bridge where people sat to fish. Cigarette butts and beer cans lay about the place. I kicked a couple of cans to clear the sand, then just about fell on my face. Dizzy like I drank too much. Next I knew I was out, dreaming. Dreaming a lot. In this big dream I was married to a pretty blonde; and there was a nice house with a fireplace, a new car, and a dog. I worked in a high school as a guidance counselor. Ha! Ridiculous. It was so real, though. Even saw my wife visiting me in a hospital after surgery, get-well cards from students on the wall. So realistic, all the details.

It was raining when I woke up. It didn't look like it would last. What dreams I had. I checked—the new scar was still there. I knew that was no dream. I felt dizzier than ever, head stuffed with lead, damned heavy, pulling me down, burning like an oven.

The rain let up. I got out from under the bridge, feeling vaguely troll-like, then began walking. The streets looked familiar. *Stupid.*

You've never been here before. I got to a church doorway just as the rain started dropping in waves. Didn't feel like a sermon any more than I did when I woke up in that flop. The door wasn't locked. A minister was in the foyer. He looked like someone I knew. Can't be. Not here. My head was fire, molten heavy lead dragging me down until I was falling to the floor. I fought to stay conscious. A gray cloud closed around my vision. My brain swirled and floated away on the sea of molten lead.

The minister spoke..."Seth? Seth Camden. Your wife...."

That's all I heard, then black silence, relief from the pain....

"Seth? Seth, honey, it's me. The doctor says you'll be okay. You're looking better."

Things were swirling, head heavy. I was rising from the pools of molten lead, seeing things, remembering bits. "Elizabeth? My car...."

"Yes. dear, it's me. They found your car, stripped, of course. You've been missing four days. I was sick with worry, going crazy wondering what happened." She cleared her throat, near tears at the feelings tangled up inside. "I thought I'd never see you again."

"I was trying to get back to Starnes Point."

"Your old college town? It's been fifteen years since you were in college. You took me there once. Who is Sylvia? You said her name a lot before you came to."

"I...I don't know. I must have lost some time, I guess."

"I guess you did if you thought you were back in college. They did a scan on that banged-up head of yours. The car-jackers must have hit you hard. You had a partial blockage to your brain, like a mini-stroke, they said. You're very lucky, hon."

"I was working."

"Huh?"

"I was working construction a couple of days. I didn't remember you, or home, or... I thought you were a dream. I'm sorry." I started crying, remembering more things, dark curtains moving away from the pictures in my mind.

"It wasn't your fault. You're with us now."

"The police were looking for me."

"Of course they were. It's their job to look for missing persons. Why did you run away from them?

"I thought I was in trouble, maybe I'd gotten into a fight or something."

"We'll piece things together eventually. You need to rest more, and I do, too. I've been here for 14 hours waiting for you to wake up. I would have stayed forever." She kissed me on the cheek and walked out.

Right after Elizabeth left, a nurse came into the room and began her routine—checking temperature, pulse, blood pressure, all the while holding my forearm to her hip. "Hello, Mr. Camden. We need to check your vitals. You've certainly improved since you were brought in last night. You look much better. We're changing shifts, and I'll be in charge of the floor tonight. If you need anything, use the call button there on your bed and ask for me. My name is Sylvia."

Marilyn Orr Cruz

Bio

Marilyn Orr Cruz is a Native New Yorker, born in Manhattan and raised in the Bronx. She went to John Dwyer Junior High, Morris High, and Monroe School of Business. She married twice, was divorced once and was widowed from her second marriage at the age of forty. She returned to school at Fordham University and studied Psychology. She left Fordham to pursue a career in the fashion industry, in which she spent 25 years working for nurturing and generous employers who encouraged her to grow with the company. She traveled to England; to many Middle Eastern countries—including Egypt, Turkey, and the UAE; and to Pakistan—doing production coordination, product development, and enforcing U.S. customs regulations and compliance laws.

Always involved with children and community, she co-founded "St. Margaret's Little Theater" in the South Bronx, in which she adapted vignettes of lavish Broadway productions, such as Chekov's classic one-act play "Swan Song." She exposed the gifted youth to every aspect of Theater Arts, including acting, costume and set design, promotion, and publicity. Several of the youngsters went on to pursue careers in the arts and are professional authors, artists, actors, and playwrights today.

Marilyn spent 15 years on the Board of Directors of the Parkchester-Bronxdale Day Care Association, which governed three nursery schools that implemented the mainstreaming of mentally and physically handicapped pre-school children into the same classrooms with non-handicapped children in the NYC Public School system.

During these years she also attended NYU where she pursued programs in Creative Writing and Journalism, receiving her diploma and certification in the latter.

She has three sons—Craig, Mark, and Edward; five grandchildren, eleven great-grandchildren, and three great-great-grandchildren. She currently lives in sunny Florida with her mate of 40 years, Carl Feoli, enjoying writing and time with family.

Three novels of Marilyn—*Mackey: A Different Kind of Love Story*; *Cops: A Bronx Tragedy*; and *Bridgewater State*—have received five-star ratings.

A resident of Kings Point Golf and Country Club, Marilyn enjoys the collegiality and friendship of the talented writers, poets, and artists of the Kings Point Creative Writers Club.

It Rained in Central Park Today

It rained in Central Park today.
Soft rain. Rain barely wet.
Water beads my windshield.
Clouds looming ever yet.

Ah me, I love the rainstorms,
When Heaven rages war.
Thunder's din 'n lightning's flash.
Those furies tap my core.

This gentle rain is you. Not me.
It falls with grace and calm.
Touching down upon the earth.
Too mild to ever harm.

My car spins down the winding road.
Your smile comes back so clear.
Our passions were so different,
Thus.... The reason you're not here.

At first the pain was sharp and deep,
You left without a fight.
I thought you such a coward then.
To sneak off in the night.

But time is such a healer,
And hearts do mend anew.
Now mornings just like this one.
I smile and think of you.

It rained in Central Park today.
Soft rain. Rain barely wet.
I smiled. And thought of you, and rain.
Ever grateful that we met!

Ode to a Suicidal Friend...

You dwell too much with death, my friend.
There is no mystery.
So rapt you are by the unknown,
You spin your fantasy.

Deep intrigue,
And rituals,
Mahogany
So neat.
Marble Angels...
Profound words,
Etched around their feet.

Oh! How we tend to glamorize death...

Remember Camille...
How beautifully she passed,
Smiling, gardenia in hand... From tuberculosis.

I think not!

Romeo and Juliet...
How wonderfully romantic,
To die from love! And Poison.
I think not!

And Jesus Christ,
The Ultimate Love and Sacrifice...
Dare you compare!
I think not!

You dwell too much
With death, my friend...
Yes much. And all for naught!
It is, for every creature,
The fate that Nature's fraught.

Let go, my friend, of Lady Death,
Let go her magic charm.
Your union's sealed in destiny,
Your end... No great Alarm!

Celebrate your life, my friend,
With things you've yet to know,
The passion from within you,
That makes your juices flow!

With Joy! Embrace the wonders,
That each new day imparts.
Laugh a lot. And Cry a lot.
Live only by your heart.

Dwell not too much with Death, my friend.
The Lady waits.... Fear not.
She waits, and waits, and you'll be there,

When she selects your lot.

Time

How faint we walk, through valleys worn
O'er fragile beings... time has tom
Remember her... remember them
Oh yes! Recall! Remember when

Youth is so quick, to come and go.
Those wasted years, how could we know
That time would pass at such a pace
Caring not what we must face

Regrets? Not me! It's been great fun
I have to laugh at things I've done
Some days brought tears I do recall
Thank God I can't remember all

The children run and play so free
This moment being all they see
Tomorrow seems so far away
They live today. For just today

You nurture well the seeds you sow
You watch them grow and then let go
You pray to God that you've done well
But know that only time will tell

There is no way to let them know
That they might face a life of woe
You watch their journey up and down
And sometimes pray it turns around

Some day they'll reach this place and know
The time has come for them to go

For those faint walks through valleys worn
And praise God's gift of each new mom

Vacations... Apart

Hello,
I hope you're doing well,
The weather here is fine.
The kids are having loads of fun,
I'm sad you chose to stay behind.

We did the beach this morning....

I watched the children laugh and play,
Their balls of color filled the sky.
Balloons on string against the clouds.
With glee they let them soar and fly.
Their tiny hands held on so tight,
Afraid they might get free.
I felt their joy,
I felt their fear,
I thought of you and me.

My Darling,
It's your balloon I am, you know.
Your breath has filled my body so.
You gave me life... to float and fly,
To tease the wind, and soar the sky.
There was no limit to my height,
Secure your hand would hold me tight.

Stormy days... Time did unfold,
To test your heart, and dare your soul.
To weary your hand, and loosen your grip.
To make the ties that bind us slip.

Though winds grow strong,
And challenge your might,
Please don't let go.
I need you so.
Conduct.
Control.
My flight!

Irresolute

The pain is sharp and deep
Much too deep to know.
How to open up one's heart
And how to let it go.

It bums the gut like fire
It grips the throat, what pain!
It spirals upward to the head
Electrifies the brain.

Breathe deep and hold on tightly
Push forward with your guile.
Swallow hard, clear your throat
Then force that neat tight smile.

Your eyes connect, and lock
You dare not be the first to blink.
Your chest is pounding wildly
Your spirit starts to sink.

He waves in recognition
New female friend in tow.
And heads directly toward you
There is nowhere to go!

His hand is gentle on her arm
Her smile is broad. Her eyes are clear.
Her head tilts slightly toward his chest
His lips touch gently on her hair.

She grabs your hand and pumps it
You're frozen there in pain.
He smiles and takes your other hand
And softly says your name.

His lips touch on your fingertips
The din of nightlife fades to still.
You stand there rapt, under his spell
Devoid of your own will.

"I'm so glad we met," she says.
"He speaks so highly of you."
You nod and then step backward
Not knowing what to do.

He touches your bare shoulder
His hand against your skin.
Brings back a flood of memories
Since, buried deep within.

And as they slowly move away.
His eyes are locked with yours.
A look you shared so many times
That rocks your very core.

Your head in conflict with your heart
Is this a game of lure?

What does this mean. Is it done?
Or dare you pray for more.

And When I'm Gone...

For my sons, my grandchildren, my great-grandchildren and my
great-great-grandchildren...and the extended family that I love.

Do not scream and tear your hair.
Weep gently for Our loss.
For I will miss you just as much,
Until our paths re-cross.

Reluctant as I leave this life,
My time has come to part.
I bid this body sweet adieu.
My soul will host my heart.

Another place, another form,
For somehow life will always be.
I promise to watch over you.
Cling tight to memories of me!

Look for me in the morning dew,
I'm cool damp grass beneath your feet.
And do not shield the midday sun,
It's my warm hand...upon your cheek.

When glasses touch 'n church bells chime.
It's nature's laughter that you hear.
Recall, our silly giddy times.
And the pleasures that we share.

You'll see the sparkle of my eyes.
In the diamond glints on snow.
They shine with pride I can't contain.

As I watch you grow...and grow.

I dwell with all the works of God,
The autumn rain, the winter storm.
I'll follow you through every day,
It matters not my form.

The day will come we'll meet again.
You'll join my world so new.
And help watch o'er the ones we love,
Till they...then join us too.

Looking Backwards...a Longing

There was a time that I thought I could recapture the solace of my childhood by visiting my old neighborhood. I was losing loved ones so fast that I needed to turn time backwards to a more secure time. I needed to be able to see them and hear them and smell them. I was sure I would find peace evoking the memories of my childhood in that old house.

I scaled the gray slate stoop two steps at a time and pushed open the large glass and wrought iron door. I almost expected to see Mr. James, the elevator operator, in his black pinstripe suit and blue shirt sitting on the high stool in front of the elevator. *Over the years whenever I saw a Charlie Chaplain movie, I thought of James; they could have been twins.* Instead, when I opened the glass doors and stepped into the lobby, it was deserted and I hardly remembered having been there before. The interior was dark and dingy. The only window in the corner by the stairwell was boarded up, denying entrance to intruders and to the sun's bright rays that used to splash across the marble interior, outshining the glow of the incandescent chandeliers. I felt extremely uneasy and quickly exited back to the street and daylight. *It was an insane idea.* I thought, as I stepped over crack vials, looking over my shoulder every few steps. *Whatever made me think that I could go back?*

I guess it's something that tugs at all of us, wanting to see again what we remember so clearly as the best times of our lives. When everyone was young and innocent.

I crossed Seventh Avenue at 110th Street to the entrance of Central Park and slowly walked down the familiar path that had been my childhood playground. On either side of me there were corrugated cartons that represented makeshift shelters and blue plastic tarps covering bodies huddling for refuge from the bitter cold. I sat on a nearby bench and admonished myself for having made the trip. *Some things are lost with time, never to be recaptured.* But I sat there on the bench for a while, remembering how good it used to be.

We were a large family and lived in a huge apartment across from Central Park. We had four bedrooms, kitchen, dining room, and the family living room where we would gather around the old console radio and listen to the squeaking doors of the Inner Sanctum. The living room also held our piano and was where we entertained each other and our weekend guests. My Aunt Lily and my cousins Richard and Vilma lived only a few doors up the street, and they were always at our house and did everything with us.

Saturday was the happiest day of our week. After piano lessons we were allowed to go across the street to the park. I had three siblings, my sister Shirley and my two brothers Carlton and Bernard. We all took piano lessons. I was the youngest and the last to play. Mrs. Woodward, our instructor, told my parents that I was her most difficult student. I think she just couldn't understand my objection to being whacked across the knuckles with a baton. My sister, brothers, and cousins took it like troopers. I, on the other hand fought back, one time taking the baton out of her hand and flinging it across the room. After that my lessons ended. It was obvious I was not going to be a pianist. Shirley taught me to play "Claire de Lune" without lessons, and I was so pleased. *For more than twenty years, ironically, a piano was a part of my own living*

room and my sons took lessons, but each time I sat on the bench I
could only remember "Claire de Lune."

Hands clasped, dragging two sleds, pails, and shovels, we would
head for the park across the street. Bunny and I always carried lots
of old newspapers to make boats. Even in the winter we would fold
the paper into sailboats and float them between the chunks of ice
on the lake, guiding them until they sank. We broke long switches
from the trees and used them to guide the boats long after they
were out of our reach. After boating we would take turns sledding
down the snow-covered soft slopes that surrounded Meer Lake.
We often played there until dusk. When evening fell and the comer
lamppost lights went on, we would grab our belongings and head
for home. Being in the house before dark was a rule, and breaking
it meant severe punishment, so we would diligently watch the
changing sky and the comer lamppost.

Sunday dinner was earlier than other days. It was always in mid-
afternoon after church service let out. Every Sunday our dining-
room table was filled with aunts and uncles and cousins. Later in
the evening when dinner was over, we would retreat to the living
room where my mother played the piano while my aunt Rose sang.
Shirley and Vilma would play piano while Carlton and Richard
took turns singing. Even Bunny played the piano and tried to sing.
It seemed that everyone had a special talent except me. I felt like a
misfit. I was the youngest, but I was the tallest, the skinniest, and
felt like the most useless because I wasn't able to master piano,
voice, or dance lessons like my siblings and cousins.

Although it was not in our Parish, the family attended St. Ambrose
Episcopal Church. The Vicar, Father Durant, had migrated from
Barbados with my grandparents; and the families bonded. Every
Sunday we all took the bus uptown to 130th street to go to mass.
Every year the Church held a recital and all of the Sunday school
classes were compelled to participate. I remember the year
they celebrated Mother Earth and the growth of the "Vegetable
Garden." Talented or not, every student was assigned a part in
the performance. My sister Shirley got the coveted position of

the *center of the radish*. She stood there on tiptoes, dressed in sparkling white, the gold locket that Daddy gave her gleaming around her neck. The girls surrounding her were dressed as the red radish peels and as green leaves dancing around and waving their arms to and fro, as though wafting in the breeze. I stood there in the wings watching everyone perform, nervously waiting for my cue. When my turn did come, the music director Mrs. Woodward touched me on the shoulder, and I froze. My feet were glued to the floor and I couldn't breathe. She gave me a gentle shove and I was on stage...terrified and still clutching the curtain.

I quickly looked over to my sister and she looked back and smiled and nodded. I slowly let go of the curtain and stood frozen on the stage staring at Shirley. The huge round spotlight rolled around the ceiling, then across the velvet curtain, then fell upon the stage in front of me. Shirley looked at me, lifted her foot, and pointed her toe. I nervously followed her lead lifting my foot and pointing my toe, I stepped into the glowing circle of light on the floor in front of me. Together we raised our arms and the spotlight's bright rays bounced off the colorful jewels that studded my butterfly wings. Suddenly I was beautiful. Shirley smiled and nodded again, I pointed my toe and took my first dance step. I could hear applauds from the darkness in front of me. And I danced. That was the first time Shirley saved me. The first of so many times to follow over the years.

I pushed my hands into my pockets and rose from the park bench. The sun was going down and the air was getting nippy. I walked back to Eighth Avenue, slipped into my freezing car and turned the heater on. I headed north and took the local streets towards the highway entrance at 125th Street. At the corner of 114th Street I passed my grandfather's shoemaker shop, which was now a Chinese take-out restaurant. The Morningside movie theater on the next block was boarded up. I smiled remembering the free movie theater passes we used to get because my grandfather let them place their advertising placards in his shop's front window. I turned right on 125th Street and got back on the West Side Highway heading north.

Everything changes, I thought, and you can't ever go back. The car was warm; I unbuttoned my collar and loosened my scarf. My hand brushed against Shirley's gold locket at my neck, and my eyes burned with tears. Shirley's gone now, as are Bunny and Vilma and Mom and Dad.

I realized that day that I didn't need that old house to find my resolve. I carry it in my heart forever, along with the people that rooted it there.

Laurie Faber

Bio

After a 30-year career teaching and evaluating middle school students in Harlem, I turned back fully to my passions of music and writing. Prior to having my son I had composed lyrics and arrangements for piano and guitar. I had sung on Telegraph Avenue in Berkeley in the '60s, in bands, in Manhattan clubs, and overseas. What fun!

Serious prose writing came later for me, starting when I had a sabbatical from my job, took a creative writing class, and received positive feedback from my professor. The first chapter in what has become a novel appeared in our first anthology two years ago. The tentative title is *Hope in Harlem: One Family's Story.*

I am a Jewish, bisexual single mother by choice of a 34-year-old son whom I conceived by anonymous donor insemination in 1985. Evan grew up to be a well-adjusted and successful man, who was able, through much research (this was before Ancestry.com) to identify his birth father. Their first meeting couldn't have gone better, and I met the father soon thereafter. He and Evan continue to stay in touch and Evan has a fuller family tree now, including half-siblings he has met through the years. Getting to know his birth father has had a profound and most positive influence on him.

My story in this anthology, the first chapter of a second novel, was inspired by my LGBTQ community, experiences through the HIV/AIDS epidemic, and by my son who continues to be my most cherished dream come true. It took place in 1983 and, as such, does not reflect the medical and social advances that have subsequently occurred.

Don't Drown at Dawn

We waken to the drip of dark, dank rain
Smearing the windows of our minds
Although the sky is clear many thoughts of dread
Keep us drowning and down

What is there to fear besides life itself
And all it can do to us
How much strength we need
To get us through the scary hours

I hold you, we're warm
You hold me, we're safe
Together, for always, we'll make it

We each don't want to leave yet
The smog of sleep still here
Reaches out to strangle courage
And keep us in frozen panic

Who will hurt us somewhere out there?
Who will burn our fragile flint of hope?

If we stay right here
And speak to no one else
Will that stop the dreadful despair
We've both so often felt?

I hold you, we're warm
You hold me, we're safe
Together, for always, we'll make it

You've gone now, my day must start
Our dreams for tomorrow
Must remain in our hearts

But reality calls to break us apart

Some small clutch of fright
Then a smile and a sigh
I go to face the world
And hope I'll get by

I hold you, we're warm
You hold me, we're safe
Together, for always, we'll make it

Ease My Mind

Ease my mind
We'll float above the clutter of the day
Ease my mind
We'll be together knowing what to say

'Cause easy minds don't need a reason
And easy minds don't need a game
We can have this time together
Ease my mind

Try to hear my heart beat
Give your hand to me
Walk beside the river
Sing your melody

Feel me melting to you
Tender reverie
We can have this time together
Ease my mind

Hear me laughing with you
Feel me sigh inside
You know all about me
I won't try to hide

Show me that you want me
Love me with your eyes
We can have this time together
Ease my mind

We can have this time together
Ease my mind

Lyrics to "If The Flowers Learn To Cry" by Laurie E. Faber ©1978

If the flowers learn to cry
Will that be our final sign?
If the flowers learn to cry
Will the world have lost its rhyme?

We used to live with our Earth Mother
Sharing Nature all as friends
But if the flowers learn to cry
Will our planet ever mend?

Flowers live so short a time
Yet they're forever with the Earth
Flaming colors blooming wild
And how wondrous are their births.

We used to live with our Earth Mother
Sharing Nature all as friends
But if the flowers learn to cry
Might that be the very end?

No, the world would not rejoice
Hearing weeping above the ground
But can you see there's still a choice?
There's still time to turn around.

If the flowers learn to cry
Their tears might be a drowning sea
Or a burst of sparkling rainbows
One more chance for you and me.

If the flowers learn to cry
Will that be our final sign?
If the flowers learn to cry
Will the world have lost its rhyme?

Will the sun then close its eyes
Darkness flooding through the skies?
Let's not lose this precious time
Don't let the flowers learn to cry.

Harmony with our Earth Mother
Don't let the flowers learn to cry.

It Just Might Be

"What was the Earth like when you were a child?" my Lizzie
wanted to know.
"Was it always so gray out and smoky and dark? How did the
concrete grow?"
Up in the attic I found an old book and took the child on my knee
Hoping to show her a bit of the old life, a good life that once used
to be.

As I turned each page and read aloud
My tears started falling inside

For the ways we had lost, the terrible cost
Of the "progress" for which we had tried.

"On a hillside near the farm is a field of colorful, wild flowers and
sounds of bees and crickets, birds and mice fill your ears. When
the warm breeze blows by and the sun glows through snowy white
clouds, all the sweet fragrances of this unblemished setting are all
around you. The puppy runs and plays all day while the cows graze
in the grass. There's a rainbow of colors caressing the Earth and a
feeling of peace all around."

"When can we go there and see all these things?
When can I breathe that sweet air?"
If I only had answers to my dear daughter's pleas
If only we all had just cared.

The field would still be here, the trees would yet grow, flowers
around every gate.
The piles of rubbish and smoke-filled balloons wouldn't have been
our fate.

Night on the Porch by Laurie E. Faber ©1993

I'd never slept outdoors before.
Well, it was a porch with screens
But I was only six and the sky was big.
The wind came through my sheet
And blew my hair as I tried to sleep.

I didn't want to be there.
I volunteered because no other kid would.
Too much company sleeping over
And the grownups didn't want to be out there either.
And now I wonder why.

I wasn't even home.
Stayed the whole summer with cousins
While my folks crossed the country.
It was great fun but not this night.

The warm August breeze made apples fall
With uneven thuds onto the roots,
Sometimes onto the roof.
Those were louder,
Sometimes like awkward footsteps.

The full moon sent shadows through the trees
Onto my cot,
Ever-changing shadows as the breeze swept the leaves into a dance.
That would have been fine if I had company
But I was only six and real became weird,
Leaves became monsters,
And everyone seemed so far away.

Even the crickets couldn't soothe me
With their rhythmic song always the same.
In my mind it became another:
Why am I here?
Why am I scared?
Why can't I tell?

I'd never even slept alone before.
My aunt would be upset
Even forty years later
When I told her the torture of that night,
And all the nights since when, again,
For one reason or another, I couldn't say "No."

Lyrics to "Open The Chains Around Me"

How do I turn my life around
How do I dare to change
When will I give up the suff'ring
And look at myself as a friend

Now is the time to make memories
I need some ways to be free
Patterns have got to be broken
Open The Chains Around Me

Won't be easy to find the answers
Often easy to be left behind
Seldom easy to seek a new way
Open The Chains Around Me

Will you turn your life around
Will you dare to change
Can you share my new-found fantasies
And look at yourself as a friend

Now is the time to make memories
We need more ways to be free
Patterns have got to be broken
Open The Chains with the key

Yes, Open The Chains with the key

Sun and Lovers

Swirling stars of snowflakes
Danced all through the dawn
While wild winds blew crispy leaves
From trees to ground they'd swarm

Like insects on a rampage
Attacking on the fly
Shadowed, crushed, and splintered
'Neath the watchful sunrise eye

Cozy by the fire
The lovers lay all curled
Blankets smoked with marshmallow
Joyous in their world

Light from scarlet embers
Glowing through their eyes
Echoed the reflections
Of sunlight in the sky

With the warmth the snow melts
And love grows fast and strong
But will they long remember
They're where they both belong?

The Crystal Vase

Awakened by my crying cat
Six-thirty Sunday morning,
My body tensed, eyes swollen
From last night's heartrending sobs.
I recall sleeping visions of the car
Weaving wildly
Brakes slipping
The children terrified
The plans ruined.

And now fully awake,
I feel a horrific familiar terror.
I am like an exquisite crystal vase

Wrapped carelessly for shipping
And as I travel and the road gets bumpier
I am vibrating from my inmost recesses
And tiny fissures begin to spread all through me.

If I cannot control my own journey
Not only will I fail to reach my destinations
But will not be there to guide my son toward his.
I need a special glue made from my very guts
To squirt delicately but firmly into those cracks
As I rest just a bit while I mend.

Lyrics to "The Mirror"

This time's going be different, she said
As she looked for agreement in her eyes
Staring before the mirror
She knew the stirring of feeling inside

And she pointed a warning finger at the face
With such changes it brought her surprise

This time's going to be different
Honest and trusting and kind
This time's going to be different
Better somehow and mine

Can I learn to learn to love without an ending
Can I learn to give without expecting a return
Can I learn to care about both women and men too
I'm tired of the games
Not willing for the same again

I want to live my life for real now
Find a smile to mirror in my mind

I want to laugh and dance and try to catch the sun
Find a space to mirror with my smile.

And she pointed a warning finger at the face
That too often had told herself lies

This time's going to be different
Honest and trusting and kind
This time's going to be different
Better somehow and mine

Lyrics to "The Struggle"

He struggles with his genuine convictions
Stimulates the passions of his mind
Reflecting projections of a spinning reality
Oh my, my

How will he find a peaceful time
When will a focus come
Might people destroy his inborn innocence
Will he change for anyone

So easy to laugh it off
So easy to cry
So good to feel his pain easing
Oh my, my

'Cause when a truce comes and it will for a while
He'll smile again, then sigh
For the loss of the anguish he chose not to avoid
Oh my, my

How will he find a peaceful time
When will a focus come
Might people destroy his inborn innocence

Will he change for anyone

Don't think he'll change for anyone
Don't want him to change for anyone

Lyrics to "Time To Make New Memories"

Every time we say hello
Seems we never said good-bye
Seems we always find an easy way to share
You can tell me what you're going through
I can read it in your eyes
We can laugh and sigh about the days gone by

Time to make new memories
Time to find new ways to care
Time to leave the old scrapbook
On the shelf behind the stairs

Time to make new memories
There's so much that we can do
Let's go on a brand new ride
You know I'll go with you

Every year that passes by
All the dreams we've shared so long
Seem to close the distance in our way
And with the choices that we've made
Our friendship will not fade
And that's all I need to face another day

Lyrics to "Until Soon"

You just said goodnight
Your smile surrounds my mind
Inside myself again

With our melodies entwined.

Not so long ago
We were as distance is to time.
In between arrivals
Gave us little chance to rhyme.

Until Soon, my friend
For although I've only known you a little while
Seems you've always been here.

Until Soon, my friend
For although you've just been gone a little while
It seems you're gone so long.

But together we have captured the secrets of space
Made a mockery of distance and time.
I can touch the traces of your tears and your smiles
Just so long as you are here in my mind.

Until Soon, my friend
Although our caring knows no boundaries of time.
Until Soon, my friend
Just so long as I can dream your eyes in mine

I can wait Until Soon
I can wait Until Soon

Lyrics to "What I Never Had"

How can I let another man take your place
How will I let another man touch my face the way you do
Don't you see it was wrong

To try to make me hold on
To someone I never really had

You were cruel without knowing
Now the pain just keeps on growing
And my mind has no place to stay

So I wander around looking for someone
But all the time I'm looking just for you
Trembling inside I say
There must be a better way
But what do I do
I try to hold on to What I Never Had

How can I ask for what you won't give to me
How can I lie and say I want to be free
Tho I know you do
Don't you hear that it's hard
To learn that now you're moving on
To someone you'll meet along the way

You've been free without knowing
Yet your pain I feel it flowing
And your mind's got no place to stay

So you wander around looking for someone
But all the time you're looking just for you
Trembling inside you say
You know that it's the only way
But what do *I* do
I try to hold on to What I Never Had

You never made a promise
You didn't try to fool me
You told me where it's at in so many ways

But I got caught in my own lies
Just refused to realize
And what do I do
I try to hold on to What I Never Had

Holding on to What I Never Had

The FOPA Club

Gabi was in only one of Steve's twelfth-grade classes at Harriet
Tubman High, in the Class of 1987, but he had taken notice of
her right away. *Tall, nice body, spectacular smile, long shiny
golden hair,* thought Steve. *She sure seems comfortable for a
new student. It's just two weeks into September and she's already
making friends with some of the cool girls. She seems really smart,
too. I can't remember the last time I paid so much attention to a
girl. I better snap out of this or I'm going to miss the homework
assignment.*
When the bell for dismissal rang at 2:30 p.m., Steve suppressed his
urge to wait and watch for Gabi, and instead headed straight to the
bulletin board near the cafeteria. Clubs and teams were forming
and the dean had posted the final lists of members. It was pretty
crowded but, at six foot three, he could see over the heads of almost
everyone else. He'd been on the track-and-field team for three years
already so he knew that was a no-brainer. He skipped competitive
athletics and looked for the lists of the other activities. He had
been one of the first to sign up for the new club called "Friends
Of People With AIDS" (FOPA) and was looking to see if he had
gotten in. He glanced down the alphabetical list of nine names and
saw his right away as number three.
All right! I'm in. My Uncle Fred is gonna be so proud of me.
Then he continued to look down the list and felt a hot rush of
excitement flood his face as he caught sight of number six.

Martin. Gabi...Gabi Martin. Gabi! Oh. my God. she's in the club too. I'm finally gonna get to talk to her! His mind immediately went to fantasies of becoming her boyfriend.

"Yes!" he whisper-shouted as he pumped his fist. He looked around and realized his friend Dave had seen him and was coming over.

"What's up, man? What are you so excited about?"

"I, uh, I got into the FOPA Club. It was my first choice and I think it'll be great."

"Oh, well THAT's exciting." Dave smirked sarcastically. He gave Steve a quizzical look, as if to say *What's so exciting about that?*

Steve rolled his eyes. "Ok, you got me. There's this girl I think I like, and she's in the club too. I've been crushing a little bit. This is my chance to get to know her."

"Haha! That makes more sense. That's cool, bro. It's been a while since you liked a girl. I was even beginning to wonder if you were gay."

"Sorry to disappoint you." They both chuckled. They had been friends since kindergarten and knew just about everything there was to know about each other. Last year Dave had come out to his family and Steve had been very supportive. It had gone easier than either of them had thought it would.

"I think I'm straight, at least right now," Steve said with a smile. "But I see your point. Other than you, most of my friends are girls. I find most boys are obsessed with trying to be cool and outlandish but they aren't funny or much fun to be around."

"Yeah, well, I know you're talking mostly about straight guys. Plenty of them are either loud assholes or lame losers, nerdy, and weird. But I don't experience gay guys like that, not most of them anyway."

"Yeah, I guess not. And if you're any indication, then you're right, many gays are probably very different. Still, I do think girls are just smarter, more interesting, and easier to talk to."

They both looked over at two of the football players doing a demonstrative theatrical handshake.

"Girls are like clever-funny instead of dumb-funny." Steve looked right at Dave. "You, of course, are not 'most guys.' You're cool. And we gotta find someone for you. Maybe in one of *your* after-school activities. Did you get into any that you wanted?"

"Yeah! After two years as a reporter I'll finally get to be one of the editors of *The Newspaper Club*. There's always gays in newspaper, so maybe I'll get lucky too. I'm also on the bowling team this year, so that should be fun." They exchanged smiles.

"Good luck with your girlfriend," teased Dave, as he patted Steve's shoulder and turned around to leave.

The next morning just as the bell ending their AP European History class rang, Steve jumped out of his chair and walked up two rows and over one seat. *Well, here goes. I hope I can keep it together.*

"Hi, I'm Steve, Steve Gould."

"Uh, Hi," Gabi replied. Steve thought from the surprised look on her face that she probably hadn't noticed him before. "You're Gabi Martin, right?"

"Yeah—do we...?"

"I saw that we're both in the FOPA Club, and I thought I'd say hi."

"Oh! Hi!" she said with a big smile. Steve was flooded with relief.

"Do you have lunch next period?" Steve asked. "I-I-was wondering if you'd like to maybe get a bite to eat?"

Gabi smiled coyly. "Yeah, sure. That would be nice. I'll just tell the girls I'll see them later. Catch up with you in the caf." Steve watched as Gabi got up, slung her backpack on, and walked toward the door.

Well, that wasn't so hard. But what am I going to say next? Just gotta be chill. Go with the flow. Just be me.

They met at the cashier line.

"You've got good taste," Gabi said as she looked at Steve's tray. Both of them had chosen a tuna-and-greens salad platter with whole wheat bread, a bottle of water, and a piece of fresh fruit.

"Just trying to stay healthy!" Steve said. *That's amazing. With so many other choices we got the same healthy food. That's really important to me in a girlfriend. Whoa, calm down. She's not your girlfriend. Not yet anyway. Just stay in the moment and relax.*

"Wanna eat outside?" Gabi suggested. "It's still very warm for September."

"Yeah, sounds great."

They walked outside to the grassy area of the school's campus, away from the long picnic tables and loud kids, and found an empty table for two.

"This sure is different from my old school across the bay in San Francisco. The only outside area was a fenced-in concrete yard. I love living in Berkeley. I've only been here since July and I already feel like it's home."

"That's great, Gabi. I'm happy for you. I've lived here all my life and, except for going away to college. I think I'd like to stay here forever.

"Do you know where you want to go?" Gabi asked. "We have to start working on our applications!"

"I don't know for sure yet. I might wind up in a big coastal city or I might want to try something really different like the Midwest. What about you?"

"I think I'll probably end up somewhere nearby. We don't have a ton of money and I've heard good things about some of the state colleges. Maybe I'll even get into Berkeley."

"You're sure you want to stay so close to home?"

"Well, my mom and I are close. Pretty much the only thing we butt heads over is curfew. So far she's winning. Gabi rolled her eyes.

"When do you turn eighteen? She'll probably loosen up then?"

"I'm really hoping she will. My birthday is in November, so that's pretty soon. In the meantime I oiled my back door so it doesn't squeak. I think I might try sneaking out some time."

"What would you do?"

"Just go hang out with whoever is up late, I guess, like maybe at the park. Or, if it's on a weekend, maybe I'd come home early from a house party and then sneak back out to it again. I bet my mom would be really pissed. She doesn't get annoyed a lot and we really get along well. But being home by eleven on the weekends is just lame."

"Yeah, but I don't really know what that's like. I have no real curfew on the weekends. My mom just wants me to wake her up with a kiss when I get home. Sometimes it's two or three a.m."

"That's pretty neat. I'm envious. Of course, you're a boy so you can take care of yourself, not like us girls," Gabi said sarcastically. "Some of us, you know, are trained in self-defense these days. I'm a brown belt in karate. Do you practice?

"No, you probably could take me in a few seconds."

"I don't know. With your height and muscle strength it might take closer to four," Gabi said with a mischievous smile. "Your mom sounds pretty cool."

"Not so cool during the week when she gets angry over things that aren't her business, like what time I start my homework. I like to relax with video games first after getting home at six. She doesn't get it. Then we go at it until she either gives up or grounds me. Too many power struggles. But my parents trust me. Then again they don't know some of the things my friends and I do. But don't worry. I'm not a thief in the night or a drug courier. I do smoke grass, only after school and on weekends. We're just having fun."

"I smoke too, but only on the weekends and not much. It sometimes makes me feel really anxious."

"Yeah." said Steve. "It really depends on the grass; but I also think my frame of mind when I smoke enhances whatever mood I'm in, good or bad. This isn't a good segue, but I need to tell you something. I hope you don't think I'm being too forward. I was surprised and very happy to see your name on the FOPA list. I already had wanted to meet you."

"You mean your friend Dave didn't tell you I was asking about you the other day?" Gabi asked with a hint of a blush. "It's hard to miss the guy who asks such interesting questions in class and looks like he could do almost any sport at all except for horse racing."

"You mean you never saw a six-foot-three jockey?"

They both laughed.

"So. Gabi, can I ask you something personal?

"Sure you can. And I can decide whether to answer you or not." Gabi said in an easy-going tone.

"Always." replied Steve seriously.

What a nice guy, thought Gabi. *Instead of going on and on about himself he's genuinely interested in who I am.*

"So." Steve asked, "would you tell me more about your family? Like, do you ever see your dad? Was it really hard, the divorce. I mean. Whoa. I'm sorry, that was way too personal. I just want to get to know you better. Please tell me when to shut up. Maybe we should head back early?"

"No, don't be silly. It was a fine question. Actually, my mom is a lesbian and neither of us has ever met my birth father. She had anonymous donor insemination and this is what she got!" Gabi said with a mischievous smile and pointed to herself. "Surprised? Shocked? Spellbound? Or am I the fifth girl you've met like me?"

"You're actually the first *girl* I've met who was conceived that way. I know two brothers who have two dads. Both dads used the same surrogate mother. She agreed to give them any address and phone changes. Neither of the boys has shown any interest in getting in touch with her. I've wondered how it would feel to not know half of my family background. Can you tell me what it's been like?"

"Well, mostly it's been just fine. Mom told me the truth from the very beginning, As soon as I first asked 'Where's *my* daddy?' when I was two. She said, 'Some families have daddies and some have uncles and a poppy, like you do.'"

"That satisfied me for the moment. There were a few times I got sad and once, really angry. I'll tell you more about that another time. But you didn't say anything about *your* dad. Are you close?

"Not really, but we used to be," Steve replied softly as he hung his head for a moment. "We've all been under a lot of stress because his brother has AIDS and has been living with us for several months. He just keeps getting worse. More than five years and over 16,000 deaths already and they still don't have any treatments. My Uncle Fred needs help with everything and has an aide on weekday mornings. Dad gets him ready for bed around 8 p.m. Then he goes into his study for the rest of the evening. Around 10 p.m. I knock on his door and we have a five-minute, maybe less, conversation. Then he dismisses me with a 'Goodnight, son.' When I try to talk with him after I have an argument with my mom, he's been like 'She's your mother. Just do what she says,' so I stopped trying. He hasn't been getting along so well with my mom either. She's quite homophobic, so he stays away as much as possible. It's upsetting, to say the least. Well, that's enough about my family. I want to hear more about yours and how you guys keep it mostly peaceful."

"Sorry, that'll have to wait until next time," Gabi said as she looked at her watch. "The warning bell is about to ring and we have to walk all the way back to the cafeteria to empty our trays. My next class is at the other end of the building, so I'm going to rush on ahead. See you tomorrow. It was really nice meeting you, Steve."

"Hey, hold on a second, Gabi, okay? I'll keep up with you. Can we do this again tomorrow, before the FOPA meeting? I'd like to know how *you* got interested in it."

"That's okay. I'm sure the leader will want to know that about everyone. Besides, I'll be having a French test right after lunch so I'll be cramming instead of eating. Bye, Steve. See you in class." *Why am I feeling like things didn't end so well just now? Maybe I shouldn't have said so much about my family. She probably wouldn't want someone with serious issues. But, with a test*

tomorrow, she really had a good reason for rushing off so fast.
Don't make a big deal of it. And, remember, you had a super
conversation. Stop doubting yourself, stupid. And don't care too
much too soon.

"Hi, everyone, please come in." the FOPA leader said, as nine
students gathered outside the Group Therapy room of the Guidance
Department. The kids seemed impressed as they walked in and
looked around. The walls were painted a deep orange and large
framed abstract prints were arrayed around the room. There were
ten upholstered recliners and armchairs of various sizes set up in a
large circle. The color scheme was chocolate brown, forest green,
and rich rust. The students were told to leave their backpacks
in a corner, find their names on the table, and take any seat they
wanted. Steve and Gabi sat next to each other in armchairs.

"My name is Moses Jones. You can call me 'Moses' or you can
call me 'Jones' or you can call me 'Mr. Jones' if you really must."
The kids laughed. "I'm a social worker with an organization that
helps people with AIDS. It's called Open Hand and was started in
1985 by an amazing woman named Ruth Brinker. It began when
she tried to help a friend who was living alone and not able to shop
or prepare food for himself anymore. She got some of her friends
to take turns bringing him hot meals but sometimes they forgot or
even went out of town, and the man died. She then started feeding
meals to seven people by herself and the word spread quickly.
People thought she was crazy to expose herself to their germs, but
she wasn't afraid. There was already solid evidence that AIDS isn't
spread through casual contact such as shaking hands, sharing a
toilet, sneezing or coughing, or by social kissing. But it takes a long
time to change hearts and minds.
"There are FOPA clubs like ours in two high schools and two
colleges in the area. They started last year and have been working
out very well. Your principal, Ms. Singh, came to us over the
summer and said there was a need for some help here. She was

obviously aware of some people's stories and hoped there'd be
enough interest to attract others. You're here for different reasons
I'm sure, but one thing you have in common is a more-than-casual
interest in HIV/AIDS. This will be a support group, yes. You'll also
study the history of the AIDS epidemic—the medical, political,
and social aspects. We'll talk about the effects on families and
friends. You will have the opportunity to make home visits with an
adult volunteer if you wish.

"Before you start doing the talking, however, let's be clear. This
is a very sensitive subject for a high school club. You may even be
the target of homophobic remarks. I doubt it would go further than
that. I know you've all spoken with your folks about this when they
signed permission for you to join. I hope you'll feel secure enough
to tell an adult if you sense a perceived threat.

"*Here* is a safe place to talk about any past or present feelings,
and the key word is 'here.' By joining this club you are agreeing
you will never divulge information you learn about any of the
other members to *anyone* in this school. You can't say to your best
friend, 'Listen, I'm going to tell you about so-and-so but you have
to promise not to tell anyone else.' Right, not even your best friend.
You all need to learn to trust each other so you can feel safe to
open up about your experiences and your emotions. If you don't
think you can keep everything in the room, please see me when we
break in a couple of minutes and I'll find another way to get you
help. I'll be in the Social Worker suite outside and to the left.

"Be sure your name tags are clearly visible. We all want to hear
about why you've decided to join. You can give us an overview
of your situation for up to about five minutes or you may pass if
you're too uncomfortable to share yet. But if you don't participate
within the first two or three sessions, I'd like to meet with you
privately to see if the club is really a good fit for you. Now please
take ten minutes to stretch, introduce yourselves to each other, use
the facilities at the end of the room, or think about what you want
to say. As I said, I'll be sitting in the Social Worker suite if anyone
needs to see me now."

[A short interval passed.]

"I was very pleased to have had those last ten minutes to myself. No one came in, which means you've all made the decision to follow a main rule: personal information about someone else stays right here. Of course you will be talking amongst yourselves sometimes. I'm counting on you to find private places to meet.... Okay, who wants to go first?" Out of nine students, four raised their hands. Four of you? What a wonderful predicament. Okay, whose last name is closest to 'Z'?"

"How about 'Zitter'?" said Larry as he raised his hand high. "Is that close enough? I've never been called on first in my whole life because of my name. Thank you so much, Mr.... I mean, Moses."

"You're quite welcome. Anyone else with a 'Z'? No, all right then, lets get started. So, Larry, seriously now, why do you want to be here?"

"Well, my parents got divorced two years ago when I was fourteen. I didn't know why at the time and it was a real shock. I found out why when Dad contracted AIDS last year. He'd been living a double life for years, going out several evenings a week to 'meet the guys for a drink' but also to have sex with them. Since the divorce I've been living with each of my parents for a week at a time. I'm looking for help and information to deal better with both of them. He's gone downhill the last couple of months and I feel frightened and helpless. Mom is still very angry with him and isn't supportive at all. It's almost like she feels he deserves it. I don't feel the same at all. She's been tested twice and is okay. We aren't getting along that well.... I-I guess that's enough for now."

"Thank you, Larry. That must have been difficult. I believe this club can help you, so hang in there, okay? So, who's next?"

Two girls talked about concern for good friends who were behaving like AIDS didn't exist and making bad choices about drugs and sex. One of them was really talking about herself but didn't say so. Another member was a seventeen-year-old recovering heroin addict, clean for three months so far, who used to share needles. He got tested once and was negative but he has to go back for another test to confirm that.

One boy, Jimmy, said he wasn't ready to talk yet. "I'm feeling so emotional that I know I'll cry if I talk about it. I just can't do it today, but I'll prepare something at home to read next week, if that's okay. That'll help me."

"Great idea, Jimmy." said Moses. "Two things about a support group is realizing that we're all with you and that tears are absolutely fine. They're very good for your mental health. We look forward to knowing you better next week."

A voluptuous sixteen-year-old, Sherri, knew she had been exposed and was afraid to get tested.

"I slept with a guy one time almost three months ago and soon learned he was also having sex with men. He hadn't wanted to put on a condom and I was so stupid I didn't insist. He started having symptoms just a couple of weeks after we were together and got sick very fast. I learned you can have AIDS a long time before symptoms appear. I heard last week that he'd already died."

Sherri had tears dripping down her face by then as she tried to keep her composure.

"Now I'm pregnant, but it might not even be his. I'm not proud of what I've been doing. I hope you can help with my dread of being tested. I also have to tell my parents that I need an abortion, like immediately."

Moses assured Sherri she'd get help right away and asked her to stay after the meeting.

Then a seventeen-year-old came out to the group.

"I always felt different," Max said in a quiet voice. I wasn't interested in the rough games so many boys played. I preferred to sneak into my older sister's room and try on her clothes. Once, when I was eight or nine, I put on her nail polish but didn't know how to take it off. I showed up at the dinner table with bright red nails and my family had a fit. My mother immediately took off the polish and I was sent to my room without dinner. Surprisingly, my sister brought up two sandwiches and a Coke for me. She wasn't even mad at what I'd done. In fact, she tried to make a deal with me, saying I could try on her clothes if I gave her a dollar a week. Forget that! I was young but I already knew when I was getting conned. That would have been half my allowance! Besides, sneaking into her room and making sure I put everything back in exactly the right place was part of the fun. Coming out to her later on was easy. I just knew she'd understand, and she did.

"I went to summer camp every year and when I was fourteen I met this sixteen-year-old junior counselor, Scott, who seemed to know why I was having a hard time at home. He told me his story and it sounded like mine and things started to make sense to me. We really liked each other. He introduced me to lovemaking and we'd be hiding in the woods or wherever we could be alone. But after about three weeks we were caught and he was fired immediately. He left the same day. We didn't get a chance to exchange phone numbers or to say goodbye and he went home to northern California. The director let me stay because he thought I had been a victim. I experienced my first heartache and it was powerful. Scott was so important to me. But now I'm afraid to be with anybody. It's not safe. My parents have come a long way and agreed to let me be in the club. I don't know how FOPA can help me, but I'm willing to give it a try."

"That's all any of us can do, Max. Keep the faith," said Moses, who then pointed to Gabi and nodded at her to start.

"Ok, well, my mom delivers meals to homebound people with AIDS five days a week before starting her regular work at home. She got the job through Open Hand, same as you, Moses. These men are either too sick or too poor to shop for food and cook for themselves. From the time I was about ten, my mom's gay male friends started getting sick and dying mysteriously. In 1983, almost four years ago, health officials determined that AIDS can't be transmitted by any casual contact like you said, Moses. But it's been hard to make people understand what AIDS patients, especially gay ones, go through, as they get fired, are ostracized, and sometimes shunned by their families. Many people still don't believe the scientists and continue to treat people with AIDS as if they had the plague.

"If they are up to it, my mom takes me to visit the people I'm close with. She has gone to so many funerals. When they're on Sundays, I go with her for men I've loved for years. The losses have been brutal. Nightmares. Deep sadness. Tremendous anger at our government for not doing enough early on when they thought only gay men got it. I want to learn a lot more about the disease and think I want to be a social worker for at-risk adolescent girls. I've also thought about being a medical researcher, which would mean very expensive schools I don't think we can afford. All I know is that there will be plenty of jobs because I have a sinking feeling AIDS will be around for a long time."

Steve hung onto every word Gabi said and was even more impressed with her than before. Then it was his turn.

"I have something in common with Larry. I also have a relative living with AIDS. It's my dad's brother, my Uncle Fred, and he's staying with us now. Dad and a part-time aide help him with almost everything and my mother consents to make dinner for him. I think the Catholic Church is mostly responsible for my mother's negative attitude toward gay men. She doesn't understand how two women can even have sex, so they don't bother her. Pretty funny, right?"

Almost everyone chuckled, but quieted down immediately to continue listening.

"She can't even be civil to Uncle Fred's friends when they visit. My mother walks past them with a disgusted look and leaves the living room where my uncle's bed is set up. She doesn't even offer them glasses of water. It makes me furious. My dad, uncle, and I had a good talk when I brought the permission form home. We agreed not to tell my mom about the club, at least for a while. I'm so anxious to find the right words that will open her heart and help her have some compassion. Education is supposed to be the best way, so if I can learn more here, maybe I can get through to her."

"Wow," exclaimed Moses. "That was all so very well done. These stories have helped me get a sense of what issues we're dealing with here and I'm sure they gave every one of you a lot to think about. I see you all living in difficult situations and I witnessed fear, anger, sadness, and anxiety but also heard empathy, intelligence, hope, and perseverance. I'm optimistic that listening to each other will give you some relief to know that you're not alone with these feelings and problems.

"Our sessions will be two and one-half hours long each with a fifteen-minute break. We'll first go over a short reading assignment on HIV/AIDS history and then spend the rest of the time sharing our ongoing stories and helping each other. I happen to be HIV-positive myself since last year. I am doing very well with AZT, the first medication approved for treating AIDS. It just came out this year. I'm living a healthy life style. I eat well and exercise. My partner and I have a good social network. Yes, I'm gay. I'm telling you this personal information to help you know I can be sensitive to your situations.

"We're out of time for now. I'm giving out the first reading and hope you'll have plenty of questions and comments. See you next week, on time or a little early, please. You may bring a drink and snacks. I'm also giving you my business card. If you need to run something by me, please call. I'd like you all to give yourselves a big round of applause. This was an amazing session. Have a great week."

Almost everyone smiled and clapped as they murmured to each other and got ready to leave. Steve asked Gabi if she'd like to go to Starbucks to talk about the session.

"Sorry, I can't. I have too much homework tonight. But maybe we can talk later this evening by phone for a little while?"

"Sure thing, Gabi. Why don't you call me when you take a break? Can we exchange phone numbers on the back of our assignment sheets? I have to start a paper tonight, but it's not due until Monday. I also have to practice my sax. We have our first concert coming up in just three weeks.

"Oh, what kind of music do you play, Steve?"

"Jazz and classical for the most part. Do you play an instrument?"

"No, but I like jazz and classical—and rock too, of course. I'm more of an art person: painting mostly—acrylics and watercolors.

"That's pretty cool. Hey, I don't want to keep you from your schoolwork. I'll speak with you later, Gabi."

"Okay, Steve," she said with a big smile. "There's so much to talk about!"

"Yeah, isn't it great?"

Steve walked home quickly and it didn't seem like his feet were quite touching the ground. His cheeks almost hurt from smiling so much. He found himself singing the chorus to Steven Winwood's "Higher Love" when he hadn't even realized he knew the song. He said a quick hello to his uncle, who was sitting in an armchair watching TV.

"Sorry, Uncle Fred, I can't chat now, but we'll have a good talk after I practice my music."

He rushed up to his room, took out his sax, and forced himself to concentrate for half an hour on two of the songs for the concert. He couldn't wait for Gabi's call. His stomach started growling and it was the first time he thought of food since lunch. That had been six hours earlier. He bounded down the stairs and fixed himself a turkey and swiss on rye. He wolfed it down fast enough to get a little upset stomach but ignored it as he climbed back upstairs two steps at a time. Nearing the top step, he heard a crashing sound downstairs. He raced down, calling loudly for his uncle.

"You okay, Uncle Fred? Where are you? Tell me where you are. I can't hear you! I can't see you!" Steve ran through the living room to the kitchen, then saw the door to his dad's office ajar. He opened it and screamed. "No, no." His uncle was lying face down on the rug, with his head to the side, obviously unconscious. A tall, heavy pole lamp lay across his back. Steve wondered for just a nanosecond if he should call 911 first or remove the lamp from his uncle's back. He very quickly pushed 911 on the phone, put it down, then immediately pulled the lamp off, needing both hands to roll it onto the floor. He was afraid to move Uncle Fred's head. He picked up the phone with one hand and the operator got on just as Steve put his other hand in front of his uncle's nose and mouth to see if he was breathing.

Isidore Solomon Friedman
(Sol Friedman)

Bio

I was born on November 2, 1924 in a privately-owned tenement building in the City of New York. At the age of one my parents, Sam and Fannie, bought a 50-acre farm about two miles from the hamlet of Woodbourne, New York. The farm consisted of a 30-room three-story building that the previous owner used for boarding New York City uniformed employees.

My parents began to operate the farm with the help of their neighbors. They bought several cows and a horse and rented rooms during the summer. For the winter months we lived back on the East Side. I had an older sister and brother who went to school with me both in Woodbourne and in New York City.

I was drafted in the Army and spent nearly three years training for the invasion of Japan after their attack on Pearl Harbor on December 7, 1941. After returning to Woodbourne I helped my parents with their resort hotel and obtained a job with the City of New York on the construction of earth dams and concrete tunnels. I married a guest of the hotel, Henrietta Rosen, and we had three children—Fran, Karen and Sam—that we raised in Woodbourne. Eventually I worked as a Public Works Director for several cities and as a Consultant Engineer in the Philippines and Egypt. I retired to Kings Point in Delray Beach, Florida, in 1986.

The Philippine Rice Terraces in Banaue

When my nephew Ben Nathan became a Peace Corps volunteer in 1978, he chose to work in the Philippines two years. I was working there on water systems. Henny and I were happy with the visit to us of his parents, my sister Shirley and her husband Paul, after they visited their son in his assigned village of Iloilo, 300 miles southwest of Manila. Ben was teaching the village people Public Health and Mathematics. At the same time our son Sam, who graduated the University of Wisconsin in Milwaukee, also visited us. Sam continued to travel around the world and visit friends from school in far-flung places.

I planned a trip that my family would always remember. What was suggested was a tour of the 2,000-year old rice terraces in the village of Banaue. It was a ten-hour ride by auto along a main road from our home in Makati, Luzon, to the highest point of elevation on the island. I asked my supervisor John Knowl if he could arrange an eight-passenger van and the use of my driver to make the trip. Everyone was in agreement. All we needed were reservations at the government-run Banaue Hotel. Ben said he would take care of that.

On a beautiful Saturday we drove from Magalaneus Village in Makati and headed north on the super-highway towards the 5,000-feet-high mountains of Baguio. We left together from our home after breakfast. Our driver was not familiar with the route, but I was. Baguio, the home of Ferdinand Marcos, the late president of the Philippines, was a resort city of 5,000 and was famous for wood carvings, spiritual healers, and cool dry weather. It took four hours to get there.

During the early occupation of Baguio by the Americans in 1930 the cool weather was a reason for the establishment of Camp John Jay, created as a retreat for our soldiers. Burnham Park, in central Baguio, was named after the American architect David H. Burnham, who had also planned and developed Central Park in New York City.

Having been to Baguio previously, I had learned much about its people, services, and popularity for alternative medicine and faith healers. At one of my visits I was told of psychic surgery that was going to take place at a small church outside the limits of the city. I was directed to the site by my counterpart, Luis, a Philippine student learning to be a water district development officer. As we entered the small white wooden church with pews for about 40 people, I noticed that the procedure had already started.

In front of us on a stage was a woman lying on a table with a white sheet draped over her. Its sides reached the floor. The practitioner faced us. He and two assistants were dressed as doctors with short white jackets like his. He began his surgery by drawing his thumb along the women's exposed stomach. Blood began to ooze out of it. Then the practitioner began removing what I thought were the intestines of an animal and dropping them into a pail we could see from where we were seated. After this simple operation we watched as her stomach was wiped clean and the women was helped to her feet. As Luis and I left the church, we discussed the operation. It had definitely been a fake one, but the woman seemed not only satisfied but happy with it.

The trip to Baguio was exciting for our guests, who, of course, had never been there before. I had been looking forward to this new experience as well. After one hour of driving before we approached the super-highway, my guests and I agreed we needed a break. We, therefore, stopped at a small village and I ran into a grocery shop for packages of buns, cakes, water, and soft drinks to supplement what we had brought. We arrived in Baguio and drove around the city to see the sights before continuing on the route to the rice terraces.

Banaue is located in the Ifugao Province. Its elevation is 4,500 feet. The facility where we thought Ben would arrange lodging for us was sold out and we had to register in a hostel called the Lake View Motel. We could hardly foresee how cold it would be at night. We had cots and blankets but no running water. Our meals were served in the government-run Banaue Hotel. In the evening the locals entertained us with a presentation of music and tribal dances depicting early native life.

The panorama of the 2,000-year-old, and some older, rice terraces was stupendous! The terraces were hacked from the craggy mountainside by the men and women of the Ifugao tribal nation that still engage in tribal warfare and head-hunting. It is estimated that there are about 1,400 miles of rice terraces built as early as 200 B.C. and continued ever since. The women build and maintain them, and the men stand guard and provide the irrigation from water cascading down from the top of the mountains. The terraces on one hillside were 500 vertical feet apart and approximately 5,500 feet long. Water from rainwater and natural springs was contained in earth basins along the ridges. The women extend the terraces lengthwise after the growing season for rice, predominantly, and for other vegetables as well.

We headed south to Makati the next day after taking many photos. Visiting the Banaue Rice Terraces was an experience my guests and I will never forget.

Life in California

The lifestyle of ease that Henny (Henrietta) and I enjoyed in the Philippines was different from anything we had experienced before. My contract with James M. Montgomery (JMM) as a Consulting Engineer, which included a full-time driver and a car plus an allowance for a live-in maid, ended in December 1981; and Henny and I relocated to Georgetown, a section in the District of Columbia, to be near our children, Sam and Karen. I knew it would be difficult to find a job because of my age and the specialized work in water supply, but after a few months I was offered jobs in California as a water-supply specialist in two engineering firms. The one I chose was in Santa Barbara, and we rented an apartment on State Street close to my workplace.

About a year earlier, in the summer of 1980, we visited with our daughter Fran and her husband Larry in Mendocino, California.

Henny and I drove from San Francisco before returning to the Philippines. We did some sightseeing along the way. One of our stops was Santa Barbara. It had the advantages of pleasant weather, a youthful culture, two state universities, and a Spanish Mission. The Mission was one of the many that evangelizing Spanish priests had founded along the Pacific Coast from San Diego to San Francisco from 1769 to 1833—each 20 miles apart, the distance of a day's ride with ox-drawn wagons.

The Four Winds moving company shipped our furniture from the Philippines to Santa Barbara. Henny and I enjoyed a month of world travel via such cities as Jerusalem, Athens, and Madrid—in a western, not eastern, direction.

We enjoyed our new environment and joyfully showed visitors the sights—the beaches and boats; a Sunday open market; an exquisitely designed theater in which we saw *Raiders of the Lost Ark*; the Labor Day parade on Main Street with high-school bands, parade floats, and riders in western garb on silver-saddled horses. Nearby was President Ronald Reagan's ranch. When three helicopters flew by, I knew that the President and close members of his staff were in one of them.

My next appointment was in Vallejo with its population of 100.000. As Engineer-Manager of the Vallejo Sanitation and Flood Control District, I began developing there a new sanitary sewage-treatment facility and the automation of ten existing large storm-water pumping stations throughout the city. The stations, which used activated carbon to clarify effluent before discharging it into the water that flowed into the San Francisco Bay, had failed. Much to the dismay of the State Board of Health the effluent had not met regulations. Meanwhile the sludge from the effluent was being hauled to a vacant field six miles away to be spread on pasture fields by a tractor spreader. Much effluent of the sewage plant mixed with storm-water runoff was discharged into the Carquinez

Strait during several heavy rainfalls and caused many pumping stations to flood.

While becoming acquainted with the staff and familiarizing myself with my duties, I followed the suggestions of the elected Board of Commissioners for obtaining federal funds to construct another sewage-treatment plant according to the design of James M. Montgomery, who had an office nearby in Walnut Creek.

Over the next few years I established a rapport with the engineer representing JMM and made several trips to Sacramento to cement relationships with the staff of the State Health Department. I engaged a firm that automated the pumping stations of the new sewage-treatment plant and produced a newsletter for the 45-employee staff to improve public relations. We applied for a federal grant to build more facilities after we received the necessary state approvals. Work progressed on the monitoring devices in the main control rooms of the plant. Meanwhile, having known of Rotary Clubs in the Philippines, I joined the one in Vallejo, which was popular with the businessmen there.

At headquarters sewer-service bills were prepared monthly by hand for some 22,500 clients and mailed to respective homes and offices. I investigated the use of computers with our approving office manager, but the clerks balked at learning a new system. Eventually, representatives from the computer company we dealt with tutored the clerks, overcame their resistance, and introduced the technology for the new billing system.

It was inevitable that I would be appointed to the Corps of Engineers in Sacramento. But Sacramento was 65 miles from our home in Benicia. I thus joined a van-pool for the one-hour trip from home and back. The office was not far from the State Capital Building. It was the job I always wanted.

The round trip to and from Sacramento began to wear on me, but we enjoyed our daily activities. We visited with our children Fran and Larry, who lived nearby, and attended a wedding in Hollywood with my cousins, the Plockiers (one earlier version of which had been Plotsky). I played tennis, a sport I had taken up in the Philippines. We became active in Vallejo's Conservative synagogue, which had 65 families; and we made many new friends. Henny and I prepared the synagogue newsletter. We enjoyed shopping in the new malls. During the winter we took bus trips to ski in the Lake Tahoe area mountains.

Finally, instead of moving closer to Sacramento from Benicia, we decided to retire to Florida. We purchased a condo in Kings Point, Delray Beach; and Henny and our son Sam furnished it. We bought a new car for the cross-country drive and made enjoyable stops on a detour via Chicago and New York City.

Blue Star Camps, Hendersonville, North Carolina

Blue Star Camps is one of the few children's camps in the South that observes the Jewish dietary laws. The idea of the Jewish camp was the plan of the Plotkin brothers—Herman and Ben, and Harry of Atlanta, Georgia—when they returned from serving our country in World War II. The name "Blue Star Camps," with "Camps" in the plural, was chosen, because it indicated different divisions, as well as different constituencies using the facilities.

I retired to Kings Point, Delray Beach, Florida, with my wife Henny in 1986 and applied for jobs listed in the classified advertisements in the newspapers. I noticed an advertisement in the March 15, 1988 issue of the *Sun-Sentinel* for a dining-room supervisor at the Blue Star Camps in Hendersonville, North Carolina; and I sent in my application, in which I emphasized my experience at my parent's resort, Friedman's Lake View Hotel in Woodbourne, New York.

I received a call and was asked to come to 3595 Sheridan Street in Hollywood, Florida, for an interview. During the interview I met Roger Plotkin, the son of one of the original owners, who was now operating the camp. He emphasized in particular how tough the work would be because of the difficulty of the dining room's duties. I believed at the time he was concerned about my age of 64 and about how different the work would be compared with managing a summer resort for adults. I assured him that I was in good health and was willing to take on the challenge. Then he proposed a job for my wife in the camp store. I told him my wife had served in retail as a clerk in her father's bakery before our marriage. He indicated that his wife Candy was co-manager of the camp.

The camp hosted 700 campers from age 6 to 16 and 300 employees in a 245-acre area northwest of Hendersonville. It has been a successful operation since 1950 because it was catering to children coming from all parts of the world who needed to observe the dietary laws. Two rabbis, who conducted Friday evening and *Shabbat*-morning services, were given a four-week stay at the camp with their families. Ironically, one of those rabbis applied later for an opening at my synagogue. Temple Emeth in Delray Beach, Florida, but did not receive the position.

Never having been at a camp in my youth, everything was new to me. Henny and I were assigned to a wooden-framed cabin that contained one double bed and dresser, and a bathroom with a shower. During the first week at camp there was a dance group of 140 adults who wanted fresh fruit in lemon juice twice daily during their workouts in the social hall at 10 a.m. and 3 p.m. It was a good opportunity for our staff to become familiar with the operation of the camp.

What I discovered was that the dining room wasn't large enough to serve 700 campers at the same time. Breakfast, lunch and dinner thus had to be divided into three shifts each. It meant the dining room staff had to clean and reset the dining room three times for each meal. A small dining room for the staff was open for a longer period, and the staff could decide when they wanted their meals served. It was a seven-day job for me from 6 a.m.in the morning to closing at about 9 p.m. when I left the kitchen. The camp-store hours were adapted to the free time of the campers, a couple of hours each day. We met another couple from Kings Point, the Kleins, who were also employed at the camp—the wife worked as a nurse in the clinic and her husband worked in the camp store with Henny.

The summer we were there the temperature was above average and the work was uncomfortable. We had a bat in our cabin and were advised to use insect spray to kill it. The dining-room staff came from the United Kingdom. Those who worked the entire summer received round-trip air fare and had two weeks to tour America after the summer. One of the staff was a Chinese student from Hong Kong who attended Oxford. I wrote his parents how well he performed his job as waiter. They replied, thanking me for my letter about their son's good work.

One waiter was recalcitrant and was difficult to manage. I advised him that I would have to let him go unless he shaped up. He was a poor example for the other waiters to follow. Someone else became the waiter's mentor and there was an improvement in the man's work. It was a very hard job for everyone. I was given a weekend off towards the end of the eight-week season. Henny and I traveled to Ashville, North Carolina, and enjoyed every minute of our short vacation. We came back exhausted but invigorated.

It was an experience that I would repeat. I had always wanted to go to camp, but because of my parents' summer resort it was never possible. Henny enjoyed her work as well. We managed all life's good happenings and hardships. One event made me proud. It was the annual Board of Health inspection. For the first time in the 40 years of operation Blue Star Camp received a 100 % rating for the excellent condition of the kitchen, dining room, and pantry. I gave the dining room staff all the credit for making it possible. They showed me and the Plotkins what a great crew they were. A camp staff photo was taken by a professional photographer and given to each employee before the end of the season.

I have focused in this memoir on the work of the adults, but I would be remiss if I did not describe the joys of camp life. Programs for the children included, among other activities, trips by bus to interesting sights in and around North and South Carolina. There was a lake for swimming and boating. River tubing, with truck balloon tubes, was popular. The camp was close to the Blue Ridge Mountains, where roads were constructed by the Works Progress Administration (WPA) during FDR's early years as President of our country. Trips and hikes through the mountains were a must for all campers. It is an excellent camp and has been well-managed to this very day.

Temple Emeth *Kallah*

I was the Vice President of Temple Emeth in Delray Beach in 1998 when Seymour Ugelow was President. At a general meeting of the membership, with nearly 450 in attendance, a deliberation about making the Conservative worship egalitarian took place. This change in service was moved by a small group of members. Until then women had been permitted to read a small number of verses during Friday evening services. After much heated discussion, egalitarian services received the approval of a majority of the members. Women were then permitted to receive *aliyot* (being called to the Torah) and other *Shabbat*-morning honors. Quite a few members were unhappy with the developments. Seymour Ugelow, therefore, asked me to plan an activity that would palliate the negative feelings of the unhappy members.

I consulted several educators about activities on a weekend outing to an oceanside hotel in Miami Beach. Our Rabbi, Richard Yellin, came up with the idea of a *"kallah."* I searched several Hebrew dictionaries to learn what *"kallah"* meant—a "retreat." Once I found out I asked myself what a retreat in Miami Beach would entail.

Many years ago, in Central and Eastern Europe, Jewish farmers went to the larger villages after the harvest to learn what changes had been occurring in government, culture, and science. Village leaders held forums. Such a forum was called a *"kallah."* Some of the educators I consulted and some Temple members advised me in creating one for ourselves.

Our committee made plans to have our Rabbi and a number of facilitators manage groups of not more than ten to twelve persons. We advertised well in advance for qualified facilitators to apply. In addition, we needed speakers for the opening and closing sessions. The hotel agreed to provide for us three meals daily, dance music, and Broadway entertainment every evening.

We chose as our venue the Saxony Hotel on Collins Avenue, where I had organized events as Brotherhood President; and we arranged for two buses. We gave the twelve facilitators the subjects for the weekend and asked them to research the material for their introductory remarks. We estimated that with four sessions a day everyone would learn a great deal in the weekend. We anticipated that about 125 people would attend our *kallah.*

Everything worked as planned. There was even time for our participants to swim in the ocean or the hotel pool and go sightseeing in downtown Miami Beach. The program was successful and continued afterwards for five consecutive years. Attendees were enthusiastic, relationships among members deepened, and revenue for the Temple increased.

Playing Professional Golf

What is the regimen of golfers Phil Mickelson, Jack Nicklaus, Arnold Palmer, and Tiger Woods that made them champions? They embodied the same principles in golf that they did in their daily life. They practiced regularly from morning to night. They corrected their errors in judgment. They took lessons in improving their swing and practiced some more.

Being a champion involves the following qualities: Patience— taking one's time. Perfectionism—mistakes are not forgiven, though the best players make them. Persistence—dedication and perseverance.

For many years I've watched Arnold Palmer on television playing golf. He always had a ready smile, which the audience enjoyed, even when he missed a shot. He had a following. I observed a drive of Jack Nicklaus go awry and the crowd gasped. It didn't faze him. A second shot didn't do that much better. Unperturbed, he rebounded and won the tournament. Julius Boros walked and conversed with the spectators in his carefree and confident manner and nonchalantly stroked his putt into the cup.

What the public didn't see was the long hours they had practiced before the tournament. They built up confidence in their swings and prepared for the extreme conditions they might unexpectedly encounter.

What are some things you can do to improve your game? Walk the course and observe the fairways and the greens. Make written notes of your observations of each green. Note the wind conditions of the greens. Note the surfaces. Were the greens mowed recently? Were they fast or slow? Dry or damp? Don't try to outguess them? Many a putt failed because they were too slow and didn't reach the cup. Firm putts give the balls the necessary momentum. Don't try on the tee to out-drive your opponent. Plan where your balls should be for your second shots.

Be cheerful with your audience. They paid top dollar to watch you win. They enjoy watching you and are disappointed when you miss an easy putt. When that happens, don't show aggravation. Sign autograph books and papers. Spectators may have children at home that couldn't make the trip. Watch your ball land before moving on.

If you play often, keep the same caddy. Get him involved with your game. Golfers need a "second opinion." My best wishes to all golfers. See how many principles you can embody. They can result in your becoming one of the "top ten" of a tournament.

Honor Flight

I met a fellow member of Temple Emeth in 2015 who had just returned from Washington, D.C., on an Honor Flight to see the new World War II Memorial. After hearing what he described, I became interested in learning more about the program that offered a free trip to our nation's capital.

What surprised me was the program! When a physician's assistant Earl Morris working for the Veteran's Administration and a club flyer, in Springfield, Ohio, asked his patients whether they had been to the District of Columbia to see the new World War II Memorial, the answer was, "No, I couldn't afford the trip." The doctor initiated the program with World War II veteran Jeff Miller of his club, voluntarily taking veterans to Washington. The first trip was with six private planes carrying twelve veterans of World War II in May of 2005. That's how this nationwide program was started. Escorts, air travel, and all meals were provided to the veterans to show appreciation for their service to our country.

In a few days I had the information for joining the Honor Flight from the Southeast Region serving Palm Beach County. I applied for the trip and was accepted for May 31, 2015. A couple of officers from the Martin County Police Department were my escort. They came to my home in Kings Point before the trip to explain the program. I told them I would be at the airport in West Palm Beach at 4:30 a.m.

It was early. I understood that we would return at 8:00 p.m. Photographs were taken of the 80 veterans and their escorts before boarding the Northwest Airlines plane reserved for us. As the plane took off, we could see people along the airport runway—no matter how early in the morning it was—waving their hands farewell. Little did I know what other good vibes were in store for us.

There was a 20-piece band playing for us on arrival at the National Airport in Washington. We were escorted with our guardians by bus to the following sites: The Tomb of the Unknown Soldier, the Iwo Jima Statue, a tour of the Capitol, and the Viet Nam and World War II Memorials. In a huge hall the meals in box lunches were served for the 1,000-plus veterans from all parts of the country, provided by the Odd Fellows organization of Washington.

It was the return trip that impressed me the most. After we arrived back at the Palm Beach Airport, lined up at the exit of our plane were six men in Scottish uniforms playing bag-pipes. They led us to the terminal while hundreds of families were waving and thanking us for our service. It was an extraordinarily moving moment for me.

The outpouring of people and families at the Palm Beach International Airport in West Palm Beach to thank us for our service, 72 years later, was overwhelming. To top everything off, I received a photo album of our trip from my escorts about a month later.

I had been honorably discharged from the Army after three years of service on March 12, 1945. I returned home from Japan, after traveling some 20,000 miles by ship, plane, train, and bus without any kind of reception, except from my parents. They were happy to see me, of course. How proud indeed they must have been looking down from Heaven at my welcome home from the Honor Flight!

David Jones

Bio

David Jones Folksinger and Actor

Songs of the British Isles and North America

For more information or bookings:
email: David Jones

Phone: 201 461 6137
115 Oaktree Place, Leonia, NJ 07605

[Editor's note to readers. I state unabashedly that
I am proud of unique features of this book. What
follows is one of them: *five* bios of a contributor—
for whom our writing club is *very* fortunate—culled
from different places. Each adds its own flavor, and
I have felt unable to choose a "best" one. Making a
virtue out of necessity, then, I have included all five
for both your reading pleasure and "*ad maiorem
scriptoris mirandi gloriam*" (the greater glory of our
wondrous writer)].

David Jones, originally from England and now living in Leonia,
New Jersey, gateway to the golden west, has a large repertoire
of folksong from both sides of the Atlantic. He has performed
in North America, Britain, Australia, and Europe—singing at
festivals, concert halls, clubs, maritime museums and colleges and
presenting songs from the great days of sail, Music Hall favorites,
traditional ballads, and the works of contemporary writers. He
sings both *a capella* and with guitar accompaniment and involves
his audience in refrains and choruses ranging from boisterous to
sentimental.

As well as performing solo, David has sung with Heather Wood and the late Tom Gibney as *Poor Old Horse*; with Jeff Warner, Jeff Davis and Jerry Epstein as *The Bermuda Quadrangle*; with Peter Marston and Charles O'Hegarty as *The Starboard List*. He was a member of the *Clearwater* singing crew. He has also sung and recorded with *Dan Zanes and Friends*; and his work with guitarist Bill Shute led to the award winning *Widdecombe Fair*, now available on the Dan Zanes label, *Festivalfive Records*. He now sings songs of the sea with *The New York Packet* at South Street Seaport in New York City. He still performs with Heather Wood as a duo and with Jerry Epstein, who adds wonderful piano and concertina accompaniments to the songs.

David has played feature roles in many theatrical productions to favorable critical reviews. He has performed across the USA as the featured artist in The *Victorian Revels*, a production based on traditions of the Winter Solstice conceived and produced by Revels Inc. He has played the part of the great sailor Joshua Slocum in *Sailing Alone*, with words and music by Dillon Bustin, and has sung and provided narration for a number of Public Broadcasting productions, including *A Prairie Home Companion, Africans in America,* and *Simple Gifts.*

David Jones is an English transplant. In 1965, he came to New York State on a six-month contract to work as an engineer. One thing led to another, and now, more than fifty years later, he is still in the U.S.A. He lives with his wife Louise in New Jersey, fondly referred to as "The Garden State." Over these years he has combined engineering with acting and being a singer of traditional folksong, much of which is sung *a capella*. His singing, especially of songs from the great days of sail, has led to travels in Europe and Australia, and to many venues throughout the States. He has made a number of recordings, which, along with theater performances, have been kindly reviewed.

DAVID JONES HAS LED A RICH and varied life, the highlights of which are beautifully presented in this wry and irresistibly intelligent collection. Not many people can say they've had a successful career as a structural engineer, boxed and competed in swimming and track-and-field tournaments, lived and worked in Tanganyika and Uganda, climbed Mount Kilimanjaro, sold programs at the Coronation of Queen Elizabeth II, acted and sung professionally—and written a book about all of it.

Of his entertainment career in particular, he says, "The big reward of performing has been the great people and brilliant musicians I have met over the years. I have had good times, interspersed with disappointments and, sometimes, failure. Failure in performance is usually self-inflicted, mostly due to lack of preparation.... I have had some minor success in theater and have been well-reviewed. One reviewer said, 'David Jones is a lusty old goat.' How can you beat that?" It is precisely this amalgam of sober irreverence that informs the memorable moments in the author's life and makes them so readable.

Today, the author and his wife live in Leonia, New Jersey, across the river from Manhattan. It's a "wonderful town," he adds, "and its citizenry has a reputation for fierce independence. I have lived there for the past forty years, so by now I am really a Leonian, but I still miss much about life in Old England—London, old friends, beer at room temperature—and though I have only spent a third of my life in England, I still remain at heart a South East Londoner." Visit the author at davidjones.ws

The two selections reprinted in this anthology with the author's permission are from his ***Smith Of Lambeth*** *And Other Tales: A Memoir* from: *Full Court Press, Englewood Cliffs, New Jersey,* Copyright 2019

My Friend Sydney

MY TWO CLOSEST FRIENDS AT COLLS ROAD SCHOOL were Brian Heritage and Sydney Short. We were in the same class in school—third form, I think it was. That would make us young teenagers. The three of us were members of the 1st Nunhead Salvation Army Boy Scouts Troop. Brian and I were drummers in the Scouts band, Sydney didn't play an instrument. You could be in the Scouts without being a member of the Salvation Army, as was the case for Sydney and me, and, for most of the scouts in the troop.

On Sunday mornings, our scout troop band marched around the streets of Nunhead. We marched behind the Salvation Army band, which played most of the tunes. They were a very good band. Then we would take a turn, banging on our drums and blowing our bugles, playing the five-note tunes which were all that could be managed on a bugle. We often passed by a monastery, and when we saw a monk standing at an open gate, we knew he was there to let us know that the other monks were in silent worship, so we stopped playing our instruments. The Salvation Army captain and the monk would give a friendly wave to each other as we passed by. We would stop at various locations, mostly outside pubs where the "drunkards and sinners" were to be found, and the Army captain would hold an open-air meeting in hopes of saving some of Nunhead's population from eternal damnation. He spoke fiercely of the consequences of not being "saved." Most Londoners had great respect for the Salvation Army, remembering its service during the wartime blitz. With its mobile canteens, it would be among the first to arrive at a bomb site to hand out hot tea and sandwiches to survivors and first responders.

Sydney was on the tall side and liked to box. His father had been a cook in the navy and a good amateur boxer in his day, so Sydney was taking after his dad. Brian was not a sporting type at all, while

I was passionate about all competitive sports, especially swimming and boxing.

One day, Sydney did not come to school, nor did he come the next day, and then his absence stretched into weeks. He was ill. It was something to do with his heart, they said, and he was in the hospital. Brian and I went to visit him several times, we always took him some treats—oranges and chocolate—and he always looked good to us. He was alert and upbeat, and then, one day, we got word that he had been moved to another hospital, it was a different kind of hospital, we were told, a place where Sydney could rest up until he got better and was strong enough to go home and return to school. This hospital was northwest of London, in the town of Aylesbury in the county of Buckinghamshire.

It was a long way from South East London to Aylesbury, but by bus, train, and foot, Brian and I made it out there. When we visited Sydney, we always thought that he looked fine. He was always happy to see us, and with a smile on his face he would be sitting up in bed, propped up by pillows. The nurses kept him in bed; they never had him seated in a chair or allowed him to walk around. It didn't seem to bother him, at least not that we could tell while we were there. He wanted Brian and me to give him news about school and the boys in our class, and about what we were doing in the scout group, anything we could tell him. He would tell us that he was feeling good and would be back in school very soon. I can't remember him ever complaining.

Then, one day, not very long after our last trip to Aylesbury, we were told by our teacher that Sydney had died. The headmaster made an announcement to the boys and girls of the school at the morning assembly and spoke some very moving words about Sydney. The usually severe headmaster seemed genuinely distressed, and his voice trembled as he spoke and said prayers. Though Colls Road School was a state school, the morning assemblies were Church of England religious services.

Brian and I could not believe this awful news—Sydney had looked so well, and sounded so cheerful and positive, just a week or so before. How could he have died? We didn't know what to do, but after coming up with a number of thoughts and ideas, we decided that we should go to Sydney's house to see whether it was true, and whether we could talk to the parents. We all lived within a few streets of each other.

Brian and I walked to Hollydale Road, where Sydney lived and where we knew his parents would be. When we got to the house and saw that the curtains to the front windows were drawn, we got nervous; we knew what drawn curtains meant. We walked around the block, and stopped to think for a while; we needed to raise the courage to knock on the front door. Finally, we went back and nervously knocked. The door was opened by an uncle. He looked terribly sad, and in a halting voice, Brian asked him, "Is it true about Syd?"

The uncle nodded, and then closed the door. Sydney's parents were too devastated to talk to anyone.

The funeral would be a Church of England service. In those days, as is true today, church attendance by the majority of working-class Londoners was limited to baptism, marriage, and death. Folks went to other people's weddings, or funerals, or for some special event, but not much more than that. Then, when you died, off to church you would go for one last time. Most of the population was nominal Church of England, and the stock answer when asked about one's religion was C-of-E. Belief had nothing to do with it, it was just how you identified yourself. There was one Catholic boy in my class at school. He was excused from having to attend morning assembly.

Londoners were very respectful and kind towards their grieving neighbors. Workmen in the streets stopped work, stood up straight, and took their hats off when a funeral procession went by. Neighbors emerged from their houses and stood silently on the pavement to show respect for the bereaved family.

I was given the day off from school to go to Sydney's funeral. It was to be held at Nunhead Cemetery, where, at the time, many people from South East London got buried. It wasn't raining that day, but it was one of those gray and damp days so common in London. The funerals were assembly-line affairs, so Sydney's family and friends waited in line with the other funeral parties, sitting in the cars, or on the grass, for their turn at the standard service before the burial. The undertakers, who had seen it all so many times before, chatted with each other during the wait, as did some of the family members and friends. One by one, the hearses moved ahead to the door of the chapel, until finally, Sydney's turn arrived. His coffin and floral wreaths were removed from the hearse and carried into the chapel on the shoulders of the pall bearers. There, they were placed on an iron stand in the middle of the chapel. While this was happening, the mourners were ushered in to take their seats for the service. The Church of England vicar who had been appointed for the day was waiting to conduct the service, which would be his fourth? or fifth? who knew how many, funeral of the day, for someone he never knew or knew anything about. I looked around at the mourners. There were Sydney's grieving mum and dad, some of his uncles and aunts and other family members, and there were neighbors from Hollydale Road. Sydney's classroom teacher was there, and then there was me. It was a small group, and a sad scene.

The vicar droned on, telling us what a wonderful young fellow Sydney had been; how would he know, I wondered. He read from the standard text for funerals. He got to the bit about the certainty of everlasting life, and how we would all meet again in heaven, and then, from the congregation, came a piecing, heart-wrenching cry. It was Sydney's father. He shouted, "I don't believe it! How can I believe it!" and wept, and his body seemed to crumple. His head fell on his wife's shoulder, and she put her arms around him. She pulled him tight to her and embraced and comforted him with soft words. His body shook with grief for his son.

The vicar carried on with his job. After the service, I followed the small procession out into the cemetery, to Sydney's grave, where the gravediggers waited. Two ladies—I think they were neighbors—had me walk with them. They knew that I was

Sydney's friend and was in need of some comfort. There were
further words around the grave, "ashes to ashes" and so on, from
the vicar, and then we threw lumps of earth on Sydney's coffin and
watched as the gravediggers shoveled in earth until the hole was
completely filled. Family and friends laid flowers on the grave,
with messages to Sydney tied to them. Everyone stood around the
grave for a while, thinking their own thoughts. Sydney's parents
clung to each other and sobbed. When the parents had gathered
themselves together, they left the graveside to go back to their
house, knowing they would never see Sydney again. They did have
a younger son, who hopefully gave them some comfort. Slowly, the
rest of the people left, most of them going back to join Sydney's
parents for tea and sandwiches. I walked home by myself, back to
28 Lausanne Road.

I stayed in touch with Brian Heritage, a wonderful and very
genuine fellow, until we were in our early twenties. Then we
went our separate ways. Brian had become a full member of the
Salvation Army, and he suffered taunts from his family for this,
but it did not deter him. He had ambitions of being a professional
orchestra drummer and was taking serious lessons. He had a
girlfriend who was as pretty as a picture in her Salvation Army
lass's bonnet. She was a few years older than Brian, and sadly
she was abused by Brian's family, who shouted across the street
at her to "find someone your own age." She was tough and brave,
however, and stood up for herself and fought back. Often, she
would speak at the street corner meetings along with the Army
captain, and go into the pubs to spread the word. You had to
admire her—she had spirit and spoke with burning conviction. She
was fearless and beautiful.

I know that Brian and his lady friend wanted to get married, but I
don't know what happened. I truly hope they did marry.

Many times, our Sunday morning marches would take us from
Nunhead Green, where the Salvation Army Citadel was located,
through the streets of Nunhead to Linden Grove. There, we
would pass by the gates to the cemetery in which Sydney rested.

Between the wrought-iron bars of the gates, we could see the long stone pathway, with trees, bushes, and gravestones on either side. The path led from the gates to the chapel where Sydney's funeral service had been held.

My friend Sydney was fourteen years old when he died.

Endnote

Nunhead Cemetery, with its fine views of the city, was one of "the magnificent seven" cemeteries of London—fifty-two acres of monuments, chapels, and the graves of the famous and the unknown. The last time I saw the cemetery, sometime in the 1970s, it had been abandoned. It was overgrown with weeds, brambles, and fallen trees. Many gravestones had collapsed and were lying on the ground, partially covered by the growth around them. It was a sad sight. For a while, the cemetery became a nature reserve where birds and wildlife flourished until, sometime around 1980, the Friends of the Cemetery set about its restoration. It was reopened in 2001.

The Mountain and The Sergeant: Climbing Mount Kilimanjaro

IN THE SUMMER OF 1960, I WAS WORKING as a structural engineer in the City of London, very near St. Brides Church on Fleet Street. The church, a Christopher Wren masterpiece, had a pleasant and peaceful churchyard where, when the weather permitted, I would take my lunch and read the newspaper. One lunch time, looking in the jobs column in the *Daily Telegraph*, I saw that a structural engineer was wanted in Dar es Salaam, the capital of what was then Tanganyika.

I did some research on Tanganyika and found that, until the First World War, it had been a German colony. After that war, the League of Nations, I think it was, took control of the country, and then handed it over to Britain—lock, stock, and barrel. No one, it seems, had bothered to ask the indigenous people of Tanganyika what they thought about that, but so it was in colonial times. So Tanganyika became, along with Uganda and Kenya, a part of British East Africa.

Some geography books, and a movie, *The African Queen*, sold me on the attraction of living and working in East Africa. So I applied for, and got, the job.

I set about learning what I could about East Africa and what I would need to live there. There was a lot to learn. What special items should I take with me? An article I read said I would have to bring lots of salt pills, as the heat would drain the salt out of my blood. I didn't like the sound of that, SO I got lots of salt pills. I went to a tropical clothing outfitter in Bond Street and bought a bunch of *snazzy* lightweight suits and other items the salesman said I would need. *Later* I learned that New York City could be just as hot, and that the general workday outfit for European men in East Africa was shorts, a shirt, shoes, and socks. The socks should come up to just below the knees, of course.

In September 1960 I was on my way to Dar es Salaam. I flew out from London in a British Airways prop plane that made three stops on the way. We changed planes in Nairobi and finally got to Dar. On disembarking and crossing the tarmac, I was struck by the air of Africa—it was sweet and scented. It was more than exciting, it was exhilarating.

I was met by Jeff Taylor, who ran the small consulting firm I was joining. Jeff was a burly Yorkshireman who was always threatening to thump someone in the ear. He was known as "Thump 'Em in the Ear Taylor." He took me to the New Africa Hotel, where I would be staying until I found permanent quarters. A fine old building close to the harbor, it had been built by the Germans around 1900. With walls three feet thick and a slow-moving ceiling fan, the rooms in the hotel were surprisingly cool.

I had brought my guitar with me from England, and after I had unpacked my suitcase, I thought I would relax for a while by playing some of tunes I had learned at the Spanish Guitar Center in London. I opened the case and was shocked to see what looked more like a boomerang than a guitar. No one had told me that you must loosen the strings on any stringed instrument before taking it onto an airplane. My guitar was destroyed—an unfortunate beginning to my African sojourn.

After a few weeks, I moved into a nice apartment, and it seemed that all was going well. Then I found that a house servant came with the apartment. He was a pleasant young Tanganyikan fellow named Hector. The problem for me was, I did not need or want a servant. I could fix my own breakfast and wash my own clothes. Apart from that, the idea of having a servant was an embarrassment. I would certainly get laughed at by my mates back in South East London.

The problem for Hector, and, as it turned out, for me, was that this was his job, and he was supporting a family on his earnings. He sent money home to his village. I just could not bring myself to tell Hector that I did not need his services, so I kept paying him, even though there was very little for him to do. On the upside, I did practice speaking Swahili with him, but, in the evening, I had to drive him home. So it turned out that I became Hector's chauffeur.

I soon settled in and started to explore Dar. It sits on the east coast of Africa, smack on the equator, and has a graceful natural harbor that provides open access to the Indian Ocean. The exotic island of *Zanzibar* lies about forty miles off the coast. Dar is the capital of Tanganyika, which was, along with its neighbors Kenya and Uganda, gearing up for independence from Britain. This would come to pass for all three countries within the next three years, but in 1960 there were still British governors who would have looked at home in a Gilbert and Sullivan operetta. They wore white suits and large, rather comical, white hats bedecked with enormous feathers. Dar was a very cosmopolitan town, and the population of around 200,000 was a lively mix of people, cultures, and religions.

The majority were indigenous Africans from various parts of Tanganyika. There were many folks whose ancestral home was the subcontinent of India. Their grandparents had come to East Africa to work on building the railroads, chosen to stay, and flourished. An interesting group came from Goa, a Portuguese enclave on the west coast of India. These were very handsome people, and very Catholic. The Greeks owned the sisal plantations and were involved in the rope trade. They were successful and quite well-to-do. Finally, there were the people who thought they were running the show, the British in their long shorts. I was one of them. Sadly, these different groups were not socially well-connected.

I enjoyed life in Dar, but it was hot, and air conditioners were a rarity. I can't remember riding in a car or a bus, or working in a building, that had air conditioning. Then I was introduced to the African American Institute (AAI) by an American friend who worked there named Ronald. It was a haven, and a gold mine for so many things—books, magazines, and records, even records of Pete Seeger, which were hard to come by in the U.S.A, in those days. He was on some sort of government blacklist for being a bit more progressive in his thinking than some folks in the American government liked.

There were many reasons to go to the AAI—it was a popular place, and it was the first time in my life I had been in an air-conditioned building. It was a great relief in the full heat of the day. A popular bar drew customers to hear a very good Goan jazz band. I went there with an African American named Dave Oswald, who had been a jazz critic back in the U.S. Dave said he was in East Africa to study German/East African history, although no one ever saw him studying anything. He was a great fellow. When Louis Armstrong and his band came to town, Dave introduced me to his friend Trummy Young, the trombonist for the great man; we took him to the town market to see some colorful local life. Dave and I enjoyed joining Ron and his wife, Jacqueline, for dinner at their house in the woods. Jacqueline was a magical cook and the most delightful hostess.

Some English colonial types had taken it upon themselves to show Louis and his band members around the town. They thought that these Americans would be impressed by a ten-story apartment

building that had recently been built in Dar. It is tough to impress
folks from Chicago and New York City with a ten-story building.
I did once, however, find myself sitting one empty bar stool away
from Louis Armstrong at the New Africa Hotel bar. How can you
beat that? Louis was joined by his wife, and they were both dressed
"to the nines" for dinner.

Other delights of Dar were tea rooms that could have been plucked
straight out of villages in Gloucestershire, and funky, slightly
sleazy bars where old-timers gathered, including a well-known
local smuggler named Kloser. Once, as I sat in one of these bars, a
gigantic cockroach fell from the ceiling and landed in my beer with
a splash. Those cockroaches were as big as a blacksmith's thumb.
Saturday mornings were fun, with a gathering of beer drinkers at
the Tusker Brewery, followed by an excellent curry lunch at the
New Africa Hotel—a great way to start the weekend.

Different ethnic groups had their own clubs and sports teams. The
Gymkhana Club was where British folks went. They played cricket
and football against Goan, Indian, and African clubs. The games
were well played, intense, and, it must be said, quite friendly. It
was too bad, however, that the social mores of the time and place
prevented the teams from socializing *after* a game. I wish that we
could have gathered together at the bar and gotten to know each
other and, hopefully, have a good time.

I liked to sit outside the New Africa Hotel in the late evening
with Dave Oswald when the bar was officially closed. The night
watchman would fry up some fish for Dave and me that he had
caught that day, and sing us some songs in his own language. Many
of the indigenous African people were fluent in three languages—
Swahili, English, and their own tribal tongue. This gave pause to
those of us who had struggled for years to learn some French but
still had a hard time putting together a sentence.

For my job, I traveled to many parts of East Africa, and fascinating
travel it was. In Karamoja in northern Uganda, where life was still
much the way it had been in the nineteenth century, the men went
totally naked while the women were fully clothed. I worked on a

number of interesting projects, including the design of a church in
Mwanza, at the southern end of Lake Victoria. I never got to see
the church completed, but hopefully it still stands. In Kampala, my
favorite East African town, I worked for a small consulting firm
named Roughton, Campbell, and Fitzgerald. I visited the Serengeti
Game Park, and the white sands of Mombasa. I once flew a small
plane over Lake Rudolph in Northern Kenya to see the flamingos.
I circled it low around the mouth of a volcano. I hasten to say
that I did not take the plane off the ground or land it; my flight
companion, who was the pilot, did that. While in the air, I took the
controls so he could take some photographs.

Because there were only three hundred miles of paved road in
the three East African countries, car journeys were long, bumpy,
tiring, and very dusty. When driving to a distant job site, I would
often pick up a traveler—a schoolteacher walking to the school
in the next village, or a mother, with a baby on her back, walking
many miles to the clinic. The local people had to walk to get
anywhere; they had no cars, and buses were rare. Their patience in
taking these long, necessary walks was remarkable.

During journeys into the back country far away from any town,
one could often find a cozy, old-world inn built by the British
settlers of long ago. Who would expect such a taste of Olde
England in a land where elephants, giraffe, and zebra roamed?
The inns were set in quiet spots and were surrounded by English
gardens. Traditional British fare was served. Meat pies, plum
puddings with custard, and tea were brought to your room at 6:00
a.m. whether you wanted it or not. It was impossible not to get your
pot of tea at 6:00 a.m. English people drink tea at 6:00 a.m., and
that was that.

The die-hard British colonists did not socialize with the African
and Indian populations. They criticized, and shunned, those who
liked to play football and cricket against local teams or enjoyed
the great bands from the Congo when they played at the local beer
halls. They could not accept the notion that independence for the

peoples of the East African countries was on its way, and that their days of being in charge would soon be over.

After about a year of work, during which time I learned some rudimentary Swahili, I had earned some vacation time. Many expatriates would travel back to Britain for vacations, some to visit their children, whom they kept locked away in boarding schools. They called it "going home on leave." I chose to stay in East Africa and do something adventurous. I decided I would climb the highest mountain in Africa and the highest free- standing mountain in the world, Mount Kilimanjaro. I had met an English fellow named Bill Ford who also wanted to climb it, so we teamed up to make the three-hundred-mile journey over the rough, dusty dirt roads from Dar to a lovely town called Moshi, which sits in the foothills of the great mountain. There we would find a place to stay for the night, look for a guide, and get some boots and climbing gear.

We saw some incredible sights on the journey—wildlife, spectacular landscapes, and interesting people. At one point, we were flagged down by the driver of a large truck that had broken down, and the driver, a white guy, was waiting for help, which, he said, was on the way. He asked for some water, which we gave him, along with some food, to help him through his wait. The remarkable thing was, the driver had only one arm. Driving those roads in East Africa is tough enough with two arms; how he managed, I don't know.

A constant sight was the fat-bottomed baobab trees, sometimes called the African upside-down tree. The trunks are fat and the branches look like roots. The story of these trees is that God got fed up with having them in Paradise, so he threw them over the wall and they landed upside down in East Africa. Not a bad story. Eventually, we pulled in to Moshi and could really see the mountain. Kilimanjaro, at 19,341 feet high, is sometimes called the roof of Africa. It was covered at the top with glistening ice and snow, and a ring of cloud hung just below the peak, like a smoke ring. "Moshi" is the Swahili word for "smoke." The mountain has three extinct, or dormant, volcanic cones—Mawenzi, Shira, and

Kibo; this last is the highest peak, and the one we were headed for. It was a stunning sight, especially when seen from afar. We took a couple of rooms in a local inn and asked for advice on hiring a guide and where to get climbing gear. Well, they said, they could help us right there. They would provide a guide and the gear we needed for the climb. I should have paid more attention during the outfitting, as the boots they gave me turned out to be much too big. I was to pay for this mistake on the way down from the mountain top.

Being outfitted at the same time was a young German woman named Inga. She was set to make the climb, so we decided to join forces and venture together. The next day, we were introduced to our guide, a very pleasant older man. I forget which tribe he was from, probably Chagga, a local people known to be very good farmers. He had been born and raised around the mountain, and he brought with him some porters, as, in addition to warm clothing and provisions, we had to carry our own firewood up the mountain. On the evening before the start of our great adventure, Bill, Inga, and I sat on the veranda of the inn, drinking local beer and gazing at the mountain peak. It looked impossible for us, three totally inexperienced climbers. Did we really think we could climb all the way to the top? I guess we did. We all retired to bed and were awakened at 6:00 a.m. by the inevitable pot of tea being brought to our rooms. We had breakfast and prepared for the day.

Mount Kilimanjaro does not present many climbing challenges. There are a couple of places where one has to scramble, but there is no need for driving spikes into the mountain face or hanging from ropes. It is basically a long, slow, hard slog. The problem is the altitude, and that is a big problem. Rushing straight for the upper slopes before getting acclimatized can lead to acute mountain sickness.

We left Moshi early in the morning for the starting point of the climb, where we met our guide. He took us at an easy walking pace along the trail, which soon brought us into misty rain forests. It was exciting, and the scenery was breathtaking. We were on our way! When evening came we stopped at the Mandara hut, the first of the exotically named huts that we would use for sleeping. The others were the Horombo hut and then the Kibo huts, which were on the saddle of the mountain at about 15,500 feet, directly below the peak. In those days, the huts were nothing more than rudimentary shelters with no services at all.

We were in good shape until around 14,000 feet. After that, breathing became difficult; we got severe headaches, and walking became a slow stop-and-start effort. Our hearts were racing at many times the normal rate.

As we got higher, the plant life turned from lush vegetation to scrubby, tough, short growth, and it got colder. It took three days and nights to reach the saddle, where we walked on rough and stony ground, and it was very cold. We walked slowly, "pole pole" as they say in Swahili, stopping every thirty paces or so to allow our heartbeats to slow down. In the far distance we could see the Kibo huts at the foot of the steep slopes that would take us to the top of the mountain. The plan was to stay in the huts for the first part of the night and then, in the wee small hours, get up, have some breakfast, and start the final ascent before the first daylight. It was a long, slow, and exhausting walk, and the huts didn't seem to be getting closer. Inga was strong and would pull ahead of Bill and me; I thought that if any one of us made it to the top, it would be her.

Eventually, we got to those huts. It was cold, so we lit a fire, cooked a meal, and then prepared for a short sleep. All was going according plan when—from out of the blue—a party made up of British army officers, a very loud British sergeant, and a bunch of African army cadets appeared on the scene with four horses. It was a big surprise to us. They had climbed up from the other side of the mountain and were on a training mission for the cadets.

The one giving the orders was the sergeant, a character straight out of central casting. He was very loud. After brief introductions and a bit of a chat, one of the officers asked if they could join us and use the services of our guide. I said they could, but after it was all over, I thought I had been a bit high-handed in saying so without consulting the guide. I hope they paid him something, but I doubt that they did.

We all went to bed, still clothed in our climbing outfits, and tried to sleep. In the very small hours of the morning, we were awakened by our guide, who said it was time to get up and get ready to go. It was still dark and it was very cold when we crawled out of our sleeping bags. Someone had boiled up the coffee and prepared a rudimentary breakfast. I forget what the breakfast consisted of, but we ate it, then got set to go. Inga, our German friend, who had been so strong until that point, said she would not continue. I tried to get her to change her mind, but she would not. Maybe she was upset by the additional company, or of being the only woman in a group of twenty or so men, I don't know. I am sure she would have made it to the top. So we started off without her. I learned later that, when daylight came, she made her way down the slopes, back to Moshi. We never saw her again. She must have been bitterly disappointed, and I was sorry for her. Bill Ford was still with us, if not as enthusiastic as he had been a few days before, but he was ready to give it a shot.

The first target was Gilmans Point, on the rim of the crater, about six hundred feet below the highest peak of the mountain, which was then called "Kaiser Wilhelm Spitze" after the German emperor. After independence in 1961 the name was changed to "Uhuru," or "Freedom," Peak. Most climbers call it a day at Gilmans Point, as it is about a two-hour trek around the crater to Uhuru, and two hours back—a long way for not much extra in altitude and the day quickly fading. The footing for the climb from the Kibo Huts to Gilmans was difficult—a mixture of loose stones, snow, and ice, called "scree." You would take a step forward and then your foot would slip back a half step as the stones moved. We rested in a cave at about two thousand feet from the top, then started again. It was still dark. Bill Ford had developed terrible stomach cramps and was bent over double; it was clear that he was in trouble. He said he could not go on, so we had to leave him to make his way down the mountain. I was in very bad shape and short of breath, my head pounding, and I had painful cramps. I had a hard job forcing one foot in front of the other and was about to quit. At that point, one of the young African cadets collapsed on the mountain side. He was groaning and in great distress. His comrades went to help him, but the loud and awful sergeant shouted, "Leave him! He's got no guts." Well, now I could not quit—I had to go on. We left the poor cadet to get himself together and make his way down to the Kibo huts, and we started off again. Our guide would go on ahead of us, then stop, sit on a rock, and watch us climb towards him. He had a little flute on which he played tunes. He was mocking us. Spending so much of his life on the mountain, he was not bothered by the altitude.

As the first gray light of dawn broke through, I was getting a second wind. I pushed ahead of everyone but the guide. We were almost at Gilmans Point and the sergeant was coming up on my shoulder. He really wanted to be first to the Point, but I was not going to let him pass. I forced myself ahead, leaving him behind, until I found myself standing alone on the roof of Africa. It was a good place for photos; after taking some scenic shots, I handed my camera to the sergeant and asked him to take my picture. I struck a suitably mountaineering pose, and he got down on one knee, fiddled with the focus quite a bit, then took the shot.

It was a beautiful morning, the cloud cover gone, and the sky was a startling blue. I looked down the mountain, first at the incredible view stretching for miles before and beneath me, and then at the stragglers fighting their way up. Maybe forty percent of the original party made it to Gilmans Point. The army party had decided that this was as near to the top as they wanted to go, so after a rest, they began to head back to the Kibo huts. That left just me and the guide. He was still full of energy. We took off on the long walk around the blue-iced rim of the crater to Uhuru Peak. I can't recall if, at that time, there was any marker for the highest point, but I took the guide's word for it that I was at the top. I could have been a few feet short. I was standing on top of the highest freestanding mountain in the world, and it was glorious.

I spent some time taking in the view, but I was not feeling well. The brief flow of adrenalin I had felt in the dash to be the first to stand on Gilmans Point had gone. The altitude and thin air were now taking a toll, and it was time to start back down the stony, snow covered-slope, back to the Kibo huts some four thousand feet below. We made our way back to Gilmans Point and then to the huts.

The wise thing to do is to take your time when going down from a high altitude, and let your body adjust. But it was too easy to almost run and slide down the stony scree, and I went too fast. The sudden change in air pressure gave me an intense and very painful headache. It felt as though my skull was opening and shutting. I sat down for a while to adjust, then started, with some others, to walk down the mountain. My feet were by then very painful. The oversized boots had caused mammoth blisters. I think we may have stopped overnight at the Mandara hut, but whether we did or not, we eventually got back to the Inn in Moshi. I finally took my boots off and looked at the bloody mess that was my feet. The blisters were the size of chicken's eggs. I was told of an old retired German doctor who could help me. I found him. He looked exactly like the German actor Eric Von Stroheim, and he had been living by the mountain since the First World War. He popped the egg-sized blisters on my feet and fixed me up with some bandages. I gave him ten shillings and went on my way.

I found Bill Ford, and together we drove back to Dar es Salaam, a rough and dusty journey, but I was very content. In Dar I had the photos developed. There were a couple of good shots of Bill Ford and Inga, and of the ascent, and some very good ones of the mountain. I did like the photo of the horses at 15,500 feet, and the picture I took of the sergeant standing on the Point was quite good. Then there was the picture that he took of me at Gilmans Point—what a disaster. It showed me from the waist up with a clear blue sky for a background and a serious pants problem. There was nothing to show that I was actually standing on top of Mount Kilimanjaro. In *fact*, there was no mountain at all. The sergeant had had the last laugh.

With no photographic evidence that I had actually stood on top of the mountain, you might not believe that I had, but there was a book in a box somewhere up there in which all climbers who reached the summit signed their names, as did I. It may still be there, so if you don't believe my story, you can climb up the mountain and search for that book. You will be sure to see my name.

I am glad that we did meet those soldiers and cadets by the Kibo Huts; otherwise, there would not be much of a story. I do also wish that the British army sergeant had been more careful when taking my photograph and included the mountain under my feet. But sometimes I wonder whether it really was his revenge for me not letting him get to the top first.

TODAY, CLIMBING THE MOUNTAIN has become a big part of the East African tourist industry. At any given time, there are thousands of climbers scrambling to the top, lining up to stand at the peak to have their picture taken, and, sadly, leaving trash scattered over the climbing trails. I don't think I would want to climb that mountain today with so many other people, but if I did, I would be sure to get better-fitting boots. In 1961, until we met the sergeant and the army party, we had it all to ourselves— that glorious mountain, and just our small group, slowly making our way up to the "Roof of Africa."

Ellen Korn

Nancy Bachrach
nancy.bachrach@gmail.com

Bio

Ellen Pennock Korn, originally from The Bronx, New York, is now a part-time resident of Kings Point in Delray Beach, Florida. When not in Florida, she and her husband Allan reside in New Jersey. In New Jersey she enjoys taking adult learning classes through Rutgers University and is a member of two reading groups. She is a graduate of Hunter College, with a B.A. in English, and Mary Grove College, where she received a M.A. in Education. Her fulfilling teaching career included a junior high school in the Bronx and an urban high school in New Jersey, in which she taught English, Literature, Writing, Reading, and AP courses.

Her fifth grade teacher, Mrs. Lyons, told her that some day she "would be an authoress" after reading her poetry and stories. Ellen has spent her life constantly writing, hoping to prove Mrs. Lyons correct.

In New Jersey Ellen enrolled in the Osher learning program, affiliated with Rutgers University, where she took a memoir writing course facilitated by Dr. Susan London. Dr. London's enthusiasm and excitement about Ellen's writing spurred her to begin writing a complete memoir, which she is currently finishing.

Ellen thanks the King's Point Creative Writers Club members for welcoming her into their midst and for their support and suggestions. She dedicates her writing to her two children and their families. She wants her five grandchildren to read her memoirs and really understand what their grandmother was all about. She offers three chapters from her memoirs for the readers' enjoyment.

The Caterpillar

Every summer my parents leased what we called a "bungalow" in the Catskill Mountains for the summer. It was something that

people in the Bronx and Brooklyn did to escape the heat of the city
and perhaps forget about everyday life, which, for some, was not
always inviting. My mother told me that I even took my first baby
steps in "the country," as she always called it. We went away every
summer. My parents gave my sister and me into the custody of an
aunt and uncle while they drove the three hours (before the New
York State Thruway had been built) through the various towns
such as South Fallsburg, Monticello, Ellenville, and others to find
a suitable place to rent. Since my aunt and uncle had no children
of their own, we were doted on until late in the evening when my
tired parents returned and said "we took a place."
This time they rented a place with a minimum of conveniences,
such as a pool and casino for social occasions. That year when
I was six and my sister was too young to matter, it was called
Drucker's, a scattering of cottages in what amounted to little more
than mowed fields and sidewalks. My father and other fathers drove
up on the weekends and my mother, along with the other women,
tried to make lives for themselves, temporary as it was. They too,
waited for their husbands and it was only on the weekend that true
happiness suffused the lives of the waiting families. We went to
town; we went to the movies; we were social. The children were
turned loose, for if nothing else it was a safe haven from the traffic
and perceived evils of the city. It was there that I had my first real
remembrances.

I remember the sun; it burned my skin. It wrapped itself around
my arms and squeezed. It made me feel as if I was wearing a tight-
fitting hat that I could not remove. It sent sweat into my eyes. It
made my clothes stick to me. The grass crunched hard under my
feet. I squinted. I ran to my mother for water often. But I stayed
outside, always outside. Part of it was because my mother felt that
being outside was necessary. They did not come to the country
to stay indoors, a sentiment shared by other mothers as well. So
I went outside. I do not have clear memories of my sister, but she
waited to be summoned, or thrust into my care. There I was, just

looking, waiting, and hoping whatever six-year-old girls hope in the place that offered nothing except a change of scenery and people I had never before seen and would never see again.

"Hello." He was about my age. I remember his short blond hair topping a plain but kind face.
"Hello." He was the first child I saw that summer, sent out to fend for myself while my mother unpacked and my sister watched her.
"Do you want to make mud?" I never thought about making mud. It was just always there.
"OK."
"Let's go. Come to my house."
I did not want to go into his house. I felt strange. I did not know him, nor was I really sure of where I was, nor what would happen; but as he asked, and since the sun was stabbing my neck, I followed him to his kitchen. His bungalow was larger than mine, and I thought that his family must be rich to have something so big, not realizing the relative poverty of everyone who was there for the summer. I stood near the door, silently watching as he pulled a chair over to the sink to fill a pail.

Suddenly, a large woman appeared at the entrance to the kitchen.
"Get out of my house!" Loud, deep, menacing. "Get out of my house!"
"We were just getting water to make mud." My words were unheard. "But we were just...."
"Get out! Get out of my house!"
"But...."
"Leave my house!"
I did not understand what happened. In my little-girl mind I tried to be as unobtrusive as possible. I stood as still as a statue. I touched nothing. I did nothing wrong. I was shocked into stunned silence as I ran out of the door, passed the woman on my way out, trying to make myself invisible as I did so. I followed the sidewalk up the hill to my family's bungalow and buried myself in my bed. I

don't remember if I cried, but I had felt swallowed by the relentless
sun, the endless fields, and the cracked sidewalks. I kept hearing
the voice that told me to "get out." I could not breathe. Her voice
covered me as I cowered in my bed. Now, more than sixty years
later, I can still hear that booming voice directed at a six-year-old
child standing in a kitchen while a blond boy was getting water to
make mud.

"Ellen, what's wrong?" My mother came into the bedroom the
entire family would share that summer.
"Nothing." My voice was almost inaudible.
"Ellen, why are you acting like this? Tell me. Did something
happen?
"No." Something, of course, *had happened*, but it had been too
monumentally confusing for me to understand. I could not speak.
"Answer me, I have too much to do. Take Nancy and go outside.
Find someone to play with."

If I could have stayed on that bed for the rest of the summer, I
would have done so. I needed more time, but I grabbed my sister's
arm and pulled her with me, carefully avoiding the blond boy
who was now standing in front of his bungalow next to that obese
woman with long black hair tied in a ponytail and wearing a
nondescript apron, worn black shoes, with her dark eyes staring at
me. It is the first thing I remember being afraid of in my life.

The next day I wandered around the grounds talking tentatively
to other children, some older than I, some the same age, trying
to forget my deep humiliation. I stayed clear of the offending
bungalow; the blond boy was there but I avoided him. I was still
afraid. I walked with my eyes to the ground, having no clear
destination. I heard voices and I raised my head to see a group of
women sitting in a circle of Adirondack chairs, being regaled by
the story of the indiscretion of which I was accused. Dressed in the
same gray apron, using the same booming voice, and gesticulating

for emphasis, she told the story. "She was standing in my kitchen. I couldn't believe it!" I was doomed, I do not remember my mother being there, and as she never mentioned it to me, I assumed that she never found out. I ran to the fields, my legs being nipped by bugs and spiny weeds, and stopped to watch the dragonflies, bees, and swinging wildflowers as they commanded the day. It was silent. Her voice could not reach me there. The drone of insects became my world for a few precious moments. My child's mind, at that precise moment in time, feared that the summer would never end and that I would forever be marked for I knew not what.

Later on that summer, the mud-making incident momentarily forgotten, she, her son, and several other children as well as myself were sitting in that same circle of chairs, our little legs sticking straight out in front of us, the Adirondack chairs not allowing us to reach the ground. Our bodies were tiny as we gripped the armrests to somehow keep ourselves from being swallowed up by the downward slant of the wooden seats. She was lecturing us, "G-d is all around you." No one had ever talked to me about G-d. With all of the religious rituals my family observed, G-d never seemed to enter the picture. I knew that G-d existed but He was a mystery which I never pondered.

"He is?" Someone asked.

"Yes, He is. Wherever you go or do, G-d is there."

"Even here?"

"Yes. Look at the chair you are sitting in. He is all around your chair."

"Around my chair?" I looked but saw nothing special.

"Everywhere. Everywhere you go. No matter what you do. You can't escape."

"We can't?"

"No, He is in front of you and behind you. He is by the sides. He surrounds you."

At that moment she abruptly left our group, leaving several children under the age of eight afraid. They, like me, never thought about G-d, but since we now knew that he was surrounding us, we did not know what to do. We stared at each other. Since our young legs did not allow us to reach the ground, our feet were in the wrong place; we could not move and we were afraid. We sat silently, looking around, intently looking for Him. I did not want to step on G-d, nor did any of the other children. We sat for interminable minutes, never speaking.

Suddenly, a voice called one of the children. It was someone's mother A boy who looked even more afraid than I was turned his head to look back at his bungalow. We all followed his mother's voice but did not move. The voice called again. It was more insistent, using his full name. He suddenly bolted, and as if given permission, we all did the same, rushing toward our bungalows for safety. We never mentioned the subject again, but for quite a while I moved cautiously, looking for G-d and not wanting to hurt Him.

Children have a resilience that is unsurpassed by that of adults and as the sun continued to bake the land, the people, and the happenings, I went on being the child that I was. One day, my arms again stinging from the brutal sun, as I looked for something to do, I saw a caterpillar. It was moving slowly and steadily on the sidewalk in front of the blond boy's bungalow. Its brown and yellow markings traveled up what I called caterpillar fur, and its head was bobbing almost imperceptibly from side to side. It was several inches long. I still see it in my mind's eye, unwavering, on a mission, "going home" as I now tell my grandson when he asks where a bug is going. That caterpillar suddenly became the focus of my existence. I no longer cared that I was outside of the blond boy's house. This was something grander, more infinite than the booming voice of which I was no longer afraid. I only cared about the caterpillar, the most beautiful thing I had ever seen. I was on my knees, scraping the skin raw as I moved as close as I dared to get, the singe on my arms forgotten, as I concentrated on the journey that only I was witnessing. The small creature marched

to its own inner rhythm, undulating toward an unknown place, an
unknown realm.

"Hey, hey what are you doing? What do you have?"

It was not the blond boy or his mother but three older boys who
were trying to relieve their own boredom by talking to me. They
stood behind me, squinting in the sun, trying to figure out what a
child could find so engrossing in the heat of that summer long ago.

"Nothing." But it was so much more than that. Again, I was afraid,
not for myself but for the caterpillar.

"Let's see. Get out of the way" They pushed me aside as they saw
the caterpillar. They knelt beside me.

"It's mine. I saw it first. Leave it alone."

"We want to see it. You're just a girl!"

"Leave it alone. Don't hurt it."

"What do you know about anything? Hey, wait a minute." They
left, but one boy quickly returned with a stick. "Let's try this."

He began to poke the caterpillar, gently at first, then with
more urgency. I silently prayed that he would not kill it, but
the caterpillar continued on its way, overcoming the tortured
interruption to which it was being subjected. It was as if none of us
existed.

"Hey, I have an idea." The oldest boy stood up. "Watch the
caterpillar. Don't let it get away." He ran off and disappeared into
his bungalow. The other boys just waited, and like sentries we
silently watched what should have been trivial but slowly become
one of the most important experiences of my young life.

I had, by this time, appointed myself the guardian of the caterpillar
and worried about its safety. The end of the sidewalk was in sight
and I was afraid of what would happen if it disappeared into the tall
grass. After what seemed like an eternity, the boy returned with an
empty milk carton. In those days of my early youth, milk cartons
were covered in wax and had a small lid on one corner which was
pried open in order to pour the milk. It held a capacity of one quart
and this one was empty. I wondered only much later on if he had

poured out the milk to implement his plan, and if his mother found out what he had done.

"You can help."

I looked at him. Suddenly I counted. He let me play. He let me see. He let me witness. "Watch this."

He broke off leaves and small stems and put them into the carton. I looked inside to see the milky white interior transformed into I knew not what. Then he carefully lifted the caterpillar using the large leaf and put both leaf and caterpillar into the carton, punching an air hole in the top. He closed the lid and sent the caterpillar on a new journey, one that I could not begin to imagine. It was taken from me and I felt awe and fright overcame me. Did it die? What will happen? Was it my fault? I should have let the caterpillar to its own devices. But it was so beautiful. I had to look. The boy ran to the part of the field untouched by lawnmower or even the tread of human trespass, the same field that had offered me solace when I ran from the blond boy's bungalow. His friends and I ran behind him and watched in awe as he raised his arm and threw the carton into the sky. It fell into the field among the weeds, away from our sight. We tried to locate it with our eyes but no one moved to find it.

"Did you see it?" He looked at me with a smile on his face. "Remember where it is." He and his friends ran from me, leaving me among the tall weeds and summer wildflowers hoping that the caterpillar would survive its ordeal.

Sometimes when I think about that small event in an inconsequential child's life, I wonder if I am remembering it at all, or if it is just a childhood wish to remember a miracle that happened when I was six years old. I really did not know what a miracle was or had even heard the word. I just remember the caterpillar. Looming large in my memory, it keeps trudging to its destination and keeps going to where it needs to be. But I still see it. As I gaze at the picture I took with my fellow teachers at our retirement party so far in the future from this happening, I understand that this incident is analogous to the another journey I would be starting in the next century of my life. Life is filled with lessons you do not even know you are learning.

The summer progressed as all summers do. Every weekend my father came up the experience of his tedious drive got erased when he saw all of us. My mother allowed my sister and me to greet him first, her turn followed, then news of our lives was shared among our small family circle. He brought us coloring books and crayons to be saved for after he went back to the city. We went to town, looked at the store windows, splurged at the movies in buying popcorn, and welcoming the air conditioning that was an added bonus. Too soon, he, as did the other fathers, got into his car and made the long trip back to the city to do whatever it was they did, only to repeat the same motions seven days later.

I forgot about the caterpillar. It had gone to another place and been removed to another time; and I contented myself with the things that little girls in the late 1950s did to keep busy. All of the children played games together, games we invented, rules made up as we went along, as well as games that tasked our imaginations. We played, and we ran, and we, even at such young ages, dreamed.

Then one day, when the unrelenting sun was biting our faces, the boy who threw the caterpillar into the field, that caterpillar whom I had once loved and then had just as easily forgotten, screamed loudly to all of the children. "Come here. Come here. Look what I found." We ran. No one knew what it was, no one knew why we were running, but it seemed to be momentous.
Something had happened, and we were all going to witness it.
We found the boy standing at the edge of the field, holding the milk carton, raising it above his head as if he had won a trophy. We crowded him, and he let me stand next to him. We looked at the carton and watched him open the lid, then slowly widen the opening with some effort. All of us held our breath. It was ours.

It had been resting in a field alone, being rained on and being warmed by the sun, waiting for us. Inside that old wax milk carton was a butterfly. It was fluttering madly. A shambles had been made of its makeshift home, but it was alive. It overcame its fate and was alive. The boy made the opening even wider, held the carton away from his body, raised his arm, and the butterfly broke free. It fluttered in circles, ever widening and distancing itself from its former captors. We followed it with our eyes until it flew into the sun, and a moment later, nothing left to see, we dispersed, the milk carton crushed under our feet.

We went home to the Bronx, I entered first grade, and I continued my life with my family. My parents still had money issues; I still fought with my sister; I still got left out of games played by children who lived on my block of nondescript apartment buildings; I still read; and I still dreamed the childish dreams that would make my life, I thought, better. I remember many things from those years; but most of all, even now, I remember the caterpillar.

My Sixth-Grade Teacher

My sixth-grade teacher was a bully. It was easy for him because when I was in the sixth grade, in the late fifties, it was tolerated; he could get away with it because no one complained, certainly not a skinny brown-haired girl with thick glasses that were not becoming to her and which she hated to wear. I did not like the way I looked in them but needed them to see clearly. I, and to a lesser extent, a few boys in the class, were objects of his derision, but I was the only one who suffered the extreme verbal abuse, condoned by Mr. Black, directed at me by other students in class 6-3, in P.S. 95, The Bronx, New York.

The school, a red brick edifice covering almost a square block in a quiet shady neighborhood, is still in existence. It now houses an intermediate school, which, to my surprise, one of my students in New Jersey had attended before moving away. But the bully is no longer there. Perhaps he has even died by now, but not before inflicting his own brand of horror on me and other students who came after me.

Mr. Black, a man of about thirty, with a balding head and black eyeglasses which seemed to bore into you as he stared, had been an eighth-grade Math teacher, and a good one, I was told. When the school was converted into a K-6 (Kindergarten through Grade Six) school, he did not move up to the new junior high school that opened a few blocks away but was given a sixth-grade class to teach, much to his disappointment. I had the misfortune to be in that class. My math intelligence being much less than stellar, and Mr. Black's intelligence limited almost exclusively to math, amounted to a nightmare for me, a quiet, unobtrusive girl, whose only intellectual love was reading and writing.

The room held 30 desks, arranged in rows of six, all of which were nailed to the floor, corresponding flip-up seats directly behind. Each desk had the remnants of inkwells, reminiscent of the days when students carefully dipped their pens into bottles of ink in order to do their lessons. I used to stare at these circular depressions set in the corners of all of the desks I occupied throughout the years and wonder about the students who had sat there before me. But I did nothing to the desk, not even adding to the hard dried collections of gum that lined its underside. In addition, no desk was immune to the deeply carved impressions of names and designs of its previous occupants, who turned the desks into minor works of art, the graffiti of the classroom. Their dark-brown color was uniform for every desk, and the small shelf underneath held our books and other school supplies.

The entire back of the room was lined with an enormous built-in closet, standard for most schools at that time, with hooks for our coats, and additional shelves for our belongings. Punctuating the closet's two massive sliding doors were three vertical bulletin boards, which displayed the work of selected students. Only the highest-marks papers were there, stapled or thumb-tacked for the viewing pleasure of the class as we hung our coats in the morning and retrieved them at the end of the day. No one was allowed to go to the closet after hanging up our coats in the morning until the dismissal bell rang at three o'clock no matter what the reason, except at lunch time, when students could take lunches from the closet. (Only the more well-off students did bring lunch. A catered box variety was served for the rest at a special table in the gym-turned-cafeteria). The sliding brown doors hid everything from view, and at the end of the wall stood a teacher's closet, covered with the same dark wood but with a lock and key. I once got a peek into another such closet and saw the mirror my fifth-grade teacher used for putting on her lipstick every day. It was bright red, like her hair. She had a place to hang her coat with a hangar. When I had such a closet of my own upon beginning my teaching in the Bronx, I remembered Mrs. Lyons wearing her red lipstick to a point every day as she stroked it back and forth across her lips. Mr. Black never needed a mirror, having few hairs to comb, and no lipstick to use. I never saw him even use the teacher's closet, although I suppose that he owned a coat that needed to be hung.

Mr. Black's desk was to the left of the front of the room, near a wall of large windows. His formidable appearance, dark suit, starched white shirt and dull colored-tie, has still stayed with me. His desk had very little on it, but he used it to write and take daily attendance in a special book he had; and he stored papers in the drawers. He sat on his cushioned chair like it was a throne. All of the students sat, hands folded on the carved desks, waiting for him to begin. We stared, and he stared, all of us waiting for the day to begin.

"Hey, Mr. Black, do you know what Pencil Head said?" Donald, one of the most popular and cruelest boys in the class, stood beside his desk, his overweight body looming, standing, as required for recitation, crewcut-clipped head erect, waiting for encouragement from the teacher for him to begin his latest comedy routine. He stabbed me with his words.

"What?"

"I asked her what H2O is and she said oatmeal." HO was a brand of a popular cereal at the time.

The class erupted into squeals of unrestrained laugher. I jumped up from my seat, screaming, "I did not. I never said that. I did not." No one heard me. I screamed it out again, but the laughter made everyone deaf. I sat down and became as small as I could, but I no longer mattered to anyone.

"All right, Donald, sit down." Donald did so, still smiling. Mr. Black was matter-of-fact about the entire performance. He knew that the story was a fabrication, but he let it go on, and said nothing to help me deal with the cruelty.

Mr. Black did Math. He spoke Math. He referred to Math even when he was not teaching it. He taught Math all day, giving perfunctory attention to the other subjects at which I excelled but which he seemed to loathe. He covered the blackboard with fractions, his handwriting bold and large, white chalk prominent against the newly washed board.

"Ellen, how would you compute this fraction?" He stared at me.

"I don't know."

"Try. I just explained it."

"I don't know."

Laughter erupted, while another student stood by his desk and gave the right answer while sniggering at me with his eyes as well as his voice.

"Ellen, why can't you do this? What's wrong with you?"

No answer.

There was only one time that I was relieved of the humiliation perpetrated by this man. It happened when one of the boys in the class was not wearing a tie. While we did not wear uniforms, all of the boys were required to wear button-down shirts and a tie every day, and girls wore dresses with handkerchiefs prominently pinned to the bodice so it could be seen that we were ready for any emergency. Mr. Black always waited until the entire class was seated. While it was not always easy to determine if every girl had the requisite handkerchief (some were in pockets), it was always easy to spot the boy without the necessary tie. The offending boy was called up to the desk, Mr. Black's top desk drawer would be slowly opened, and a paper tie would emerge. The boy was handed the tie and a safety pin, and the entire class watched while he pinned the tie to his shirt. He had to wear the paper tie for the rest of the day. The tieless boy would always be embarrassed and usually had a red face upon returning to his seat.

Sometimes I got a math problem correct. It made no difference, because other students loudly feigned surprise and pretended that they had stomach pains, or conveniently fell to the floor from their hard wooden seats, laughing all the way at this strange occurrence. Ellen got something right. Mr. Black was silent. I just stared at him through my thick eyeglasses and tried to ignore the antics, but even the teacher noticed my pain. I once saw it on his face. But he never stopped them.

I was ten years old when I entered sixth grade. The school cutoff date was April 30th and I made it by fewer than two weeks. Some of the students in the class were close to a year older than I, and students often guffawed about my age, calling me "baby." One of those offenders, named Sybil, lived on the opposite end of my block, but we were not friends, neither of us ever venturing to each other's end to play games. She was the "teacher's pet"; she could do no wrong. Sybil was shorter than I was and had a hairstyle that involved rounded curls symmetrically placed around her

head. She had a protruding face, which announced her when she
walked towards you, and her buck teeth needed braces. Sybil wore
a snickering smile whenever she was near me. I do remember,
however, a pink dress that she often wore, with a swirling skirt
and large sailor collar with white stripes. When I think of her
I think of that dress. Someone so mean did not deserve to have
such a pretty dress. She was Mr. Black's monitor, his secretary,
his student confidant; and her desk was directly in front of his. He
asked her for her help unobtrusively whenever he needed it. And
he did need it. Often, indeed always, Sybil had it covered. She
knew things about every student that she should not have known,
and she seemed to know everything. She was always turning
around to stare at the class, as if she was searching for someone
or something. The sly smile that she constantly wore was visible
to the entire class. Somehow, one day Sybil had in her possession
a list of the I.Q.'s of every student in the room. I do not know how
she got it, but she had it on her desk. Suddenly, all the students
knew their I.Q.s and everyone else's as well. She shouted them out
rapidly, like in a roll call. I had never known my I.Q. before but I
soon found out, as did everyone else in the class.
"Oh, I don't believe it." Donald exclaimed, when he found out that
my I.Q. was way above average.
"It must be a mistake." Robert joined in.
"It says so right here," Sybil shouted. Then she laughed.
Again fake illnesses with accompanying groans and choking noises
developed. I did not pay attention, because I was given a new
confidence. Mr. Black quickly took the offending information out
of Sybil's hands, but the lives of all of the students were impacted,
and nothing could be done about it. The ethical breach was never
mentioned.

The rows of desks were set two together, so there were three sets
of two rows each, the desks joined together like conjoined twins,
but in this case, separation was impossible. I sat next to Louise, an
almost totally blind girl who unfortunately had one of the lower

I.Q.s in the class (thanks, Sybil) but was spared taunting because of her physical affliction. Louise liked me, and I tried to help her as much as I could. I had sympathy for her limited vision, since without my own glasses on I saw only blurs and knew what a handicap she must have faced, young as I was. She was very sweet and always smiled. Her short brown hair framed a flat face, with mostly expressionless eyes. She also wore glasses, and we worked together, as long as it was not Math, to make sense of the lessons taught to us each day. One day Louise and I were working on a reading assignment, and I was actively explaining the lesson to her, helping her understand the concept at hand. I suddenly felt a presence hovering over me and looked up to see Mr. Black leaning over my desk.

"Why," he stated in an even voice, "can't you be as good in Math as you are in English?" Then he turned away.

Everyone bought a gift to the teacher at Christmas. My parents, for whom every penny counted, had little to spend.

"I bought Mr. Black an eyeglass case for Christmas," my mother said proudly when she showed me a beautiful black eyeglass case with gold threads running through the design. We were sitting on her bed, a place for important discussion.

"An eyeglass case?" I was horrified.

"What's wrong with it?" my mother asked.

"Can't we get something else?" I was pleading.

"No, Ellen, this is it."

A few days later the class was walking back to the classroom from the gym, which was on the top floor of the school (Mr. Black was also our gym teacher). I found myself walking next to him, as the straight line the class started out in had fallen apart.

"Mr. Black, do you use an eyeglass case?" I tried to sound grown up.

"Yes." He looked at me.

"Can you use more than one?"

"Yes," he repeated.

Confident that I had paved the way for my present, I contentedly walked back to the room.

The day before Christmas vacation started we gave him our gifts, gaily wrapped in bright paper and bows. His desk was piled high with a gift from each student, and, like a bride opening her shower gifts, he made a great show of opening his.

"Look at this." It was a shirt. He held it up for all to see.

"This is great, a pen and pencil set." He held it up so that everyone could see. Mr. Black commented after opening each gift.

After several gifts of obvious expense were opened, he came to mine.

"An eyeglass case," he said.

"Look at that stupid present Ellen bought," Sybil shouted.

Titters made the rounds. Her comment was echoed by some of the boys.

"Thank you," Mr. Black said and moved on.

"Did Mr. Black like the eyeglass case?" my mother asked that evening.

"Yes," I mumbled. "He said, 'Thank you.'"

Mr. Black practiced a form of physical punishment. On the days he felt the class was unruly, or broke a rule, or for some other unknown reason, he let us know that the misdeed would not be tolerated by his punishing the class as a whole. No one, not even a favorite of his, was immune. "Everyone stand next to his or her desk." We did so.

"Now when I call each row, walk to the closet and take your books and coats." We did so. "Take all of the books from inside your desks." We did so. "Stand at your desk and hold everything in your arms, and don't put them down until I say so." We obeyed. We stood still and quiet until we were allowed to put everything away and sit down.

Other days we had to stand with our arms straight out in front of us until he deemed it ready for us to place them by our sides.

In all the years I attended P.S. 95 I never saw anyone enter any classroom to observe or even check on a class or a teacher. The teachers were on their own and could run their classrooms as they saw fit, as did Mr. Black. He was loved by the administration because he did so many things that other teachers did not want to do or simply did not know how to do. One thing that made him a coveted member of the faculty was that he put on plays. He was good at it. The school had an auditorium and a large stage at which various presentations and grade or class meetings were held periodically. One time my class was standing on the stage, rehearsing a song for the play *The Red Shoes* that Mr. Black was producing. It starred Nancy, a girl who lived across the street from me who was extremely intelligent and mature and knew ballet. We were cordial to each other but never had a friendship until years later, when we had achieved a more equal footing in life. Mr. Black lavished attention on her, and she choreographed her own dancing; but as he had to do something with the rest of the class, he made us sing. We stood on the stage, in two rows; I was in the back row, singing along with the class.

"Hey, Mr. Black." Donald raised his hand.

Mr. Black stopped his direction of the group and all eyes and ears turned to Donald.

"I'm very busy. What do you want?"

"I'm trying to sing and Pencil Head is singing the wrong notes and messing all of us up."

Mr. Black moved along the line to me. "Sing," he said. His head was tilted to his left, and he listened. I sang, making my voice very small.

"He's right, just move your lips."

Mr. Black also ran the dance festival, a yearly school-wide event that showcased the ability of all of the students in their square-dancing and folk-dancing prowess. With the assistance of other teachers, Mr. Black taught all of the dances to all of the grades. On a spring day, in the huge yard attached to the school, all of the students sat cross-legged on the cement ground, as we waited for our chance to show off to the invited guests, mostly parents. A phonograph, placed near a microphone, played the music, and the boys, wearing special neckties and the girls, their biggest swirling skirts, showed off. I loved it. A boy who hated me held my hand and the girls curtsied with me as we were taught, and it was a time when I was unafraid of any hurtful words or actions. This was one occasion in which I never made a mistake.

Mr. Black was also popular for his annual Thanksgiving dinner, held in the classroom. Invited guests were Miss Flynn, our short, gray haired principal–whose only appearance other than this one at Mr. Black's yearly feast was at weekly grade meetings in the auditorium when she constantly repeated, "a lot is a piece of land" and other such bits of wisdom—and Miss Bilia, a tall, imposing woman with a loud voice and bright red hair, the assistant principal. She wore green almost every day. Each day she chose one student from each fifth- or sixth-grade class to be her monitor, someone to do her errands and anything else she needed done. On the day she chose me I had forgotten my glasses and could not find any of the rooms to which she sent me, or read any of the papers she gave me to read. I was sent back to my class in disgrace, and she commented at the negligence of a mother who would allow her child to attend school without her glasses. A special table was set up in honor of Miss Flynn and Miss Bilia with a table cloth and real eating utensils; and Mr. Black served them first, with the turkey and other dishes paid for by contributions made by everyone in the class. I watched them eat daintily, while thanking us all for the lovely meal. I ate also, served by Mr. Black just as he served the other students. It was one of the few things I enjoyed that year.

Mr. Black assigned what we all called his punishment assignments. Unruly or other objectionable behavior was dealt with by having the offenders write a paragraph consisting of 30 words (the offenders counted each word) a certain number of times.

Sometimes it was 10 times; others, it was 20 or more. The paragraphs were handed to Sybil, who marked off the homework and counted the paragraphs. She would report the findings to Mr. Black, who would nod his head and say no more about it. The assignments were placed on his desk and no one ever saw them again.

I see Mr. Black pacing in front of the room, his dark shoes making clicking noises. The students are sitting at their desks, nailed to their seats as firmly as the desks are nailed to the floor. Their hands are folded tightly on their desk tops. He stares at the class through the black-rimmed eyeglasses that are always on his expressionless face. The class states back at him.

"Here it comes," a nameless student mutters under his breath.

"Michael, 10 times." The mouths of almost everyone in the class make an O, in genuine surprise.

"Donald, 20 times." Mr. Black verbally lists his punishments. He points his finger. Not a surprise.

"But I didn't do anything."

"25 times." Mr. Black amends his punishment. The 30-word paragraph must be written as many times as directed. There was no appeal.

"Larry, 30 times." Larry adjusts his tie. He scratches his head, making no indentation in his crewcut.

"Robert, 50 times" An audible groan rises from the class. Robert puts his hand on his head. He lightly taps his hard black shoe on the floor. He turns his head to look at the rest of the class.

Mr. Black turns his head to look at the clock. There are 15 minutes left to the day. The large black hands are prominent in the heavy brown-framed clock as it holds court from its position above the blackboard, which is covered with Math problems. There is still time. The sound of a hard rain suddenly fills the air.

"Sybil, are you writing this down?" Mr. Black looks at her.

Mr. Black's student recorder dutifully writes down every assignment he gives. She holds up her pencil to show him and the class.

"Lucille, 5 times." Lucille smooths down the front of her dress. Her face shows a slight smile.

Mr. Black, looking large and fearless in his gray suit and matching tie, takes a deep breath.

"Here it comes," said the same nameless student again.

Mr. Black looks at me. "Ellen, write a two-page report on the Renaissance."

"The what?" I could not help but speak up.

"The Renaissance." He spelled it for me.

"What is it? I never heard of it." Tears creep into my voice but I hold them back.

"The Renaissance. Look it up." Mr. Black dismisses me with his voice.

Students stare at me. Eyes roll. Some look away. They pretend I am not there. I turn to look at Michael, one of the few friends I have in the class. He turns from me. Even my fellow partners in crime are in shock. But I say nothing more.

When the three o'clock bell rings, I go to the wooden Closet, which—as I described—hosts bulletin boards in between the wooden sliding doors, displaying the superior work of the students (not mine), move the heavy sliding door, and slowly take my coat. The students still avert their eyes, and I walk slowly home. "The Renaissance" I repeat, as I cross Mosholu Parkway, barely looking to see if the light is green; "The Renaissance," I say, as I walk up the hill on Gun Hill Road around the corner from Gates Place, my home. "The Renaissance," I whisper, as I climb the stone steps that lead to my apartment. I arrive home from school in tears.

"Don't worry', my mother says. I'll help you." She stops what she is doing and we both sit at the kitchen table to do Mr. Black's bidding. We take the "R" volume of *The Book of Knowledge* from its special place in the bookcase, the encyclopedia that had been an extravagant purchase made by my father a year or two previously. My mother and I both quickly become educated about the Renaissance, she, turning the pages of the encyclopedia, and me, writing down the information I think important enough for the report. We sit at the kitchen table. We read the pages together and learn about something neither one of us ever knew existed.

"Ma, I can't wait to show this to Mr. Black. It's so good. Thanks for helping me."

"You did a good job. Let me know what he thinks," my mother smiles.

I rewrite the report in my best handwriting, using my favorite blue pen, and carefully put it in my looseleaf. I bounce my way to school.

"Everyone hand in your assignments to Sybil now." Mr. Black watches us pass the assignments across the desks to Sybil's waiting hands. She busies herself checking off names and counting paragraphs. She checks off my report. I am excited. I want him to read it. I stare at Mr. Black.

"Did everyone do the work?" Mr. Black looks at Sybil.

"Yes," she dutifully replies.

Mr. Black stands in front of the class, square body still, stretches out his right hand in Sybil's direction, and receives the papers from her. He quickly flips through them, looks for names, looks as if he is reading some of them, and makes sure that all is in order. Then he holds them high, at eye level, and, with great deliberation, rips the papers in half and drops them in the green garbage can beside his desk.

College

In college I learned to love literature, learned folk dancing, wrote a play, had the play shot down by a playwright who was one of

my professors, made friends, was disliked by members of a club
I joined, dated, broke up, took long rides on beautiful roads that
skirted the Bronx and Westchester, never drank alcohol, learned
how to drive, flirted with geology, loved Shakespeare, was
introduced to a wide range of classical music for which I developed
a lasting appreciation, smoked pot, had sex, briefly dated a
professor, went to a singles weekend at a hotel in the Catskills, had
four very serious romances, met the man who would eventually
become my husband, went to parties, began a lifelong love affair
with the protest/folk music of the sixties, left my old friends
behind, stopped liking most of my new friends, learned to play the
banjo, shot a rifle, ate lunch with a group of girls at the same table
every day who largely ignored me but met one of my boyfriends
because I sat at that table, met a very sweet girl who did not know
the meaning of the word "apathetic" (in her adult life she became
chairperson of a public school elementary reading program),
developed a love for history, majored in English, minored in
Speech and Theater (mostly theater), had a very misogynistic
science teacher, grew to love acoustic guitar, lived at home but
stayed away as much as possible, forgot about my life before
college, and tried to forge an after one.

I attended Hunter College in the Bronx, now called Lehman
College. I felt it had a more beautiful campus with five main
buildings set on a sprawling lawn with a traffic circle in the center
than had most of the other colleges in the system. My friends had
all scattered, attending different branches of the City University of
New York, pursuing different majors and different agenda. I left
a comfortable life with close friends who understood me and the
problems of my life; I left the easy laughter and my three good
friends Allen, Larry and Eddie, whom, except for Allen, with
whom I was later to reconnect, I rarely saw. There was no more
hanging around the park or going to someone's house to listen
to records and talk. I had to find an anchor. Although there were
fraternities at Hunter, there were no sororities. Instead there were

House Plans, a title I have never understood. They were similar to sororities but had no national affiliation or separate places to call their own off campus. They were allotted classrooms for meetings and, for all else, a rented room or a member's own home. They pledged new members, like sororities; and I attended open houses for two of them with the one friend from my neighborhood. We were accepted to different House Plans and decided to part ways and lives to join our respective ones.

T house was supposed to be the best of all House Plans and everyone was extremely nice and friendly. I was flattered to be accepted. In retrospect, I cannot understand why those girls, who thought so highly of themselves, were considered to be desirable, when in reality they were mean and petty. I did not know that then and was happy to have the girl with the vocabulary problem as my big sister to show me around and educate me about the T House's inner workings.

It was nice to never be alone. Whenever I went for lunch in the cafeteria there was always someone sitting at what became the T house table. At first, I had friends and felt important. We all spent time together and were partners with a fraternity with whom we put on plays and had social functions. I noticed that the girls, who were so friendly at the pledge functions, had their own mini-groups within the House Plan and ignored the rest of us. These same girls, who played the guitar and sang the folk songs I came to love, rarely spoke to me. These same girls, who had smiled at me and engaged me in conversation, ignored me. These same girls blamed me for a heartache suffered by another member with which I had nothing to do nor understood.

His name was Lorenzo. He had been dating Margie, but they broke up. Lorenzo liked me. He pursued me. We were both English majors and by chance were in several of the same classes. We sat near each other. We talked shop. We compared notes. We walked through the halls together. We became good friends.

One day I was stopped in the hall. "Ellen, we have to talk to you." Susan, the president of T House and two other girls were standing in front of me.

"OK." I could not understand why they stopped me. They wore serious expressions.
"Let's go in here." They led the way to an empty classroom.
"What is it?" They made me nervous.
"Why are you going out with Lorenzo?"
"I'm not going out with him. We have three classes together, that's all.
"You know that Margie loves him. Don't talk to him."
I was in shock. "They broke up. They're not together anymore. I'm not trying to take him away from her."

"Don't talk to him. He's Margie's." They left abruptly, leaving me stunned and upset.

The next day I met Lorenzo in the cafeteria. He said that he wanted to talk to me about the charity show that T House and his fraternity were jointly rehearsing. I had a part in the show. He was the director. We sat in a part of the cafeteria that was not near T House's table. We talked about the show. We were tentative with each other but by the time our conversation was over, we liked each other. After lunch we walked to class.

I was approached by three other girls. I was warned again. I was upset but did not mention it to Lorenzo. I liked Margie but they had broken up long before Lorenzo and I had even spoken, and he was doing the seeking out. No one cared. Keep away from him. He is Margie's. Margie never indicated that she knew about these girls and their agenda, and although she was cordial to me, we never had a conversation. At this point most of the girls were curt with me, belittling me for anything I did and sneering at any comment I made. Through all of this, Lorenzo and I were just friends. We eventually drifted apart, but he never dated Margie again. The attitude of the T House brigade never wavered, however, and I know that it was one of the reasons why I let the relationship fade away. I can still picture his wavy brown hair and sincere smile. I heard much later that he eventually married, not Margie, so the machinations of the T House girls, who thought that they were looking out for a friend, had been in vain. They never knew or cared how much they had hurt me, and I remember it still. I eventually left the House Plan; it had nothing for me. When we passed in the halls, the girls ignored me; but I no longer cared, and we eventually graduated and went our separate ways.

One of the Barrys in my life shared a class with me. He approached me one day as we left the building in which our class was held and encountered a violent rain storm. He offered to share his umbrella, and we spent the rest of the afternoon together. He was tall and thin with dark hair and serious eyes that told me he was listening to everything I said. He was not a fraternity member and had no air of superiority that many of the frat boys had. He had a large group of friends, many of whom he sees to this day, and an easy way about him. He played the banjo and guitar. He loved folk music. His friends embraced me and I truly could be my own person. The House Plan faded away, and when I thought about it, I berated myself for even having joined it. I was never like those girls, but I had been searching for myself. At T House my search was never rewarded.

Barry and I spent time on campus, sharing lunch and talking. We dated for about a year. We, along with his friends, sang the folk songs they played on their guitars and banjos. I even learned how to painstakingly play the old ballad "Skip to my Lou," which I played often; Barry let me keep the banjo until we ended our relationship and I returned it. I met his family, who were very nice to me, and was happy. No one bothered me. I was accepted. I was liked. We dated often and one date stands out as most memorable to me.

It was the first and only time I held a firearm. Actually, it was a rifle, a long, heavy, rifle. I was scared to look at it but it was unceremoniously thrust into my hands and I was told to aim and shoot at a target in the direction of a pointing finger. I had hit (no pun intended) the big time.

Barry's parents owned a summer home in the Catskill Mountains; and one day, with some of his friends, we took a ride to the house, which was closed for the winter. It was not too long into our relationship, but the activity and ride seemed like fun, and I was about 20, with the freelance mental outlook so popular with the young and invulnerable. The house, a small two-story white clapboard surrounded by a porch, stood on about an acre or two of grass, trees, and fallen leaves. It was a cool fall day, and made a pretty scene, reminiscent of a picture postcard. I was amenable to any suggestions, so after a trip to a fast-food restaurant, we went to the house, along with a small group of Barry's friends. After a quick tour of the house and grounds, we stood at the back of the house, just talking, and Barry reached into a case he carried. Then I saw it. He held a rifle. I must have looked askance at the sight but I kept my cool as I was reasonably certain that I would not be the target, nor would any animal. Barry and his friend Bill, as well as some of the other people who did not seem to think this was an unusual happening, began shooting at a tree branch or other similar object, the sound reverberating in my ears while my mind kept repeating that this was not what I had signed up for. But I put on a brave face since I wanted to be a good sport and did not want to unravel the fabric of the afternoon. I watched with as much interest as I could. Before I could understand what was happening, I became a participant.

"Ellen, do you want to try?"

"No, Barry, that's all right." I tried to sound nonchalant.

"Come on, try." Bill joined in.

I looked at both of them and then suddenly found the rifle in my hands. I was afraid to move.

"Is it loaded?" A stupid question since they had both been firing it moments before.

"It's OK. The safety is on," Barry assured me, though I harbored major doubts.

"Do you see that tree branch?" Bill pointed to a group of trees. "Point the rifle and try to hit it."

Barry positioned me to fire, helped me hold and aim the gun, then let go of me. I was shaking. "Don't let me kill anything," I muttered to anyone or anything that could help me. I pulled the trigger. I did not hit the target and the bullet flew harmlessly into the brush.

"See, that wasn't so bad," Barry smiled.

"No," I grinned, "it wasn't." I tried to sound self-assured, not wanting to admit that I enjoyed doing it. I had actually fired a rifle. It really was fun. I don't remember if I fired it a second time, but I had done something entirely out of the box of my life, and I was proud of it. I had never been one to protest about anything because I wanted to please, but I was right to abandon my fears that time. Now, years later, I still have to wrestle with such conflicts in my personality. Barry later taught me the rudiments of banjo playing. But the only injury done then, was to my sore fingers, and, as in the case of the rifle, I enjoyed it but it was not nearly as much fun. We then took a few pictures, got into the car, and rode home, rifle in the trunk, and a grin on my face. A few years ago we reconnected on Facebook. Barry still plays folk music, and I still remember the good times.

I took an American History course with a teacher named Mr. Eisenberg. He was tall, with light brown hair, and wore glasses. He also wore heavy braces on both legs and walked with crutches. He was young, probably a few years older than I, a teaching assistant paying his way through graduate school. He stood at his lectern, sometimes unlocking his braces to sit, read his notes aloud, with an occasional editorial comment, and opened the door to American History to me, telling me facts that I had never known, and drawing me into his world. I always wondered about his braces, and since it was never discussed, there was no way to know. He reminded me of a classmate I had had in elementary school, who had been afflicted with polio, just before the vaccine became available. There was also a girl in my House Plan who also had it as a child. In my mind, this was also his affliction, and I admired how he never let it get the best of him.

In this class, I met Allan, the man who would eventually become my husband. We had a mutual friend, Molly, who formally introduced us, and we became good friends. We sat near each other, wrote notes to each other in our notebooks during class, and sometimes ate lunch together. We each had our separate lives, though, and did not become a couple until several years later when we reconnected in graduate school. Both of us were consumed with our own dating and daily busy lives and never considered a future with each other. Now, almost fifty years later, I laugh at the lack of full awareness which had once characterized our lives.

I took a course in Geology. I really wanted to take Anthropology, but by the time I registered for a required science course, that was the only science class open, and although I had no idea what it was, I took it gladly. I loved my first semester. The origins of the earth, the topography of the planet, and the characteristics of rocks somehow fascinated me. I thought about going into the field of Geology and I did very well in the course. My second semester was more grounded. My professor, a balding, slight man in his fifties, wearing a crown of closely cropped gray hair, and white shirts with rolled up sleeves, thinly disguised his dislike for women in the sciences, but I ignored this aspect in him as I was interested in the topic and needed this course to fulfill my science requirement. We

learned about glaciers and other earth-shaping events and went on
a visit to The New York Botanical Gardens in the Bronx, a place I
frequent to this day, not without remembering that field trip. That
course made Geology come alive. I remember how we disturbed
many couples who thought they were in a secluded spot for
assignations as we traipsed through the grass and rocky areas. One
day we were learning about hills. We were handed graph paper and
a formula to use for diagramming. I probably made my professor
happy as I had to abandon my continuation in this subject area
after the course ended. He had watched me struggle with the math,
but offered no real assistance. I returned to my love of English. Mr.
Black and my college Math teacher were right about my weakness
in Math. I was never sorry. though, about taking my geology
course and I still have an amateur's love for the subject.

I had a Shakespeare teacher who entered the room on the first day
of class a few minutes after the class had been seated, reciting
a line from one of Shakespeare's sonnets, "Let me not unto the
marriage of true minds admit impediments." I had never read
any of Shakespeare's sonnets before and began to realize that the
Honors English classes I had had in high school did not prepare me
for what I was about to encounter. Another world was introduced
to me. When I taught my own English class, this was always one of
the sonnets I taught, with a nod to Dr. Mandelbaum.

Mrs. Archer, a native Parisian, met her husband, an American
military officer in Paris, married him, and eventually became a
French teacher. I suffered with her for one semester. I was not
prepared for the class. In previous years, my French teachers had
been an extremely old man who barely stood straight as he hunched
his way into the class room, and taught us little; a very young
woman who merely had us repeat French sentences, such as *"Voici
une lettre pour vous"* over and over; and my third French teacher
who was a lovely man who did not speak English beyond the very
basic. I do not know how I did it but I actually read two books in

French in his course and understood most of what I read. He told
me that I had the best French accent in the class. Unfortunately,
none of the teachers ever taught grammar well. My French accent
may have been excellent, but it was not enough. Madame Archer
did grammar. I did not. I was in trouble. I made a good friend in
that French class, and she helped me understand French grammar
and complete the class, but Madame Archer did not like me; she
indicated that with her voice and lack of patience. She told me with
her sighs and exasperation if I phrased something incorrectly and
she constantly corrected my pronunciation. She also taught me
by her negative example about the value of good teaching; and,
although I did not know it at the time, I was taking teacher prep
courses before I knew teaching would be my life's calling.

I always wrote short stories and poetry mostly for my own
amusement, so I decided to take a writing course during my last
semester. The only one that was given was playwriting. I never had
written a play until then, nor was I good with dialogue, so I timidly
walked into the room the first day, knowing that I had to stick it
out because I needed the credits for graduation. We had to write a
play in order to get credit for the course. It was a disaster. I had no
ideas; and the professor, a lovely older woman with jet black hair
teased into a ball, did not offer much guidance. However, I loved
the play *Waiting for Godot,* and, having become enamored of the
style of the Theater of the Absurd, adopted the style for the play. I
devoted hours to writing and rewriting it, and I finally handed in
a semester's work with shaking hands. I waited for the verdict. I
received an "A." She loved it. She gushed over it. She wrote a page
of superlatives at the end of the play. She pointed out the fine points
of each scene and complimented me on a job well done. I still recall
her red lips extolling the virtues of my play when I think of the
reality of what it really was. In graduate school I took a class with
an accomplished playwright in a course devoted to theater in which
we analyzed plays and discussed playwrights. We had placed our
chairs in a circle as we discussed everything we read. I felt secure

and happy in the class because I was able to fully participate and had great respect for Dr. A., my professor. He regaled his students about the many off Broadway successes he had had and the well-known actors he had known. For most of the classes he brought his German shepherd with him. The dog spent most of his time lying by his master's side, with an occasional walk around the room to sniff the students, who for the most part ignored him.

Because I felt that Dr. A was so intelligent and a little avant-garde (after all, how many people brought their ninety-pound dog to class and actually knew actors with whom I was actually familiar?) I was stupidly brave enough to ask him to read my play with my professor's gushing comments still on it. He returned the script and said to me in a voice I will never forget, "Your playwriting teacher was an idiot."

By the time I started to immerse myself in my English major, I knew that I wanted to teach High School English. One benefit to this was that I would not have to minor in Education and take a myriad of what I saw as inane courses about the psychology and methodology of the young mind and how to teach it. My mother saw it differently. She was afraid of High School.

"Ellen, don't teach High School. Teach Elementary School. It's better."

"I want to teach English."

"The kids are too big. You will never be able to handle them."

My mother never knew how wrong she was. Managing and dealing with high school students was one of my best talents when I finally taught High School, but midway through college, I was unsure of myself. "O.K. Ma, I'll take some courses in the subject."

I took courses; I read adolescent literature, the only course I liked; I took a course in which I had to dance in front of the class to music played on an old-fashioned record player by a teacher who nodded her head while several of us pranced around the room like reindeer. I did volunteer work at a daycare center where the children truly loved me; I worked at a Head Start program when the children stood in line to get a hug; and I took a course where the teacher emphasized teaching the gifted child when I knew that it would take years before I would ever teach gifted children. It was the most seasoned teachers who usually were rewarded with these classes. I was disappointed and bored with most of my courses and took them because I was too afraid not to.

One day, while sitting at the T House table, a fraternity pledge approached me. He wanted to know if I would attend a party that Friday night at the fraternity house. He was contacted by Sam, the person who would become the last boyfriend I had in college. I convinced a friend to go with me, and we went to the basement apartment the fraternity rented as their base. Sam approached me and we began our relationship.
We spent most of our time together. At school we now sat at his fraternity table, T House, all but abandoned because of my tepid relationship with them. We had good times on Saturday nights. (Sam reserved Friday nights exclusively for his friends and did not deviate from this practice.) We went to the movies; went to Yankee games at Yankee Stadium in the Bronx; sat in the cheap seats behind home plate; had hamburgers at White Castle; took long rides along the Bronx River Parkway, a beautiful scenic stretch of road just outside of the Bronx; and had a good time with each other. We slept together, ate together, played together and smoked pot together, introduced to me by him, the least favorite part of our relationship.

Sam's father gave him 20 dollars a week above his usual school expenses. I rarely had much money above the minimum I needed to get through my days, so the expenses of our relationship were Sam's. I always wondered where he got the money for our dates. He and his friends sold marijuana. They bought it, cleaned it, bagged it, and sold it. It funded his life and the one we shared. He once took me to a friend's house where a group of people were sitting on the floor, sifting the pot. I felt uncomfortable but had no choice but to remain there and watch. Someone gave me some pot and told me what to do but I hated it. I never told Sam. Since this had to be part of the relationship, I accepted it.

Sam and I remained together until after he graduated and I had one more semester to go. I went to his graduation, spent the afternoon with his family, and we continued seeing each other into his first year of teaching elementary school. Eventually, we broke up on a friendly basis; and as I knew that it was time, I buried my disappointment and moved on.

Graduation was a bittersweet experience. I was leaving a safe zone. Things would be out of my comfort zone. I would surely grow up. I completed my four years, met and discarded many people, was liked and disliked by students and teachers alike, developed interests I still have to this day, and married the man I met in undergraduate school two months after my 24th birthday. I learned how to teach and how not to teach, and I left with a multitude of memories that forged in me dreams of infinite possibilities. It took me many decides, however, until—upon my own retirement from teaching along with dear colleagues who had endured the same "hard knocks," as well as fulfillment, both in college and in our teaching careers—I became inspired to write this remembrance.

Jeff Langer

Bio

Born: June 30, 1959

Hometown: Lombard, Illinois

Education: Montini High School, Lombard, Illinois, 1974-1978
B.A., Educational Administration, Northern Illinois University, 1983
M.A., Educational Administration, Elmhurst University, 1991

Events Coordinator, Elmhurst College, 1982-2017

Mentored in Writing and English Literature by
Northwestern University Professor Edith Marshall, 1995-2000

Author of: *Along the Road to Heaven, American Trilogy, Beautiful Reward, Bootie Patrol, Chi-Town, Guilty Not Sorry* (the Adrian Prince Story), *Murder in Miami, Pretty, Ruins to Redemption*

Avid swimmer; Collector of sports cards and memorabilia, coins, and comic books

Proud member of the Kings Point Democratic Club

Vice-President of The Kings Point Creative Writers Club

With Leah

I want
To build
A house
On higher ground,
In a world
Of splendor
Love the only sound,

High above
The road
Of shadow and doubt,
Discovering what
Sweet love
Is all about

My Bella

Sing to me
Of triumph
Sing to me of Spain,
Chase away the dark clouds
And all the pouring rain

Take me to the
Doorstep of heaven
And open up the door,
Hold me in your arms
And kiss me forevermore

For the moon
Of love will rise
A surfeit of delight,
Inflame the fire of Orpheus
The rising tide will touch the light

You're My Home

If you look into my eyes
You'll see the gypsy in my soul,
Where hope is shining
And dreams do dare to grow,
There's a happy roof above
And good walls are all around,

On the doorstep of Eden
Where miracles can be found,
So trust me little darling
I'll keep you warm all night,
Though the night be dark
Here comes the light,
You are my sky
My pleasure dome,
I need you in my life
Because you are my home

Memories Of Venice

Flickering in the
Candelabra light,
A nirvana
Of the sheer delight,
A cheery melody
Playing from afar,
From a grand piano
And idyllic guitar,
A light-hearted
Song of yesterday,
Wafting floating
Over to my way,
As heavenly skies
Are shimmering above,
And putting me
In the mood for love

The Loudest Voice

Good morning to the
Unvarnished truth,
Whispering in the

Ears of the youth,
From the bottom
To the top,
It shall not
Ever stop,
It flows like
Fine wine,
In three-part harmony
With angelic rhyme,
Day after day
Time after time

Gift From The Prince Of Peace

There is
Angelic beauty
That flies so high,
Where the king's flag
Waves in the sky,
There is
No more weeping
In the blessed hour,
For the miracle is granted
And the bloom is on the flower

In The Moonlight Of The Living

For here
The prophecy
Is spoken,
The holy prayers
Are woken,
On the shores
Of this
Enchanted land,

In the sacred sea
On the consecrated sand,
The stars
Guide me home,
As I'm no longer
Dry as a bone,
Celebrating the seascape
So very pretty,
A long way
From the sinister city,
On an island
So peaceful and forgiving,
I find my soul
In the moonlight of the living

Saving The Soul Of America

With prayers
On our lips
And a loving God above,
We need to get back
To the America we love

We're talking to the people
Of Scranton Pennsylvania,
Youngstown Ohio,
South Bend Indiana,
Duluth Minnesota,
Madison Wisconsin
And Peoria Illinois,
To the lonely girls and barroom boys

This is our wake up call
To take our country back
From the chaos, corruption, and hate,

Yes my brothers and sisters
It is not too late,
For we are speaking to
The American spirit
Of hopes and dreams,
Drawing a straight line
Toward electoral moonbeams

New York Sour

When I was nine years old
Four older boys from the neighborhood
Stole my baseball glove
The very one my father
Gave me for my ninth birthday,
When my father found out
He pulled my pants down
Hitting me four times with a belt,
Ordering me to face the boys
To retrieve my glove,
So I raced out of the house
With tears in my eyes
I confronted the boys
And they beat me unconscious,
I was in the hospital
For over a week,
My father never said a word
Until he took me home
Sat me down and said,
"You still have to get that baseball mitt back!"

The Bust On 42nd

(The Tenderloin District of New York City)

Wild Billy, here's the skinny about the
blinking red light (red light District)
My eyes glued on the Mad Gunner (street nickname) in the night
Suffering the unpleasing sneezing (high
on heroin) feeling much older
Has a monkey on his back and a boulder
(drug habit) on his shoulder
Locked and loaded (a hard on) trolling in the Indian summer
Hazy Daisy (crack whore) flashing her bedroom eve
At the slick fifty drummer (a big mouth or one flashing $50)
Mary Methhead (female methamphetamine
addict) dressed in a hurt skirt
Teasing her golden arches ready to get down in the dirt,
She's real fleshpot
A hot to trot cheeky mascot (big bootie)
A dye in the wool forget-me-not (a hooker
a john scores with over and over)
Her flame (hook or attraction) burning red hot
Wearing adolescent pink pumps (platforms streetwalkers wear)
Leaving all the Romeos down with the mumps (STDs)
Mad Gunner and Hazy Daisy collide (engage in sex)
In the alley where lust doesn't bother to hide,
Leading to squeezing and wheezing (vaginal intercourse)
Jack and Jill crashing down so pleasing (naked bodies intertwined)
As the sassy silicone sister (tart with a boob job)
Scored a 30 stack ($30) from a back alley twister (half and half)
While a squirrel in a four wheel go-cart (cop in an unmarked car)
Was checking out the weather chart (running
their faces for arrest records)
As the twirler (whore) and the Magic Rat (john)
Walked out the front door of a hello and goodbye Laundromat (jail)
The snooper scooper cuffed the jaded faded sinners in the night
Taking them to Gun Club (county jail) as
they were blinded by the light
Blinded by the light, blinding by the light, the red light

The Dating Game

Here is to the club scene
Of somebody will and somebody won't,
Of now you see it
Now you don't,
All the charming music
Under a soft light,
Of grins and kisses
While the devil tangos in delight,
All the pleasing promises
Made of honey,
Casual conversation
Eventually turning to money,
Where couples dance
And lovers romance,
Endless lines of hellos and goodbyes
Somebody leaves and somebody cries,
Welcome to the party
So very preppy and pretty,
In the dazzling neon lights
Of the naked city

Lost In The Flood

I seek divine deliverance
To shed the stain
On my soul,
Cleaning the blood
Off my hands,
Covering my tracks
Cutting off my beard (my disguise)
Cleaning my face (settling my debts)
Shivering in the cold rain,
I'm so tired

Of this death waltz,
So I'm casting
Off my shackles
Throwing away
My needles and spoons,
Leaving the blackness
Of the false dawn,
Oh momma, I'm heading
Into the light of the living,
I am begging
For forgiveness
And seeking redemption,
I'm getting drenched in the pouring rain
For I am all alone
And I can't come home,
Not like this

Where The Cottonwoods Grow Tall

In the darkness
Of our love
We scream and shout,
You clam up
But, I want to talk it out

I storm out
To come back again
Discovering pills all over the place,
You're balled up on the couch
Tears running down your face

You are walking
On shattered glass
A hostage of dirty shame,
But, I hold you tight

For I love you just the same

Midnight Blue

I play bartender out in the Nevada sands
Serving two dollar shots and settling for one night stands,
Those trays are getting heavy and the tips are getting weak
It's so late that even the mimes have learned to speak,
As the dawn is closing in
The pickings are getting slim,
I spot a blonde at the end of the bar
Her eyes shine vacancy as she hides a scar,
The jukebox plays a song of yesterday
While yet another graveyard shift surely slips away,
Had my chance at fame and glory
But mister that's a long long story
So, I'm flashing the lights and shouting last call
Out the window I see the hustlers leaving Monty's Pool Hall
I've seen so many people with ghosts in their eyes
Getting stone cold drunk to numb their lies,
Here at the Lone Star Bar all I see is midnight blue
Mill hands chasing dreams that never will come true,
Suffering pink slips of fear
And trailer parks of pain,
Sleepwalking through their lives
Trying not to get caught in the pouring rain

On The Streets Of Blood And Stone

I have pockets full of needles
And a nose
Full of snow,
I've been running all my life
With no place to go

I am stumbling
On a crooked crutch
Have only myself to blame,
Another lowdown foul-mouthed fool
Drowning in the pouring rain

Now there are
Eyes in every shadow
And I don't know who to trust,
There's a dirty wind ablowing
Of devils and dust

Paying For My Sins

After all these years I am still in Saigon
Way back in '73 a war run
By four-star clowns
Who don't know how to run a circus
Ordering around a
Bunch of rock and rollers
With one foot in the grave
Crawling through the
Sweaty soggy jungle
Like ghosts on the landscape
The longer we creep
Through the slippery shit
Charlie grows stronger
The hours of darkness
Are haunted by
Inconsolable bloody screams
The dark side slaying
The naive willing
To die for a corrupt cause
Lying in a bed of rice
M102 howitzers drop cover fire

Zippo flamethrowers burning bright
Counter guerilla gun ships
Killing friends and foes
Cutting them in half
And giving them a band aid
Hear the rat-tat-tat
Of M60 machine guns
A-37 Dragon Fly popping out eardrums
As I gag on the bombs of napalm
And the stench of burning flesh
Chicom bullets blowing my buddies apart
Their last breath in my face...
The flashbacks seem so real
The walls of Piedmont closing in
The dawn comes up as I
Suffer from the horror, the horror, the horror of war

Separated From Herself

In my estimation
Mattie is a
Lady in every way
It hardly
Makes a difference
What I think
At this point,
Once in remission
Now she's reeling
From the black clouds
And the howling winds
Suffering once more
The whirlwind of the big C,
Mattie is without
Breasts, a uterus,
Cervix, ovaries

Or fallopian tubes,
She hysterically sobs
In our dark bedroom
Wondering aloud
"Am I still a woman?"

40 Years Of Tears (For My Father)

The joint was
Quiet as a church
The church of the good hustle,
I took the job at 5% commission,
Because five percent of something
Was better than a 100% of nothing,
For over forty years I was
The ghost of the used car lot
Dressed in a suit, tie, and a slit-eating smile
And the funny thing is everybody thought I loved it

The Story Of Sonny And Bunny

My mother spent
My childhood sticking
Her finger down her throat
In order to fit into her zero size dresses
Screaming at my father
Instead of nagging like
The other mothers...
My father ranted and raved
About her outlandish spending
Drinking himself into a coma
Passing out on the living room couch...
Only to rise the next morning at five
Tanking up on Bennies
To jump start his mania

Rushing out the front door
To his self-proclaimed
AUTO Emporium in
The nitty gritty city...
A car lot built on mendacity
Of spun back odometers
Gobs of bondo
And slick paint jobs...
To sell tired and used cars
Polished to a gleaming shine
Pitching the dock workers
And hustling housewives with his
Amusing vaudeville jokes
Fueled by Dago black coffee
Chain-smoking Pall Mall Cigarettes
Always running out of cartons
With the red pack...
Working dawn to way past death
When he finally arrived home
Reeking of black label whiskey
Wearing some trollop's perfume
He was usually dead ass drunk...
All his mistresses
Haunted our house
At 873 School Street
My parent's marriage felt
Like an endless Halloween...
Sonny and Bunny
Lived a lifestyle
In the soft and sunny suburbs
A life they couldn't afford
Of maxed out credit cards
A second mortgage
And an appalling credit line
Yet that was their

Dirty little secret...
They were the envy
Of all the neighbors
With their children attending
Prestigious private schools
New cars, an ocean front
Winter hideaway in Miami
The remarkable remodeled
Kitchen and living room
Purchased on
Borrowed time...
They suffered from
The affliction and addiction
Of the Go Go 60s
Of spend and borrow
Not worrying about tomorrow...
We became preppy mannequins
Pasting a gracious grin
Over a gaunt grimace
Pretending everything
Was peachy keen...
My dad's generous
Yearly donation to
My prep school
Assured my grades
Were always top
Of the class...
That's the life I knew
But never shared with anyone
Not my first, second, or third wife
My spoiled rotten
Country clubs kids
Just you, my therapist

EDWARD R. LEVENSON

Walking With Angels

We hold the reins
To our beautiful reward,
The sky is the limit
For the believers in the Lord,
The stars are
Our inspiration,
In our
Spiritual nation,
So look
Toward the smiling moon,
And take a ride
On the silvery spoon
Walking with freeman's shoes
Dressed in yesteryears' blues
Saying goodbye to a smiling skull ring
With a happy song to sing

Edward R. Levenson
(Eddie Levenson)

Bio

Edward/Eddie grew up in Roxbury and Brighton in "Boston Proper" (that is, within Boston's city limits), Massachusetts. After graduating from Boston Latin School, he received undergraduate degrees in Jewish Education and Classics (Greek and Latin Literature) and graduate degrees in Ancient and Jewish History, Near Eastern and Judaic Studies, and Educational Administration. He taught Hebrew Language and Jewish History in college and Hebrew Scriptures in graduate school before he retracked into teaching Latin and Social Studies in high school.

He relocated in 2015 from Philadelphia, Pennsylvania, to Delray Beach, Florida, where he has been fulfilled, in retirement, in a second career as a writer. In these last five years he has published three anthologies and four multi-genres books. His *Personae of Ed: Literary, Psychological, and Spiritual* is in the works. A newlywed of four years to prolific writer Reva Spiro Luxenberg, he has edited nine of her books.

He is a proud member and officer of our Kings Point Creative Writers Club and Kings Point Writers Club Supplementary, considering them both outstanding models for emulation.

These Are a Few of My Favorite Things

Edmond Jabès
Great Inspiration
Particles
Wordplay
Edward R's Personae
Have their say
"Occude" and "Qvell"
How very apt
Check Wordnik out
And you'll be rapt
Reva my Diva

Love of my life
Quippes
Be you sure of that
Scrabble
Win-to-lose ratio's flat
Quite pious wife
With heart of gold
Enduring joy
We'll never grow old
Rob my brother
And Loudell
Gifts from Heaven
I don't tire to tell
Children give *nachas** much
A cornucopia I'm not going to touch
Cousins getting along
As it is such

Natalie, Barbara,
And Judy, too
Judys do number three
Judy W., Judy B., and Judi Z.**
Colleagues in Writers Club
Wondrous exemplars
At 1 p.m. on Wednesdays a happy hub
Almost all of the time
"Good People"
Testifying I'm
Exciting production
Excellence of expression
No need for reduction
Proud editor
Accomplishment significant
Fulfillment extraordinary
No problem with creditor

Aggravations some
Irritating messings
They pale in comparison
To the overwhelming blessings

*Yiddish. A parent's emotional satisfaction and pride
**Of Blessed Memory, Deceased on June 26, 2020

Introducing Édouard Zola ben Zola: His "I Affirm!"

First, a *bissel* (a little) biography. As I just hinted—and did not intend as a tribal wink, loving all as I do, just wanting to create an alliterative thread—I *am* Jewish. Émile Zola was my great French forbear, but I am not his biological descendant. I have taken his last name and added a metaphorical patronymic to convey my spiritual indebtedness to one of the world's greatest fighters for freedom, honesty, and truth in all of human history. Readers need no introduction to him.

I must state at the outset that I am not "cheap" or "stingy." The name "Zola" did not derive from the Hebrew "*zol.*" Nor am I a glutton—Hebrew "*zolel*"—through I have been finding it hard to diet.

Enough preliminaries, and no more humor. I just needed to get your attention for the serious things I feel impelled, nay driven, to say. Please sit down firmly in your seats.

I AFFIRM that everyone everywhere should respect the legacy of Émile Zola.

I AFFIRM that self-interest can stifle "the better angels of our nature" (Abraham Lincoln).

I AFFIRM that democracy is the best form of government and of social organization.

I AFFIRM that citizen of countries, cities, towns, and villages—and members of associations—need to maintain vigilance against the subversion of noble values for elitist, antidemocratic purposes.

I AFFIRM that one must oppose close-minded selfishness and the power-seeking of the few.

I AFFIRM my belief that readers young and not-so-young, near and far, female and male, athletic and less-so identify with my affirmations.

Bonjours! Á Toujours!

Edward R. Levenson
May 14, 2020

How Has the Pandemic Affected Me?

(submitted to pandemic@palmango.com)

My title is interrogative, because, as the question in the call is multi-faceted—How has Covid-19 pandemic affected your life and your thoughts about the future, life in general, and the world?—my response is far-ranging, multi-leveled, changeable, and even self-contradictory. Since an essay requires the imposition of logical order, however, I proceed from (shocking and unabashedly, but honest) self-centered considerations to stoic ones to subjective religious understandings. The latter requires clarification at the outset. A believing Jew/Judaist, I have traversed more versions of Jewish religion and culture than many people know exist; but I also have universalist strivings, having taught Religion for eight years at a Catholic university (Villanova) and having been the Latin teacher for a subsequent eight years in the two diocesan high schools of South Bend and Mishawaka, Indiana.

My self-centered considerations involve guilt, but perhaps not as much as they should. For my wife Reva and I are deriving benefit from the new "social distancing" rules. We actually enjoy staying at home more. We have no communal obligations, such as our weekly writing-club meeting. We play many more Scrabble games than before. We take longer naps. And we are writing more. A serious pitfall for me in the situation, to be sure, is that my diet has gotten "shot to hell." After having lost 25 pounds by the end of 2019, I fear I put back 35 in the month of April 2020 alone. It is not a consolation that the gain in my midriff's volume is inversely proportional to the decrease of my desk's piles and piles of papers because of my more disciplined "de-cluttering" in the greater amount of free time that I now have.

Other benefits are economic. We each have gotten stimulus money, though our writing "businesses" are not suffering financially. Any more than usual, that is. And our expenses have lessened. We don't go to restaurants. And with our staying at home more our vehicles consume far less gas than before.

Tempering these complacent reflections of personal benefit is the recognition that my wife and I in South Florida—and our children, grandchildren, great-grandchildren, and my brother and sister-in-law in or near the metropolitan areas of New York City, Philadelphia, Chicago, and Jerusalem—can catch the disease at any time and even be felled by it.

Complacent thoughts give way to stoic ones, which involve skeptical resistance to ideas of the virus's having a "higher purpose," objectively speaking—for example, a reaction to human indifference to global warming, or overpopulation, or wealth inequality, or xenophobia and other kinds of moral hubris. I incline towards accepting the scientific judgment that a biological organism such as a virus has a single overriding purpose—to reproduce. Its spread owes its need to find more and more lungs in which it can procreate, mutating as much as it has to in the process, just so its species will not die out. For once it can no longer reproduce that is what must happen. The obvious does not even need to be stated. We practice "social distancing" to deny the virus fertile "spreading places." And if wayward germs do somehow penetrate the gates of our condo community—as has happened, resulting in the deaths of a small number of people—well *c'est la mort!* (That's the death!). At least they only zapped a few of us here.

Instead of my ironic French exclamation, I was about to write, "But for the Grace of God go I." I caught myself, realizing that would be a contradiction of my emphasis of disbelief in the disease's having a higher purpose. I, analogously, don't believe that the Holocaust was the supernatural punishment of God for the sins of the Jewish people or a prerequisite provided by God to motivate the United Nations to create the State of Israel, the reestablishment of the Jewish Commonwealth of old.

Here, however, is where religious understandings, subjective ones, are vitally important. Plagues have occurred throughout human history. They decimated the Israelites in the Sinai desert, not just the Egyptians in Egypt. The Talmud relates the deaths from a plague of 24,000 students of Rabbi Aqiva in the years of the Bar Kokhva Revolt (132-135); and whereas there is a scholarly interpretation that many of them actually were killed in the fight against the Romans, a large number of them, if the interpretation is correct, may have been infected by the plague as well. Shakespeare knew of plagues, as is vividly attested in *King Lear*.

As we fight this contagion, I write this with much emotion, our need is to bring our own meaning to our lives—as individuals, in our families, in our communities, in our cities, and in our nations. We need to be as united as possible in pooling our resources and in supporting both our medical specialists and caregivers on the front lines and the recuperating victims and their families as the pandemic runs its course.

I mentioned the Holocaust earlier. Having been born in 1942 in Boston, I escaped the Holocaust only because my paternal and maternal grandparents had emigrated to America at the turn of the 20th century from Kovno (Kaunas), Lithuania, and from Slavuta in the Ukraine, respectively. Thinking about surviving in the death camps has been ingrained in my consciousness since my earliest youth. A cousin I recently reconnected with revealed to me that she is alienated from religion because of the Holocaust. In my expressing my own point of view to her, including the emphasis that no one should self-righteously presume to understand a supernatural rationale for it, the need is for people to embody the best possible moral behavior in the face of what appears to be evil, human as well as natural.

Namely, a starving concentration camp inmate who shared a portion of meager rations with another in the hope that the other would have a chance of surviving was a far more commendable human being than the one who didn't and left the other to fend for self in hopelessness.

Chief Inspector Dreyfus

(Eddie Levenson, for Adam Sword's FAU
Fiction-Writing Course, January 2019)

It was Sunday afternoon, June 25, 2000, I was a Social Studies teacher in a challenging high school in the Philadelphia School District. The spring term had just ended, and summer vacation was beginning. At that time I had not begun summer-school teaching; and I was about to switch from part-time weekend cab driving to driving-as-many-shifts-as-possible during July and August. In the same time frame of the previous year I had been crippled with debt—to the tune of $30,000 with no way, so I thought, to whittle it down; but I began teaching in the afternoon "Twilight School" of the District in addition to my day teaching; and I took up a sometimes-grueling moonlighting job—cab driving—30 hours on weekends. I received a little money from the will of my Mother of blessed memory, who had passed away in January at the beginning of the year; and I was gaining a new optimism that I would not succumb to economic disaster.

Divorce, if you're not aware, is a "killer"—with its pressures of child support payments, lawyer's fees, and one's own household maintenance costs, not to mention emotional trauma. At one point during the year I compared myself to a Nazi concentration camp survivor who wrote that one of his coping strategies in the camps involved giving free rein to his curiosity about what unprecedented extreme trials he would be compelled to endure—and try to survive—on each passing day. I had been in great distress about my troubles, but cab driving was to prove an important part of the solution for me. The company I worked for, I might add, was Service Cab.

I was scheduled for night shifts that summer, that is, from 5 p. m. to 5 a. m. six nights a week. On the Sunday afternoon as my summer routine was to begin, the phone rang and the caller asked in a pleasant voice, "Hello, is this Ted?"

"It is," I answered. "What can I do for you?"

"Ted," he replied somewhat enigmatically, "You don't know me, but I know a little bit about you; and that is why I have called."

His statement could have alarmed me; but, as I just said, his voice was pleasant and I was curious to hear more. So I asked. "Who are you?"

"I can't tell you exactly yet," he replied. "We'll have to meet face to face first; and, if you're interested, as I hope you will be, that could be soon."

"But I'd need to have an idea who you are and why you want to meet me," I said.

"I can't tell you on the phone, for discretion's sake," he continued. "Let me just call myself for now "Chief Inspector Dreyfus." Do you remember him as the Paris Sureté Bureau Chief who hounded Inspector Clouseau in the Pink Panther movies."

"Of course I do. But that name doesn't exactly recommend you to me," I quipped. "Chief Inspector Dreyfus in the movies was a bumbling idiot whom Inspector Clouseau continually outsmarted."

"You're quite right," he responded. "That's where the comparison ends. I don't get outsmarted; and, for that matter, no one—at least no one who isn't a criminal—wants to or needs to snooker me. The name I gave you simply suggests that I am a top official in the Philadelphia Police Department. We have had you under a kind of "surveillance," for want of a better term, during your part-time cab driving this past year, and that's what I want to talk to you about."

"Me!? I am scrupulously honest. To a fault. I have never broken the law, except that once I 'squeezed a yellow,' went through a red light, and nearly got a ticket for it. The cop who pulled me over said that, since I make a living driving he'd 'let me off with a warning this time.' Why, once a young woman inadvertently paid her fare with a 'Benjamin' instead of a 'Jackson' at Thirtieth Street Station, and I ran down the stairs after her to exchange the bills. I caught up with her just as her train was pulling in."

"We well know what a 'good guy' you are, Ted. I was being facetious when I used the word 'surveillance.' Look. I want to present a Win/Win situation to you. At the upper echelons of the Police Department we've put together a picture of a small number of cab drivers who we think can assist law enforcement this summer in important ways. You're one of them. If you will volunteer to be part of our 'project,' you will be compensated for your time. If you will be available one night this week. I'll be able to describe the details more fully."

"How can I possibly 'be available' at night? Nights are precisely when I work."

"Here's how, Ted. I probably should wait until I know you better before explaining more; but in truth, I already know a lot about you—more than I indicated earlier—and I feel good vibes with you now. One, and only one, manager of Service Cab—knows what we are doing and is cooperating with us. It's top-secret work, and it even could be dangerous. But I don't want to scare you. We think you can handle the challenge. The person-in-the-know can override cabs' computers and give special dispatching instructions to individual drivers. She's a woman. She could, for example—if you give me your OK now—send you, after you get your cab, to my point of origin in Northeast Philadelphia, such as a Seven Eleven, for your first job of a shift. I will have listed on my cab order a destination in Center City. But we would not be going to Center City. Instead we would just be going on a long ride to places I might want to point out to you, if we would pass near them. My main purpose would be to explain to you how we think you can help us this summer."

"Well, I feel good vibes with you as well," I responded, "but I would like to know just what you claim to know about me. I'm a little nervous, in fact, whether you might be holding something over me to pressure me to acquiesce in this 'project' of yours."

"Don't be silly, Ted. There's nothing negative at all. On the contrary."

"Well, I want to know the stuff you've gleaned about me from your 'surveillance.'"

"All right. I certainly understand. I'll reveal it to you if you'll agree to take that ride with me. Two good incentives for you, I think, are that I've arranged with the manager I mentioned that, after the particular 'job' will be completed, you 'will have gotten a severe 24-hour flu' and have to bring the cab in. You'll have the remaining hours of the shift off and I will pay you the fare of $300. Don't worry about where the money will be coming from. You'll be able to pay your waybill to the Company. It will be for a half-shift, which they will willingly accept; and you'll make a decent night's profit as well. What do you say, Ted?"

"I accept—on one condition!"

"What's that, Ted?"

"It's that, since you've put me on a first-name basis with you, the reciprocal must be the case as well. I have two quick questions for you regarding Chief Inspector Dreyfus. Do you know the name of the actor in the movies who played him?"

"That's a no-brainer, Ted. It was Herbert Lom."

"Right. 'Herbert' happens to be the first name of my accountant. He's the 'best in the business,' if you want to know. But do you know Chief Inspector Dreyfus's first name? It does pop up in the movies every now and then."

"You know, I'm at a loss on that. It probably would come back to me sooner or later."

"OK. Let's proceed tonight according to your plan. I'm putting you on the honor system. Don't search on Google for the name. I don't need to know your real name. But be prepared for my calling you by the character's first name. It's French, as you might expect. It does have an English analogue. I'll leave the pronunciation, French or English, up to you. See you later, alligator. 'Alligator' comes from Latin, by the way."

I shaved and showered quicker than ever. I often do shower after I shave so I can wash off in the shower all the remaining shaving cream on my face and in my ears; but this time I was in and out of the shower so fast that I didn't get it all off and had to feel around to do so while I was driving to work. I arrived at Company headquarters on Frankford Avenue twenty minutes early. My vehicle was waiting for me on the street out front.

If you saw the unassuming storefront where the Company was located, you might have thought that the word "headquarters" was an overstatement; but it was an apt descriptor, for the layout extended from the front room with its banks of computers for the four dispatchers, to the middle room for the supervisors, to a lounge area in the back, to a long backyard where about fifteen vehicles—cabs and drivers' cars—were parked. The cabs themselves were "perpetual motion machines" in that they were in operation round the clock. When they didn't need to be taken for repairs to nearby garages, such as one on Torresdale Avenue, a driver completing his or her shift would park on the street up or down the block. When I arrived at the Company, I saw my assigned cab out front to the right of the entrance. There was a space behind it, so I parked my car in it; went in to get the keys for the cab—it was a Lincoln Town car, billed as a "luxury sedan"; made a little "small talk" with the dispatchers, such as asking whether anything unusual had happened during the day and inquiring about the weather; and made it a point to go over to the one of the three managers who was a woman, who I knew was getting over a cold, to ask her how she was feeling.

"I'm feeling much better, Ted. It's good of you to ask. It's a coincidence that you came over to me, you know. I was going to

send you the first job of your shift on the cab's computer, but now
I can say a bit more about it face-to-face. A special client of the
Company has requested your service in particular. He ordered
a cab for 5:15 at the Seven Eleven at 1900-10 Welsh Road at the
intersection of Old Bustleton. I've kept his order private, so a cab
that's closer to that spot now wouldn't get the job automatically on
the computer. I, of course, do everything I can to accommodate
customers. This person must know something about you. Your
reputation of being a considerate and street-smart driver, as well
as a humorous and interesting conversationalist, seems to have
preceded you. He may not have picked up the scuttlebutt that you
sometimes talk too much, but that's another matter."
"Thanks, Mary. I appreciate the compliments. I know I talk too
much, and it's not just 'sometimes.' I feel it's involuntary. I'll try
to be more restrained this time. I'd better be off now to get to the
Seven Eleven on time."
"Be well, Ted. I hope you'll have a good night."
"Thanks, Mary. See you tomorrow."

I met "Chief Inspector Dreyfus" at 5:15 as he had ordered—
that is in the sense of "filling out an order for something,"
not "commanded." My vehicle was a Lincoln Town Car, as I
mentioned; and the "Chief Inspector" took his seat in the back.
"When we both get more comfortable with each other," he said, "I
think it would be OK for me to switch to the front passenger seat."
"OK," I concurred. "I wonder," I promptly asked, "if you have
recalled Chief Inspector Dreyfus' first name in the movie."
"I'm not sure I ever actually registered it," he said. "I have no idea
now what it was. Give me the answer, please."
"It was 'Charles.' And, as I mentioned, the first-name basis must be
reciprocal. If you want me to use the French pronunciation—with
a silent 's' at the end and a softer 'ch.' at the beginning, that'll be
your call; but, since we're both obviously American, the American
pronunciation with a 'z'-sound at the end and a 'tch'-sound at the
beginning seems preferable. What do you wish?"

"I'll go with the American pronunciation, Ted. But consider yourself lucky that I can't make you jump through hoops over the pronunciation of *your* name. As for our route tonight, just drive around Northeast Philadelphia for a while. I'll describe the 'mission' we foresee for you, and we'll work our way southwest towards South Philly before doubling back."

"Don't forget, Charles. I want to find out what you know about me from your 'surveillance.'"

"Of course," he answered. "I'll start with the 9-1-1 operators. Several recognize your voice, though they don't know your name. They value the information you call in, such as about potholes, broken-down vehicles and stranded drivers, flat tires, and vandalized street signs. Do you remember last January the 'One Way' signs on several blocks on Wolf St. in South Philly that, as you indicated, had gotten pointed the wrong way? An operator contacted us about them and we corrected the situation quickly, perhaps averting a few accidents.

"We've learned about you from different sources. The most important one. I think, was an off-duty detective you picked up in front of a bar on Castor Avenue near Oxford Circle. Do you remember telling him about policemen covering the clubs on Delaware Avenue on a Saturday night? You were perplexed why they hadn't taken away the keys from two staggering drunks getting into their cars. He answered that he thought they might have been assigned the far more serious responsibility of arresting revelers who were high on Ecstasy. Your sharp question and your social concern impressed him, and he suggested to us that drivers like you could assist our law enforcement efforts in new ways.

"He and others have praised your personal qualities, which, in sum are what give you a leg up on others. You are in a nutshell, worldly-wise, friendly and compassionate, well-mannered, scrupulously honest, refined, knowledgeable, and modest. You can hold your own in intellectual conversations with professors, and yet you relate well to all manner of diverse individuals. You love ethnicities and languages, and you have a wealth of teaching experience with students on many different age levels. Need I say more?"

"Well, I try to give people a fair shake and I have always been inquisitive. How do you see me helping the Police Department?"

"Hold on. There was another source of information, different from the detective. That one was highly important for us. You had an Asian prostitute as a passenger, not once but twice. The first time was in November last year; the second time was last month."

"How can I ever forget her? What's her connection with the Police Department?

"She was an informer for us."

"You said 'was.' Is she no longer in touch with you?"

"I'm afraid not, Ted. She's dead. She apparently got discovered and was brutally murdered and dismembered just a few weeks ago. Her body parts were found in a dumpster near her house in the Grays Ferry area. Positive identification took the lab a long time."

"Oh my God. The two times she was my passenger I remember feeling bad about her hardships in making a living."

"She picked that up and told us about you."

"Do you know about that first ride of hers? She and her john were going from Five Corners to a motel in Feltonville. They were completely quiet at the beginning, but then all of a sudden, completely out of the blue, the lowlife began to yell at her and accuse her of screwing things up. I had a sense that he was setting her up for a savage beating in the motel. I called 9-1-1 after they had left the cab."

"Your instinct was 'right on.' We did get that information and were able to intervene. Perhaps, though, our speed in getting to the scene made the criminals she had to deal with suspicious of her. We know, at any rate, that she appreciated your instinctive alertness to her plight. The policemen who rescued her did also. We had them find out from the Company who you are."

"Her second ride in the cab was just as memorable for me. It began at 2:15 a. m. early Saturday morning just a few weeks ago at her house. It was on Grays Ferry Avenue near the intersection of 24th

Street. I can't say I find it hard to believe that she's been murdered. Not from what I am about to tell you. After she got into the cab, she said exactly what you often hear in movies, 'Step on it, cabbie!' She continued, 'I have a 2:30 appointment, and I can't be late.' You know, I was a 'sheltered Jewish boy' when I was growing up and, for the life of me, wouldn't have known back then what kind of an 'appointment' she meant. But I have seen enough in this business 'to make a sailor blush,' to use a cliché. It's no more 'naive Teddy.'

"The memory of the earlier ride months back was so unsettling to me that I didn't mention it and I sensed the same was true for her as well. But, as is said, 'the silence was pregnant.' I don't like to mix metaphors, but 'it spoke volumes.' And. further, we were 'on the same wave-length.' I felt a deep human compassion for her, and she knew it.

"I conversed much less with her—sometimes I say 'conversated'—than I generally do with passengers; but as we were approaching the destination and there were a few minutes to spare, I said, 'You know, it's dangerous out there at this time of night, be careful.'"

"Don't I know it, mister. I have a secret weapon. No one will dare mess with me.'

"And to my complete surprise, and even horror, she stuck out her tongue to reveal a razor blade taped to its underside! Getting out of the cab, she paid me the fare and added a 40% tip. 'Bye now, mister. Hope to see you again soon.'

"Charles, I am deeply saddened by the news of her death."

"Ted, I have seen many terrible things in my line of work, but her murder has been one of the worst. I know exactly how you feel! But it's time for a break. Let's stop and stretch our legs. There's an IHOP open until midnight in Olney up ahead on Roosevelt Boulevard. Let me treat you to a coffee and danish. When we resume our ride, I'll switch to the front seat."

"Sounds good to me. Except that I'll have to pass on the danish. I need to watch my sugar. I'll see if they have a low-calorie sugar-free yogurt."

We didn't 'talk shop' in the restaurant, nor did we talk about our families. But since I, as a matter of fact, was teaching then at Olney High School, which we happened to be quite near—I later transferred to another high school—I related a humorous story how I had avoided a confrontation with a student there a few years previously.

"The student's name was James. I was standing at the doorway a few minutes before the end of class when he attempted to walk 'through me' out of the room. 'Out of my way, pussy!' he exclaimed brazenly.' 'Why are you insulting your mother, James?' I challenged him."

"'I'm not insulting, my mother,' he replied. 'I'm insulting you.' But, pausing, he switched gears and asked, 'What did you mean by that?'"

"I knew that he had given me a 'teaching moment' and that every student in class, especially the young women, were waiting with rapt attention to hear my reply. 'You used a metaphor, James, a poetic comparison without the word 'like.' You used a 'girl word' in a negative way. Your meaning was that I am an 'interior female.'"

'That's ridiculous.' he said. 'Pussy' means 'cat.'

"Not the way you used it, it doesn't. It refers insultingly to that special part of a woman's anatomy; and, as such, you were insulting not only your mother, but also every young woman in this room."

"The bell rang at that moment and I extended my right hand to James. He extended his to me, and we shook hands. I said, 'See you tomorrow, James. Have a nice day!' And we parted amicably."

"That was quite a story, Ted. You're a very skilled teacher and communicator."

"Thanks for the compliment, Charles. You can bet that whatever capacities I have developed are the product of years of blood, sweat, and tears. But we need to get a move on. I need to hear about the 'mission.' I'm not sure, you know, whether I'll commit."

Back in the cab with Charles now in the front passenger seat. I picked up the thread of the discussion where we had left off. "Can you tell me the name of the murdered prostitute?"

"Yes I can, Ted. Her name was Rose Huynh. You can probably tell that the last name is Vietnamese. 'Rose' of course, is Americanized. She wasn't a hardened whore in a brothel. She 'free-lanced' getting to clients in cabs. One might even say that she sacrificed herself 'altruistically' to support an extended family of parents, aunts and uncles, and children numbering 20 or more people. Her yearly income of $250,000, earned in twenty 'tricks' a week, was more than yours and mine combined.

"But her murder brings us to the subject of the evening—what we need to begin to discuss: crime in Philadelphia and how we think you can help us. Let me emphasize at the outset that we are confident we are making inroads. Mob bosses fear us more than ever. Violent crime rates are decreasing from year to year, although our success is not as widely publicized as it should be. Schools are improving, as you well know, thanks to excellent teachers and role models like yourself; and more and more teenagers are finding alternatives to delinquency.

"Our police work is becoming better-focused, and our enlisting select cabdrivers like yourself as volunteer 'eyes-and-ears-in-the-street' is an example of an innovative promising new program. I'll describe to you an endeavor that we feel you would be very good at.

"We have identified about ten organizers of criminal networks out there. They have the false confidence that we can't touch them. They are woefully mistaken about that. But for now we are 'spreading the nets as wide as we can' to pull in much larger hauls later. They take cabs and we know many times who they are; from where, to where, and when they go, and in their periodic round-trips how long they stay where they have gone. Your manager in the Company shares with us the details of their rides. What she can do is plant among your nightly 'jobs' a few such rides. It would be safer for you not to know whether particular 'jobs' are automatically generated on the computer or assigned as overrides by her from the office. In other words, you wouldn't know which rides are the ones we want to know about. That lack of knowledge would preserve your 'nonchalance'—or better, 'harmlessness'—in the thinking of criminals. There would be less in your manner to tip them off. You could, of course, also get good information from an occasional madam.

"Your genial manner and 'gift of gab,' Ted, puts your taxicab passengers at ease. After ten minutes in your cab, as happens very often in taxis in general, they start revealing personal information, partly because they think they are anonymous to you and that you will probably never see them again. Some nervous people are so pent-up with emotion that their unburdening to cab drivers is one of the only forms of release—and relief—that they get."

"I think I see what you're 'driving at' (no pun originally intended), Charles. What will my first task be?"

"From my innermost heart. I thank you, Ted. A priority of ours is catching the murderer or murderers of Rose Huynh. For starters we'll give you a preponderance of 'jobs' within a two-mile radius of a Grays Ferry Avenue point of origin. Will you help us?

The Cabbie Sleuth

(Eddie Levenson, for Adam Sword's FAU Fiction-Writing Course, February 2019)

Wednesday afternoon June 28, 2000. The ride in the cab with the police official the previous Sunday evening made a deep impression on Ted, but he grew increasingly uncomfortable with what he came to recognize was the "beating around the bush" of the situation, and he sought to be more in charge. This was on his mind as he checked in at Service Cab at 4:50 to begin the night shift.

"Mary, can you arrange a cab ride with me for the officer tonight, or tomorrow night, or as soon as it will be possible?"

"Well I know he's willing. Stick to Northeast Philly for a while. If I send you to that Seven Eleven, it'll probably be to him. If that won't be happening, call me on my cell in three hours; and I'll be able to tell you whether to stay close or go where your fares take you. We may have to try again tomorrow night."

From 5 to 6:30 Ted had three fares to restaurants: Jack's Deli at Bell's Corner. Gallo's Seafood on Roosevelt Boulevard, and Las Margaritas on Welsh Rd. Then the location of 1900-10 Welsh Rd. popped up on the computer, and Ted knew it was the ride he was waiting for.

Sure enough "Chief Inspector Dreyfus" was at the front entrance of the Seven Eleven and he didn't hesitate to get in the cab on the front passenger side. "Glad to see you, Ted. How are you? Do you have any leads to talk about?"

"Not quite. I'd like to discuss ground rules."

"Of course, what's on your mind?"

"First of all I don't think you should be calling me 'Ted.' Someone might put a bug in the vehicle. Using a false name for me might give me a layer of protection. With all of the conversations in the first shifts of the week, a listener might lose track of who is who. As a matter of fact, you might want to use different names for me in turn for that reason. And we might want to speak cryptically about locations and situations, such as referring to Thirtieth Street Station as 'The Bar' and Grays Ferry Avenue as 'The Stadium.'"

"Good idea! We can work out a system as we go along, and we can even develop hand signals."

"Glad you agree. We can't be too careful, I feel. Next, the name you went by—"Chief Inspector Dreyfus"—has got to go. I know you used it disarmingly, no double-meaning intended, in self-deprecation and I played along in calling you 'Charles'; but this is not a matter for 'cuteness.' I don't need to know your real name and position, but I want you to give me a strong pseudonym that I can relate to.

"Above all, I would prefer your role to be that of FBI-man Mark Felt, who was the source for Woodward and Bernstein in the

Watergate upheaval. Felt's persona. 'Deep Throat," was, in fact, 'cutesy'; but between the two of us as individuals, we don't need to replicate it. In essence Felt did not give specific prescriptions to Woodward and Bernstein about what they needed to do, just general advice, such as 'Follow the money' and negative suggestions, such as 'You're getting cold' or 'You're barking up the wrong tree.'

"So, in sum, I would like to be the main sleuth for information about Rose Huynh and her sister prostitutes—that is, about the extent she was in a network, the criminals who frequented them, the more violent ones who liked to beat them up, and the one or more who might not have scruples about killing them. I think we can be sure that more murders occurred than even the police have been aware of.

"I will be eager to learn as much as I can. As we discussed, passengers reveal all kinds of things to cabbies, thinking the encounters to be completely random and casual. I may well glean valuable knowledge about the seamy side of, shall we say 'nocturnal city living,' which I will be able to share. You will be able to steer me in certain tracks of interest. But I will be a 'self-starter' and not a 'police operative.' *Capisce?*"

"Yes I do, Ted. And that's the last time I'm calling you that. For the rest of this ride it's going to be 'Mike.'"

"And it will be a good idea to vary the point of origin. Let's try places like the Dunkin' Donuts at 8902 Frankford, the Northeast Racquet Club on Krewstown Rd., an apartment house on Nandina Road, and Kelly's Seafood on Old Bustleton Ave. I'll be alert when I'm sent to those places that you'll probably be the passenger."

"Sounds good to me, Mike. And I'll see what supporting information I can glean from the police reports and the scuttlebutt in the Department. I may be able to pass along some tips, but I do understand your wish to be your own man. I'm like that myself. I work better that way, not feeling that I'm under someone's thumb. So double back to the Seven Eleven and drop me off."

It only took ten minutes to reach the starting point, during which Ted suggested a few names for the officer. "'Clancy,' I suppose, is too old-fashioned, even if you might happen to be Irish."

"Very funny. You're right about the 'old-fashioned,' Mike; and you're not even close about the 'Irish.' I'm half-Greek and half-Italian. So I was impressed by your '*Capisce.*' I think it reflected an uncanny sense on your part about people. At any rate. I see the Seven Eleven up ahead. Be well. I hope to see you again soon."

"*Ciao*, Guglielmo. How about if I call you the derivative 'Will' for that name. And. speaking of 'uncanny,' are you aware that '*ciao*' means 'goodbye' in both Italian and Vietnamese. That word is a new bond between us, as is the memory of Rose Huynh. In relating to your half-Greek identity, I majored in Greek Literature in college, if you want to know. I'm going to be thinking of a Greek name, also, that I can interchange with 'Will.' What do you think of 'Themistocles'?"

"Keep thinking, Mike. Good night. Keep safe."

And they both exchanged "*Ciao*" as the officer left the cab.

After a couple of local fares and one to the airport, the computer sent Ted to a high-rise on Pennsylvania Avenue near the Art Museum. A stylishly dressed young woman Ted figured was about 25 got into the cab and said, "Take me to Positano Coast at Second and Walnut, please. I'm meeting friends there for dinner."

The woman had Asian features that Ted couldn't quite identify with confidence; and fascinated as he was by the rich variety of Philadelphia ethnicities and estimating that the ride would take 20 minutes, he began a conversation with her as follows: "You know, I'm a high school teacher during the year and I have a veritable United Nations of students."

"You do strike me as being more refined than the average cab driver, and the word 'veritable' gives that away."

"Well, I have to be me. I can't 'dumb myself down,' as the expression goes. Unfortunately, some passengers get the wrong impression about me and, because of my academic vocabulary, think I'm putting on airs."

"On the contrary, you're friendly and by engaging in small talk with passengers you make them feel more comfortable than otherwise. I'm already feeling that this will be an interesting ride. And after the day I've had I sure need the lift."

"What happened? Do you want to tell me?"

"Sure. My dog got hit by a car and I had to take him to Bree's to set a broken foreleg in a cast."

"Sounds as if it could have been a lot worse."

"That's true. But I feared internal injuries. Fortunately, the dog's OK on that score."

"The dog of a friend of mine had a broken leg and the vet said that after the bone would heal, it would be stronger than before."

"I sure hope that will be the case with my dog."

"Me too. But can I change the subject?"

"I'll be glad if you do."

"Actually, I want to resume the topic I began to suggest earlier, ethnicities—in the plural. I see that you're Asian, but with a variation that I can't quite place. I have a lot of Cambodian students in my high school; and, familiar with Cambodians' faces, I'm able to detect subtle differences between them, and between Vietnamese, Japanese, and Philippino students' faces, in turn. I have more difficulty identifying Chinese ones. They seem to me to have a wider range of features.

"By all means, continue."

"Of course, I respect your privacy and I don't mean to pry. But I want to ask your permission to try to guess your identity."

"Go ahead. You have it."

"Thank you. You strike me as being Japanese, but not completely. I am guessing that you're half-Japanese and half-American."

"I'm absolutely amazed, cabbie. Yes, I *am* half-Japanese. It's impressive that you got that. But I'm not half-American. I'm half-Korean. My father is Japanese and my mother is Korean."

"Wow! I sure appreciate this conversation. Now I'd like to ask a further question. You strike me as being a strong person. Might you say that your strength derives more from one parent than from the other?"

"You better believe it! I'm impressed with this insight of yours also. My father is the introspective, soft-spoken, cerebral parent. My mother is the powerhouse! I'm a mix of both of them. Who could have believed I would be telling you so much in such a short ride?"

"I'm very grateful to you. I think I'll remember you for a long time."

"And I, likewise, won't forget you soon either."

"You know, I'm Jewish. I wonder if Korean mothers are tougher than Jewish mothers. Have you heard of Jewish mothers' guilt-tripping?"

"Who hasn't? I have Jewish friends. But their mothers I'll tell you can't hold a candle to Korean mothers!"

"I'm not so sure about that. But we're arriving at the restaurant. Have a great evening. I hope we'll meet again some day."

"Me too. Bye now."

Next Ted received on the computer a "rush order" to transport a frozen liver from Frankford Hospital in Frankford to the Frankford Torresdale branch of the hospital on Torresdale Avenue in the Far Northeast. The job irritated him for three reasons, in increasing order of discomfort. First of all, the hospital paid for the ride—on a voucher—only half the regular fare, perhaps on the assumption that less work was involved. Certainly the liver did not involve dealing with luggage, just carrying the ice packing in its box. Secondly, it was a busy night. It would have made less difference on a slow one in which all fares were appreciated. And, thirdly, he couldn't make conversation with the liver, although he did make the attempt, as he was conscious of Shakespeare's Hamlet doing so with the skull of "poor Yorick."

On the way to the Frankford Torresdale Hospital Service Cab dispatcher Mary called Ted on his cell with the heads-up to stay in the Far Northeast. He knew what the call meant, and, sure enough, after he had delivered the liver, duly wishing it the happiness of a new host body, the computer directed him to the Dunkin' Donuts on 8902 Frankford Avenue. It was to be the second ride of the evening with "Will," and Ted sensed that something important was up.

"Will" was waiting for him and the first thing "Mike" thought of was the coincidence of his derivative from the Italian "Guglielmo" and of the nickname for Shakespeare's "William." He vividly remembered a fare a year and a half before from quite nearby at the Rose Brier Inn, and he described it to "Will" before any other subject could be discussed. That showed something about what animated him in his consciousness over and above other matters of concern.

"Can you see the Rose Brier Inn sign a block to the west, Will? It's on the left side of the shopping center up ahead. It was Saturday evening January 2. I have a very good reason for remembering the exact date. Three big guys got into the cab, one in the front passenger seat and two in the back. They were from out of town. The guy in the front was the leader, and he said, 'Can you take us to a sports bar downtown, cabbie?'

"When I heard they were headed downtown, a $30 fare, I did not quibble about his sitting in front. Besides he looked peaceable enough, as I sized him up, no double-meaning intended. I asked if Dave & Busters on the Delaware would do."

"No, that's too big and noisy. We're thinking of a small quiet place to have a drink. Then we want to turn in early at our hotel. We have a big day, tomorrow. We're staying afterwards at the Marriott on Filbert Street. We stayed at the Rose Brier last night because we wanted to avoid the crowd downtown and also to meet old friends for dinner."

"Well, there are a few places on Chestnut St. I can suggest."

"Right you are, cabbie. Say no more. I remember the scene now from an earlier visit. Take us to First and Chestnut. We'll be OK from there."

"Are you guys athletes?" I asked, judging from their bulk and their request to go to a sports bar."

"Not exactly," the fellow in the back diagonally to my right said. "We're coaches. Kenny in the front is the head coach, and we're assistant coaches."

"Oh my God! Ted exclaimed to himself. *I've got the fate of the Dallas Stars National Hockey League team in my hands. To my right is the nationally famous Kenny Hitchcock and in the back are the team's two assistant coaches.*

"I can't believe it," I said. "I sure know who you are. Every cab driver in Philadelphia would give his eyeteeth to be in my seat right now."

"I knew, Will, what the 'big day' mentioned by the coach was to be. The Dallas Stars were in town to play the Philadelphia Flyers the following afternoon. They wanted to continue an amazing twelve-game unbeaten streak, whereas the Flyers needed to snap a twelve-game winless streak. Each team had had a tie or two in between."

"'Tell me, Mr. Hitchcock," I asked him. What's wrong with the Flyers? We Philadelphians don't know what to make of them, and we're very frustrated.'"

"'Not to worry,' he replied. 'They're a good team. They just need confidence.'"

"The Stars did win the next day and the Stars went on to win the Stanley Cup championship that year. I felt ever since that I had been in the presence of greatness during that cab ride and that Kenny Hitchcock's profound understanding of motivational psychology exemplified that. I also have mused that if I myself had wanted to self-destruct that evening, I could have destroyed the Dallas Stars with me.

"In future conversations, though I'll have to relate how cab driving must not be glorified. It's often a pretty grungy job. I can't tell you how many times the windshield wipers haven't worked or the vehicle has broken down and I need to be towed in. Another time my forward gears failed, and I had to drive a mile in reverse to get back to headquarters. Once my starter failed, and I had to keep the ignition on for the entire shift. If I had turned it off, I wouldn't have been able to restart the vehicle. But those stories have to await other times."

"Didn't I tell you that you have the gift of gab. That sure was an interesting story about Kenny Hitchcock, Mike; but I do have another priority now, so listen up. The arrangement you suggested in the earlier ride has to be modified. I didn't want to 'pull rank on you' or 'steal your thunder' so I didn't interrupt you. I in fact, enjoyed listening to what you had to say. But, by sheer chance, I had gotten a call from the Commissioner at 8:30 and have new information that I must share with you immediately. So here I am again."

"Let me just add, Will, that I had an ulterior motive in going on and on for the length of time I did. I sensed very well that you arranged a second ride this evening because something important has undoubtedly come up. I wanted to illustrate indirectly that my running on and on will not fail to put criminals off their guard. They'll think. *This blabbermouth is so into himself that he couldn't possibly have the slightest interest in us,* and they'll reveal things. Besides, you know how much I love to talk. I partly couldn't help it."

"Well said, Mike. Here's what I need to tell you. Our sources tell us that the Mob is having a big meeting in town all day on Saturday, two days from tomorrow. They're planning big things, including rubbing out about five people, some of whom we think we know. Rose Huynh 'serviced' one or two of them, as well as others. By the way, they're by no means all Italians; and, being half-Italian myself. I resent unequivocal 'Italian-mob stereotypes.' The murders are being planned not only for suspected informers, but for rivals in the power struggles as well as non-entities who have fallen out of favor for one reason or another. One unfortunate is simply the hapless boyfriend of a boss's daughter.

"We have no love for any of these people, but we have been trying to clean up the city and we would like to prevent unnecessary bloodshed. That's why I'm being more directive to you now than earlier. We want you to get as much information as you can from random passenger conversations in Northeast Philly, North Philly, Frankford, Kensington, Center City, South Philly, West Philly, Southwest Philly, and Grays Ferry. Different people of interest to us live in every single one of the nine areas I just listed, and they are interlinked. You may learn a great deal indeed, and our teams can put together the bigger picture. Imagine, for example, your picking up a tidbit from an angry Kensington passenger that someone in West Philly has 'just about had all he can take' from someone in Frankford.

"*Capisco molto bene* (I understand very well), Will."

"You suggested that Mark Felt of Watergate fame was indirect. That's the impression conveyed by Woodward and Bernstein. I'm suggesting to you, Mike, that Felt had a more direct involvement than the duo indicated. He had personal grievances against Richard Nixon and a deep passion to 'do him in.' I feel convinced that Felt provided more actual leads to Woodward and Bernstein in the underground-garage meeting place than the team ever actually indicated. But because he felt it necessary to provide himself with the defense of 'deniability' in the matter of undermining the President and with the pretense that his role was merely peripheral, he wanted to be presented to the *Washington Post* as a mere 'adviser.' "Adviser" my ass. Mike, I think he was a 'major player' all the way through."

"You don't want to approximate what he was, do you, Will?"

"Not at all, Mike. I want to reassure you that in your cab you're the boss. Use your head. From your vantage point as a teacher on summer vacation, mention subjects like guns confiscated in schools, students you've had who had to wear ankle bracelets for tracking their movements, flash mobs of students summoned on cellphones to Center City department stores, passengers high on Ecstasy, and actual whorehouse locations. Also, for our purposes, high-class expensive hookers who travel to houses in cabs.

"You're a likable fellow, Mike. Believe it or not, criminals also want to be liked. In seeking your friendship, and not being threatened by you in any way, they'll let down their guard, as you indicated so well, especially if they've had a few drinks. So we don't want to discourage your initiatives in getting information. Occasionally, though, we may learn that a suspect we are surveilling needs to be in a certain place for something we want to know about and, for purposes of anonymity, wants to take a Service Cab to get there. Mary may arrange that you will be the driver for just such a ride.

"You may wonder if we're gonna need you to wear a wire. I certainly hope not, Mike. That would be too dangerous. Criminals spot wires, and we absolutely don't want your dismembered body to wind up in a dumpster like Rose Huynh's."

Reya Spiro Luxenberg

Reva Luxenberg

Bio

REVA SPIRO LUXENBERG embarked on a writing career after she retired as a school social worker. She has written 21 books—mysteries, dramas, non-fiction books, anthologies, and humorous versions of two of the books of the Bible. She is married to Dr. Edward R. Levenson, who has edited nine of her books. She is a member of Florida Authors & Publishers Association. Her hobbies are reading, painting rocks, and taking care of her tortoise Mordy. She is a proud grandmother of seven and great-grandmother of seven.

A Fragile Female

Cornelia had been teased relentlessly in grade school by the students who had called her "Corny." As a result she became introverted and sometimes downright nasty, but Joy overlooked her character flaws and remained her friend. Cornelia had black stringy hair, never wore makeup, and with her small mouth she resembled a fish. Barely accepted by Carnegie Mellon University, she failed all her subjects in her freshman year. Afterwards, she remained home with her wealthy parents and kept busy doing needlepoint.

Her older sister Monica was just the opposite—gracious, pretty, and sociable. It was Monica who introduced Cornelia to a pimply youth named Brad, who was a bookkeeper. Brad proposed after three dates in an attempt to marry into a rich family. In two months he flew to Reno and divorced Cornelia, who had watched cooking shows on TV but never found her way to the kitchen.

Monica's husband Walt successfully invested in the stock market and accumulated a significant fortune. With some of the money they purchased a beautifully renovated home in Key West that had five bedrooms, four bathrooms, and a wondrously appointed kitchen with wraparound windows. The living area overlooked a kidney-shaped pool and tropical grounds. There was a guest house rented to George Harris, an elderly man who went deep sea fishing when the weather allowed. He had a trimmed short white beard, wore thick glasses and paid his rent on time.

One April day Monica called Cornelia, who was depressed after her divorce from Brad. "Hi, Sis. I met a guy who's a widower with no children. Steve Hawk is our real estate agent and is very lonely. Stay with us and I'll introduce you."

"How tall is he?"

"Does it matter?"

"Sure it does. I'm short and I don't want a man who's short like me. I also don't want a man who is tall and bulky and will overwhelm me. I'm fragile and I want someone who will take care of me. My former husband expected me to cook and take care of him. It's time a man looked after me."

"Steve is about Brad's height. I don't know how he relates to women. I leave it to you to judge."

Cornelia screwed up her fish mouth. "I don't like the name Hawk. I wouldn't want people addressing me as Mrs. Hawk."

"Nowadays women can keep their own name if they want."

"All right. Can I bring my friend Joy with me?"

"Sure, I like Joy. You can fly down to Key West and rent a car. I know you don't drive but Joy does. Bring summer clothes and shorts and a sweater, as the evenings are cool."

"I don't wear shorts. My legs look like sticks. I'll wear dresses and slacks. Bye now."

When Cornelia and Joy entered Monica's home, they were surprised that the only room that was completely furnished was the study. They noticed that there were two black leather armchairs, a matching couch, a black ebony desk and desk chair, and a bookcase filled with books about finance and mystery novels. A Picasso hung on the wall. Outlines of three other paintings that had been removed showed marks around them. Monica said the Renoirs were being restored. She added, "Our house is up for sale. Now that our father has died, Walt and I will be moving to England where he has family." She brought the two women to adjoining bedrooms that were furnished with one bed, a night table with a lamp, hangers in the closet, and nothing else.

The next day Steve showed up and Monica introduced her sister to him. Cornelia looked at him with displeasure. He was just an inch taller than she, but his belly protruded like a cantaloupe. He had a waxed mustache and wore yellow Bermuda shorts that clashed with his bright orange and blue print T-shirt. "I'm pleased to make your acquaintance," said Steve. "The weather is nice. Would you like to go parasailing? You'll be 300 feet above the water and you'll have the opportunity to see the whole island. You take off and land right on the boat. If you want, you can dip in the water or stay dry. It's up to you. It's a marvelous experience that you'll remember the rest of your life."

"That's not for me. I want you to know at the outset that I'm not the athletic type."

"Okay. How about going to the Key West Aquarium?"

"All right. Will you drive?"

"It's hard to park on Whitehead Street. We can take the trolley. It's called a trolley, but it's really a comfortable sightseeing bus."

Cornelia got on the bus reluctantly. The windows were open and she hated the warm breeze that swept through her open window and messed up her hair that was unsightly to begin with. Inside the aquarium Cornelia refused to pet the small sea creatures in the touch tank. She strode quickly past the fish tanks. Steve remarked, "The lion fish are picturesque, don't you think?"

"You can't eat them, so what good are they?"

Steve's eyes widened but he kept silent.

Cornelia asked in a whiny voice, "Did you take care of your wife in her ill health?

Steve face clouded over. "I did. I loved her. I miss her. She also took care of me.

"I need a man to take care of me. I'm fragile, very fragile," Cornelia said as she looked with disgust at the sharks circling in the pool in the center of the room.

"Would you like to go home since you're so fragile?"

"Not yet. I want to go to the Surf & Turf Restaurant. I'm hungry and I could eat a full meal."

"Sorry Cornelia, I have to skip lunch. I need to leave to feed my greyhound racing dogs."

The back door of the house was never locked, and when George returned from fishing he entered the kitchen and presented a string of mutton snapper fish to Myra the cook, who was built like a pear. She wore her salt-and-pepper hair in a bun and was dressed in a creased housedress with an apron tied loosely around her ample waist. She took the fish with an ingratiating smile, cleaned, and placed them in the freezer.

The humid night was foggy but it didn't stop Cornelia and Joy from dangling their feet in the pool. She spoke to Joy in a confidential tone, "I want you to know that Steve Hawk is a narcissist who is hooked on dogs and, who knows, maybe drugs? I'm fragile and I need a man who would be devoted only to me. Besides he's too short and has no taste in clothes. He left abruptly without even taking me to eat."

Joy assumed that Steve had been turned off by Cornelia and her rigid demands. But she had gotten used to her bristling brusque comments about people and hardly paid much attention to them.

Everyone retired at 10:30 p.m. and at midnight Joy was awakened in a stupor by an eerie scream in the next room. It took her a few minutes to awaken completely. She crawled out of bed, put on a cotton robe, and opened the adjoining door. The lamp was turned on. She shrieked when she saw Cornelia lying on top of the coverlet bleeding profusely from a wound caused by a knife that was sticking out of her chest. Joy bent over her body. Cornelia's eyes were open and glassy. Her blood stained Joy's robe, but she was so frightened that she became oblivious to it. She could tell that her childhood friend was dead. She knew from watching crime programs on TV not to touch her body.

Racing downstairs Joy grabbed the landline phone in the kitchen. Her hand shook as if she had been stricken with Parkinson's, but she managed to call 911. "There's been a murder at 1125 Seminole Street. Send the police." She couldn't answer any questions that the operator asked, as she started to weep. Her heart began to beat rapidly. She felt faint and panted like a race dog. She was panicky, anxious, unbelieving. *How could this have happened to Cornelia? Who would have hated her so much that he or she had to kill my admittedly difficult friend?*

Joy flung herself down on a kitchen chair and let out a cry of anguish that alerted the rest of the people. Unaware of what she was doing, she bolted up the steps and entered the scene of the murder. The resident cook Myra came in as well as George Harris, the older man from the guest house. Then Monica and Walt added to the number. Monica yelled, "Oh, my God!" when she saw her sister. Walt placed his arm around Monica, whose tears were rolling down her face.

A squad car screeched into the circular driveway and the sheriff entered. "I'm Sheriff Nelson Rodriguez," he said. He was dressed in navy slacks and a matching polo shirt with a police logo. He looked with a poker face at Cornelia's dead body. "Go back to your rooms now and don't discuss anything with each other while you wait. We will question everyone separately. Detective White and Crime Scene Investigator Castellano will be here shortly before the body is removed."

After the forensic team arrived and concluded that Cornelia's death resulted from the stabbing of her heart, hemorrhaging, and cardiorespiratory insufficiency, Sheriff Rodriguez advised that everyone present in the house is a "person of interest" in the homicide investigation. He read them their Miranda rights. "We'll question you back in the station and give you time to lawyer up."

Myra immediately said, "The knife was in my kitchen, but I didn't stab Cornelia and that's my final word."

Monica's eyes kept tearing. "I need to know who killed my younger sister."

Cornelia was my friend, Joy thought. *I don't know what to think— but someone here is a murderer.*

Detectives White and Castellano decided to question the cook first, as the murder weapon came from the kitchen. White took over the interrogation. "What's your full name?"

"Myra Welsh Waddell."

"How long have you worked for the Johnsons?"

"I didn't kill Cornelia. I ain't no murderer."

"Please answer the question."

"Six months since they bought the house."

"Did you ever know the victim before she stayed at the house?"

"No. I never seen her before."

"Do you have a prison record?"

"Yeah, but I was innocent. I didn't steal the old lady's pearls."

"How did you get the job with the Johnsons?"

"My probation officer helped me get it. I've been a cook for thirty years and a darn good one. You can ask anyone."

"When was the last time you looked at kitchen knife block? Did you see the knife that was used in the stabbing?"

"I saw it the evening before when I put it back after slicing tomatoes. The next time I saw it was when it was sticking out of Cornelia's chest."

"When was the knife block bought and who bought it?"

Myra looked nervous. She folded her hands tightly. "The boss gave it to me last week. I complained about how dull my knives were. He was kind enough to get me snappy-looking expensive knives."

White nodded. "The murder weapon has been identified as a high-carbon stainless steel 8"-slicing-knife which has its blade forged right into the wooden handle. The German Pakka wood block had 15 assorted knives. Miss Waddell, that's all for now. Just sign this statement. You may go back to the house, but don't leave Key West."

After Myra waddled out of the interrogation room, White and Castellano conferred with each other. Castellano said, "She signed the statement with her right hand. The killer was right-handed. She could be the one."

White shook his head. "What's the motive?"

"I don't know. Why don't you now question the woman who found the body?"

They brought Joy into the interrogation room. She shivered from the coldness of the air-conditioning combined with her probably being a suspect in Cornelia's death. She sat at a wooden table opposite both men and folded her hands over her stomach. She thought, *I should've worn slacks instead of shorts and brought along a sweater.*

After the preliminary questioning of name and address, White started asking serious questions. "What brought you to Key West?"

"I knew Cornelia since we were kids. She asked me to go with her so she could meet some guy that her sister knew."

"Don't you work?"

"Yes. I'm a teacher. I have the summer off. I had never visited Key West before and I was anxious to see it and help out Cornelia at the same time."

White cleared his throat. "In your own words tell me about why you went into the victim's bedroom. I want to remind you that what you say is being recorded."

"I heard a scream in the room adjacent to mine. I looked at my watch and it was 3:00 a.m. It takes me a few minutes to wake up. I put on my robe and when I entered the bedroom I saw Cornelia lying on her bed with a knife stuck in her chest. I ran downstairs and called the police. I yelled and woke up the other people, who then came into the room."

"Who came in?"

"Monica and Walt, Myra the cook, and George Harris, the elderly man."

"Do you have any idea who would've killed her?"

"No. She could be annoying and selfish, but she was childlike and had no enemies."

"I think that woman may be our killer," White said after Joy left the room.

Castellano raised his eyebrows. "I saw that she's young, healthy, strong, and is right-handed, but what makes you think she's a murderer?"

"I believe she was lying. She hesitated before answering questions. She knew the victim most of her life. She called her annoying and selfish. She *is* right-handed. She clasped her arms to her chest like she was keeping something back."

"It's cold in here," Castellano said as he shrugged his shoulders. "She was trying to keep warm. We should talk to the old man next and give the sister and brother-in-law time to recuperate from the shock."

"All right. I'll reserve judgment."

George Harris didn't wait for the detectives to ask him questions but plunged right in. "I think I know who killed that little woman. My guest house is thirty yards from the back door where the kitchen is. The back door is always left open. I saw a short man with a big belly and yellow shorts hanging around the house at about 6 p.m. He left and could've come back later, grabbed the knife in the kitchen, and stabbed the little woman. He's the guy who took Cornelia out for a date."

The detectives immediately learned the name and address of Cornelia's date and brought him in. Steve Hawk squirmed in his seat in the interrogation room.

White said, "We have a witness who saw you at 6 p.m. at the back door of the Johnson house. What were you doing there?"

"I was there walking around the house deciding if I should ask Cornelia to go out to dinner with me. I thought it over, decided not to pursue the matter, and left.'

"Did you return at about midnight, enter the kitchen, and kill Cornelia?"

"What? You're accusing me of murder? Me—a man who never even got a traffic ticket? Cornelia didn't appeal to me and when she asked to go out for lunch, I said I had hungry dogs and that I had to go home and feed them. I felt guilty about lying to her and not taking her out to eat and that's why I came back."

"So you admit you're a liar, and that the woman didn't appeal to you."

"I'm not talking anymore until I have a lawyer."

Monica's eyes teared when she spoke to the detectives about asking her sister to come to Key West to meet Steve Hawk, a potential suitor, and how it didn't pan out. She kept wiping her eyes when she revealed that her mother had passed away a year ago from a heart attack and that her father had died in a car crash just six months ago. She couldn't continue talking about the three close deaths and as a result the interview was terminated. Walt was asked to return after he brought his wife back to their home.

"We need to keep our suspects under surveillance," White said.

Castellano agreed. "Let's go. Maybe we can wind up this case today if we're lucky."

After Walt put Monica to bed, he went to the study. "What do you think you're doing?" he shouted when he spotted Joy scrutinizing a paper that she had found in his desk drawer.

"I was looking for a motive for murder and I found it. You invested foolishly in options and in buying a house you couldn't afford. Monica and Cornelia inherited a large fortune that they split, but it wasn't enough for you so you murdered Cornelia to get her share."

Walt snickered, "Sure I needed money, but you can't prove I murdered to get it."

"I didn't see you heartlessly plunge the knife into Cornelia, but there must be a way to prove you did it. Sometimes circumstantial evidence is enough to put a person behind bars and that's where you belong." Joy began to yell at the top of her lungs.

Monica must've heard her because she came running down the stairs and entered the study. "What's going on?" she asked.

"Your husband is the one who murdered your sister," Joy said.

Walt laughed. "Joy is delirious. I would never kill anyone. If I see a spider in the house, I take it outside. I'm not a hunter who shoots deer with a rifle."

Monica looked from Walt to Joy and back again. "Do you have proof that Walt killed my sister?"

"No, but he's greedy and that was his motivation."

"I don't believe you," Monica said. "I'm gonna take a hot bath to calm my nerves. Then I'm going to bed. Will you be coming, dear?"

"Of course, sweetheart. I just need a few minutes to straighten my desk. Joy messed it up."

Walt waited until Monica was gone. Then he tore off the cord from the Venetian blind. He clamped a hand over Joy's mouth so she couldn't call for help. He used electric tape to tape her mouth. Then he tied her hands behind her back and led her to the back door which he opened. When he pushed her out, Detectives White and Castellano were standing there. They put cuffs on his wrists and freed Joy.

Joy should've gone home the next day, but Steve Hawk came around and asked her to go parasailing with him. It was an exhilarating experience that she'd remember for the rest of her life. Later they went to dinner. He wore attractive clothes, told her he didn't have any dogs, and asked her to stay in Key West so that they could get to know each other better. They day after they planned on going on a glass-bottom boat and getting to know each other better. She thought, *I don't think I'd mind changing my name to Mrs. Joy Hawk.*

A Homeless Man

Every day when Alice visited her father in his semi-private room in Memorial Hospital she brought him a chocolate-chip cookie. The patient in the next bed looked with longing at the cookie. Alice noticed that and soon after she brought two cookies and gave one to him.

The patient had thick oyster-white hair and a razor burn on his face. He was very depressed. When Alice's father nodded off, the patient said, "I'm Nick and I thank you for the cookie. I have no visitors and I think that you're a wonderful daughter. I wish my own daughter would pay attention to me but we're estranged."

"Well Nick, there's always hope."

"No, not in my case. Right now I'm homeless. When I get medically discharged, I don't have a home, an apartment, or even a room to go to."

"Why can't you check into a hotel?" Alice asked in a soothing tone of voice.

"I have no money and all my credit cards have been canceled. When I was young all that mattered to me was making a lot of money. First I opened one garage and cheated people by telling them their cars needed parts that were unnecessary. I was a successful crook. I was able to open more and more garages. I married a woman for her money and I had a daughter who I paid no attention to. My wife divorced me and got custody of her. Then I got arrested and jailed for my crimes. After my sentence was up, I gambled all my money away. I never helped anyone in my life. When I had some money, I didn't support any charity. Two weeks ago I got sick with bleeding ulcers and here I am. I deserve the position I'm in. What is your opinion of me?"

"I happen to agree with you and I'm tempted not to bring two chocolate-chip cookies tomorrow."

A Skull

Brooklyn, March 31, 2018. Detective Jonathan York received an anonymous call. A man with a raspy voice said, "At midnight go to the first level of the Kings Plaza parking lot and you'll find a suspicious bone," and then he hung up abruptly. York decided to follow up on the possible clue. He was working on the mystery of the murder of the janitor of Midwood High School and he was anxious to solve the crime. The janitor had been a nice fellow who had been friendly to all who knew him.

The detective drove to the parking lot. It was dark. The weather of that early spring evening was cool. Gingerly he stepped out of his Ford and checked his gun in the holster on his hip. He shone the light of his flashlight around the cement paving. He noticed a skull in the illuminated area. He bent down; picked it up with his gloved hand; and, intending to give it to forensics, he put it into a plastic bag. Then he returned to his car. After his shift was over, he headed home for a good night's sleep.

The following day he handed Millie the technician the evidence he had found. "As soon as I have the results of my exam, I'll phone you," she said.

All day long the detective wondered if the clue he found would reveal who killed the janitor. And who was it who had tipped him off? Could it have been the killer? So far he had no other clues about the murder.

At the end of the working day Millie called him.

"Have you learned anything?" he asked insistently.

"You'll be surprised. First of all the janitor wasn't murdered. He died from a massive heart attack. Secondly, the skull you found isn't a human skull."

"Is it from an ape?" he asked in a quivering voice.

"No. It's a synthetic hard plastic. It's April 1st, April Fool's Day; and someone has played a trick on you. Bye now. Next time bring me something real."

An Exchange Student

Benny Kawano and Laurence Walker, who shared a room in
the dormitory in Northern Arizona University, had become fast
friends. Admission had been highly competitive. When 700
students had applied to the Physical Therapy Degree Program, they
were 2 out of the 72 who were accepted. Laurence's father was a
cardiologist in Phoenix while Benny's father was a sheep herder in
the Navajo Nation.

Laurence teased his roommate when he declared. "You're an
exchange student."

"I'm a Native American," Benny answered with a frown.

"Yes, but you come from an entity within the United States
which is considered a nation—therefore you can be considered an
exchange student."

Benny mulled over this explanation which seemed to be true on the
surface but somehow didn't sound right.

Laurence asked. "What do you like about my country?"

Benny smiled, "I like the education I'm receiving. When I graduate
and get my license as a physical therapist, I can return to my
reservation and help the people of my tribe with their ailments,
especially my grandfather who is the chief. My uncle is a medicine
man and he and I can do much good by alleviating pain."

"What else do you like?"

"I like my tribal dances but additionally I like your dances like the
waltz, the foxtrot, and the tango."

"The tango is not an American dance."

"Maybe not, but I still sure do like it.."

Both students were dressed in their pajamas, sitting on their twin
beds opposite each other, when Laurence asked another question.

"What do you dislike about the United States?"

"I don't like being teased when I wear my turquoise necklace and
bracelets."

"What else?"

"I don't like speaking English all the time. As a matter of fact, my Navajo language was utilized as a code during World War II by those who were known as the 'Code Talkers.' The Japanese couldn't break it."

"Teach me some Navajo words and I'll speak to you in your language. What's the worst thing you don't like about being in the U.S.?"

"The food. I'm used to boiled mutton and goat meat and all I can get here are hot dogs and burgers."

"Sorry, my friend. My father says being a vegetarian is good for you."

"If that's true, how come my meat-eating grandfather is 105 years old?"

Boxed In

Me and Moish, hand in hand, were walking along Lexington Avenue minding our own business. Right in front of Bloomindale's department store, I seen a wallet on the ground. I picked it up, put it in my knapsack, and me and my boyfriend pushed off.

When we got to the alley, it was empty so Moish said, "*Bubeleh* let's see what you got there."

He calls me *"Bubeleh,"* even though my name is Delores. We've been an item since Chanukah. I took out the high-end woman's leather wallet. It was stuffed with *gelt* (money). Moish counted $550. "*A gezunt ahf dein keppele*," (health upon your little head), he said, wishing me good health.

I looked further. There were three credit cards and a picture of a fancy lady, a man, and two kids. There was also a driver's license with the dame's address. "We have to give this up!" I said strongly. "My old lady taught me to be honest and most of the time I is."

"Are you *meshugga* (crazy)?" Moish said. "We ain't never seen so much *gelt* in our lives. This rich dame don't need this, but we do."

I begged Moish to return the wallet and everything in it. I even let my eyes get teary, but he wouldn't listen to me. He's a real donkey.

We were starved. Moish took me to a restaurant in a hotel and we ate like millionaires. We went to Macy's and he bought clothes for him and me. He spent a total of $535. Then he said, "No way am I using the credit cards. They ain't puttin' us behind bars no more."

"What should we do?"

He said, "We'll put the picture, and the credit cards, and the driver's license in an envelope and mail them to the dame."

We went to the post office and that's what we did. "What should we do with this expensive wallet?" I asked.

Moish said, "Maybe it's worth a couple of bucks. We'll bring it to the pawn shop."

Can you guess what happened? They traced the wallet back to us and booked us for theft. Life ain't fair! After all, we did return everything but the money. We should get a reward for that.

The Pawn Shop

Her name was Rho and her father, who was a chemist, named her after the element Rhodium which has the atomic number of 45. In fact Rho's father was both pleased and amazed that at the age of 45 he had his first and only child. Rho romanticized her name as signifying the atomic number and as being associated with the Greek word "*rhodon*," which means rose. Her mother was an inventor in the line of improving military weapons.

Rho's brilliant parents taught their precious daughter to be kind and thoughtful to all people. When her mother gave her a doll, she taught the little girl to say, "Thank you." When she asked her father for a ball, he said, "Say 'please' when you ask for something."

When Rho had been playing outside at age four, she came home sobbing and showed her mother bite marks on her hand from a girl next door. Her upset mother approached the child's mother and related the incident. The mother of the three-year-old girl said with remorse, "My daughter has a terrible habit of biting children. I'll hold her and, Rho, you bite her back."

"I can't hurt a girl who is smaller than me."

Rho's parents were proud of their child's kindness. The only disappointment they experienced was that their beautifully behaved daughter hadn't inherited their genius gene since she had only average intelligence. The report cards she gave them to sign had all "A's in Deportment, but only passing grades in academic subjects. She was outstanding, however, in Phys Ed; and they provided her with ice-skating lessons in the winter and dancing lessons the rest of the year.

After Rho graduated from business school, she went to work as a typist in a law office in Manhattan. She had high cheekbones, a big heart, and a striking appearance; and Madison Strauss, one of the legal clerks where Rho worked, became entranced with her. He rubbed the back of his neck and shifted his feet when he first approached her. "Would you like to have a coffee in Joe's Italian restaurant around the corner after work?"

Rho, in a light tone of voice, said, "Why yes, thank you."

They sat opposite each other at a table with a checked red and white tablecloth and Madison nervously nibbled on the knuckle of his left hand. Rho's stomach growled with hunger. Madison asked in halting stilted speech if Rho would like something to eat. She hesitated since she knew Madison was not earning much and had heard that he was supporting his sick mother. "No thank you," she said. "My mother has prepared dinner at home."

Madison subsequently made it a habit for both of them to drop into the restaurant for coffee after work. It took a few weeks before he got the nerve to ask her to go to the zoo on Sunday. They dated steadily for a year—strolling in the park, sitting on the boardwalk at Coney Island, and roller skating. One evening under the stars on a bench in Central Park, Madison said in a quivering voice, "I love you. Will you marry me?"

"I don't know," Rho said, as she clenched her fists. "You'll to have to ask my father."

With a high-pitched quick laugh Madison said, "But I don't want to marry your father. I want to marry you!"

Rho's father met Madison and approved of him. After he gave his permission, Madison said to her, "I'll give you an engagement ring. I don't have much money so it'll probably have a small diamond with a flaw."

"I have an idea," Rho said. "I don't want you to spend too much, so why don't we go to a pawn shop and look for a ring there. I don't mind if someone else has worn it before me."

"I've never been to a pawn shop," Madison said, raising his eyebrows.

"Me neither, but there will be many rings to choose from and checking out the situation ought to be interesting."

Snow was floating down from a gray sky when Rho and Madison entered the Crown Pawn Shop. It featured guitars, typewriters, and record collections. A clerk who wore a toupee that was askew approached them. "We're looking for an engagement ring," Madison said, as he tightly held on to Rho's hand.

The clerk guided them to a glass showcase. Rho tried on some rings that were too large and some that were too small. "Here's an unusual antique ring," the clerk said.

Rho smiled. "May I please try it on?"

The ring proved to be a perfect fit. It was gold with one diamond in a centered triangle resting on a larger triangle. Leaves were encrusted with eighteen shiny diamonds. Rho's eyes shone with pleasure.

"If you buy this ring now," the clerk said, "I'll deduct ten per cent."

"What do you think?" Madison asked, taking out his wallet.

"It's beautiful. I love it, thank you."

On Rho's birthday the couple returned to the same pawn shop. This time Madison bought Rho a pearl necklace. The next trip to the pawn shop was on their first anniversary and he bought her a gold bracelet.

Soon after that Madison enrolled in a two-year program at a technical school and graduated with honors. He learned enough to open his own business. He prospered so much that they were able to buy a home on five acres of land.

When Rho gave birth to a 7 lb. 6 oz. son, Madison bought Rho diamond earrings from the same pawn shop. They named the son Andrew.

Two years later Rho gave birth to Jessica, and Madison showed up at the hospital with a thick gold necklace that he got from 'their' pawn shop and with a large jewelry box that he bought in Macy's. Rho showed her sister-in-law Denise all her precious jewelry, and her sister-in-law dragged *her* husband to the Crown Pawn shop. Denise never revealed to her friends how her husband had been able to afford all the diamond pieces he continued to buy there.

When Rho encouraged her father to buy jewelry for her mother, her father agreed but her mother demurred, "I don't like jewelry. I'd rather wear scarves around my neck."

Her loss for sure.

When Jessica and Andrew were old enough to go to intermediate school, Rho joined the PTA. She willingly shared her privileged information with the women she became friendly with. They all frequented the Crown Pawn shop like bees in a flower garden.

The time came when Andrew was an adult and had chosen a young woman to marry. "Tell her you can get a good bargain for an engagement ring at *my* pawn shop," Rho advised her son. The girl was a snob, scoffed at the idea, and broke off the engagement. Andrew never listened to his mother again about pawn-shop shopping.

Jessica had the opposite result. Her fiancé was thrilled when he saved thousands of dollars on an engagement ring for her.

As their business expanded due to the many recommendations by Rho and Madison, the Crown Pawn Shop bought the stores on either side of it, added upper stories on top of them, and opened a mid-size department store. The manager was so thrilled with Rho and Madison that he sent them birthday and anniversary cards and gave them huge discounts.

When Jessica gave birth to her twin boys, she was blessed not only with healthy babies but gifts of a ruby and diamond necklace from the pawn-shop owner.

Time marches on and after 20 years a now-white-haired Rho had accumulated tons of precious jewelry. She collected treasures the way Madison collected stamps. Madison installed a safe in their bedroom to protect Rho's collection.

At their 50th-anniversary gala Madison, with a champagne flute in his liver-spotted hand, rose to his feet and addressed the 250 assembled guests. "My dear family and friends, I offer an unusual toast to the owner and the manager of the Crown Pawn Shop. 51 years ago Rho and I entered a small shop and I bought Rho the engagement ring she still wears to this very day. It started as a habit and turned into a tradition that on birthdays and anniversaries we shopped for fine jewelry at the same pawn shop. We spread the word around about how pleased we were with the shop and more and more people patronized it. On my son Andrew's birthdays I bought him the watches he admired, and on my daughter Jessica's birthdays I gave her the necklaces she cherished. My darling wife always selected something lovely from the growing amounts of jewelry the shop featured. Many of our friends here have followed the tradition we created. And so the business has thrived beyond anyone's wildest dreams. The store provided win-win solutions for the problems of what to buy for loved ones.

"When I met Rho, I was a poor struggling fellow with no prospects. I couldn't even get the words out when I proposed. As I matured, I attended a technical school and afterwards started my own business. It became successful. I really don't expect that *my* customers will invite Rho and me to their anniversary parties as we have invited the owner and manager of the Crown Pawn Shop to ours. Now gentlemen, please stand up now and take a bow."

The men in their tuxedos stood as the audience recognized them and clapped hands very enthusiastically.

"I hope that all of you who are here tonight will continue our tradition."

The applause which followed was deafening.

Caterpillars: A Three-Act Play

CHARACTERS
Reva, a four-year old girl
Mama
Daddy

SCENE 1, An apartment in Brooklyn in the summer.
Mama: "Reva, it's sunny. Go play outside. Don't cross the street."
Reva: "I have no one to play with. The children are across the street and I won't cross it. Mama, can't you go out with me?"
Mama: "Not now. I have to prepare dinner. Daddy will be home soon. Go out. You'll find something to do."

SCENE 2, Outside a three-story apartment house. Maple trees in full bloom line the street.
Reva: "What should I do? The kids across the street are playing ball. I'm all alone. Ooh! I see so many caterpillars. They're yellow and furry and they look so cute. If I had a jar, I could collect them and put them in the jar. I'll go up and ask Mama for a jar."
[Reva comes down with a jar with holes in the cover. She bends down with a twig and puts twenty caterpillars in the jar along with leaves from the trees. She smiles with delight.]

SCENE 3, A gas station in Suffern, New York. A model T-Ford pulls up to the pump. Inside the car Daddy is at the wheel, Mama is beside him, and Reva is sitting in the back with the jar of caterpillars on her lap. All get ready to get out of the car. Reva has forgotten about the jar. As she leaves the car, the jar of caterpillars falls to the ground and shatters. The caterpillars scatter all over.
Reva: "Oh my goodness!"
Daddy: "It's all right. The caterpillars are free, and that's how they should be."

A Twinkle in Her Eye

When my father asked my mother to marry him, she cast her dark brown eyes downward and then, looking up at the handsome man facing her, she smiled. "I need time to think it over."

The next morning she went to her brother Morris, who was known in the family as "Morris the Millionaire." He said. "You turned down the well-heeled men I sent you and now you want to marry a poor jerk who sells advertising signs?"

"I had good reasons for refusing them."

"Like what?

"One had a big stomach. Another smelled of garlic. And another talked only about himself. Ben is kind and, more importantly, he loves me.

"I won't give my approval until he gets a steady job," Morris said firmly.

For reasons I never fully understood my mother had problems making decisions. Many times I saw her decide to do something and then change her mind. Meanwhile my father took the test to become a clerk in the post office and he passed with flying colors. He went to work in the general post office in Manhattan. Still my mother hesitated. She was attractive and dressed fashionably, but she was now 36 years old.

Finally my father approached her. "I have a steady job. I love you and want to marry you, but you keep putting me off. I have no choice. We've been going together for five years. If you won't agree to marry me, I'll have to break off our relationship and look elsewhere."

"I'll speak to my brother Morris tomorrow," my mother said. "If he'll accept my marrying you, I'll agree to it."

"Don't you have a mind of your own?" my father protested.

"Not in this case. It's too important a decision. I need my brother's blessing. If my father were alive, he'd be the one I'd ask, but he died years ago. Since my mother approves of you. I think my brother will too."

When my mother spoke to Morris, he said, "If you marry a postal clerk, you'll be poor the rest of your life. Will you be satisfied living in poverty?"

"Yes, I will," my mother answered, with a twinkle in her eye.

Relaxing with Rocks

My mailman hates me. Every day he stuffs my mailbox with catalogues. I get more of them than anyone else. I love catalogues and peruse them all at my leisure.

I received a book catalogue, and something in it caught my eye. It was a book on how to paint rocks. I used to paint pictures but I stopped. How many canvases did I have room for? But rocks? Rocks are small. You can paint hundreds and they don't take up much space.

I bought the book. Then I purchased the rocks, the acrylic paint pens, and the black regular pens; and I went to work. I've thought that this is more fun than I've had in a long time. My husband is verbose, to say the least, and can expatiate at any time on any subject for an hour or more. Meanwhile I paint my rocks and I'm not as bored as I might be otherwise as I listen quietly to his perorations.

I've given rocks to my friends and my family—and also to a policeman of my acquaintance who told me his wife is sick and would appreciate a rock with her name on it. It was a pleasure to design another rock with an owl and her name RITA on top.

A woman in my creative writing club wrote about how she took up Yoga and this changed her life for the better. I won't be doing Yoga, but I will positively be continuing my relaxing with my rock painting.

Reva Luxenberg's Painted Rocks

Faye Menczer

Bio

Faye Menczer lives in West Bloomfield, Michigan, but winters in Delray Beach, Florida. She has been writing and publishing since 2014. She began as a writer of children's books for her two grandchildren. After six of these she began to write "How to Publish" books and teach classes. She now primarily publishes other people's books and has had in print 55 books to date. Check out her blog at FRM Publishing, as well as her website and new blog, *Tales of Israel*! If you like what you see, become a subscriber and get the latest updates.

The Loss of Son Brian

"Mom, are you home?" David asked from his phone.

"No, Emily and I are at the mall shopping. What's up?"

"I have something really important to tell you. When will you be home?"

"Probably in an hour. Can't you tell me now?" Thoughts of a new job, a business opportunity, some good news passed through her mind.

"No. We'll talk when you get home."

Faye and her twelve-year-old granddaughter finished their shopping and headed back to her house for dinner. When they entered the house, they saw sitting in the living room her children—Miriam, Emily's mom, who was an attorney; son David; and his wife Sandy. Taking off her coat, she dropped into a comfortable chair waiting to hear the good news. Noting how grim their faces looked, Faye realized it was not good news. She wondered, *Was someone sick? Was it Sandy's dad?*

"Mom, I have some really bad news about Brian," David began.

Faye waited, thinking *There is always bad news about Brian. He gets into more accidents and incidents than all of us combined.*

"The coroner called...."

"The coroner," she screamed, feeling hysterical, "Is Brian dead? Is Brian dead? He's only 51. He wasn't sick. What happened?" She covered her face with her hands and began to cry softly, "My poor Brian. What could have happened?"

"I got a call from the coroner that Brian was found dead in his house in Oakland this morning by his friend Franklin. The coroner said it looked like natural causes with no foul play, no drugs, or homicide or suicide. From the meds on Bri's nightstand it looked like it could have been a heart attack. They won't know for sure without an autopsy, but they don't feel one is needed."

"Oh my God," she sobbed into her hands, "What else do you know? What happened? Did you talk to your brother Mike?"

"I called Mike right after the coroner called me. We have spoken several times. Mike spoke to some of Brian's friends in Oakland. Mike had met some of these guys when he drove up from up LA to visit Brian last summer. They had gone up to Lake Tahoe and met Brian's boss and family. Apparently, Brian missed two days of work without calling. The boss knew this was not like Brian and asked Franklin, who lived closest to Brian, to stop by the house and make sure he was okay. Franklin did so. He found poor old Ronin barking loudly in the yard. The back door was propped open. The dog's food and water dishes were empty. Frankie fed Ronin and, sick as he is, cancer-ridden Ronin led Frank upstairs to the bedroom where Brian was lying on the floor next to his bed. It was obvious that he was gone. Frank went downstairs and called the police. They took a long time to arrive. Frank was left in the house, upset and beside himself waiting for them. It was a terrible experience, which will probably haunt him forever. When the police finally arrived, they saw Brian and called the coroner. The coroner examined him, checked the medicine next to the bed, and called me. That's all I know," said David, his own voice beginning to quiver.

"How did they get your phone number?"

"You and I were both listed as next of kin somewhere. I don't know where. The coroner, apparently learning your age, said he thought it was better to call me," David responded quietly.

"Who else knows? Whom have you called?

"We haven't told anyone else, but the news is spreading among Brian's friends and they may start calling the various family members. We need to tell people."

"You are right. Divide up the family heads and please make the calls. Tell them I can't talk to anyone. I can't take phone calls. They can email or text and I will respond as well as I can. Did you know, I spoke to Mike two or three times today? I don't know if it was before or after you spoke to him. I don't know if he knew about Brian when we spoke. He didn't say anything. Maybe it was before he knew. Oh my God! Oh my God! It is such a terrible shock. How is it possible? We know Brian had diabetes and took insulin shots. He told us a few years ago that he had been diagnosed with MS and was seeing specialists, but he did not yet seem to have too many issues that I was aware of. The last time I spoke to him was two weeks ago before my trip to Italy. He told me that he hadn't had electricity for a week. P&G had turned off service because of the fires. That for a whole month the power was on and off. He said the smoke was terrible and the air-quality rating was really low. That was the last time we spoke. When I returned two days ago, I texted all of you that I had returned safely. Brian never responded. He may have already been gone…," her voice trailed off, her mind wandering through the series of events.

Faye started again, "Did he have heart disease? Do any of you know if he had a heart problem? I think he had high blood pressure. He didn't take very good care of himself. He didn't trust his doctors and wasn't very compliant about eating healthy…." Again she drifted off into thoughts of her son.

"It's possible, Mom. Brian did not always share his medical situation with us. I called the Dorfman Funeral Home to make arrangements.

"They will send someone to get the body and bring our brother home," said Miriam. She had been very quiet the whole time. She too was crying softly.

"I don't want to use Dorfman. I want Hebrew Memorial. They buried your dad and will bury me. I want Brian to be near *us*. Please call Dorfman and ask them to arrange it with Hebrew Memorial," Faye said.

Miriam made the necessary calls. The arrangements were made.

"Otto at Hebrew Memorial said it could take three to five days for the coroner in California to release Brian's body. California has the most difficult bureaucratic regulations for moving a deceased out of the state. He said there can be unexpected holds, but he did not elaborate."

"When is Mike coming?" Mother asked.

"Saturday morning. He'll stay a week here with you," David answered.

It was late. Everyone was tired and grief-stricken and wanted to go home. Each one in the family was thinking of Brian, their son, their brother. The mood was somber. Death was on their minds. Mourning and deep sadness had begun for them privately, all coping in their own way.

Faye gathered herself together. She had a cup of tea. She had a large glass of some type of leftover wine. Many thoughts of Brian filled her mind. Her second son Mike was adopted, so Brian was the first from her body. She thought of this first pregnancy, his infancy. Very many memories flooded through, hundreds of images. He was taken by the *Mal'akh Hamovet* (the Angel of Death) on Monday November 4, 2019. He was too young. He was so full of life and laughter and stories. He had so many friends, so many plans for himself. There was no wife, no offspring, no significant other that she knew of. But Brian kept so much to himself that she didn't really know.

She thought about his visit in May for her 80th birthday. How her kids had all gathered and laughed and told so many stories.

The weekend was spent with them sitting around various tables revisiting family lore, sharing their adventures. Brian's many exploits were chief among the tales. He was a great story teller and he loved to share his tumultuous experiences. They all either cringed or roared, and they repeated the stories eagerly. He was their "Devil-may-care kid," living on the edge, experimenting with life. The family had been telling "Brian Stories" ever since he was born. He always loved that and when David started a book of stories about him, maybe 20 years ago, Brian was thrilled.

It is time to finish that book, thought his Mother, through her tears. *That will be my project for this coming year. That would be my memorial to my boy, my son, soon to be buried next to his father.*

In Memoriam
Brian Philip Menczer
November 28, 1967— November 4, 2019

Gayle Spanier Rawlings

Bio

Throughout the years I have always enjoyed writing and reading and I have participated in numerous writers' groups. My father was the one who taught me to love reading and writing. He took me to the library regularly and he loved reading.

In the 70's I founded a writers' group that developed well in its diversity. We decided to publish a literary magazine that included poetry, prose, and art. The writers' group met monthly. The editorial board members met separately, and we created the magazine in our basements.

As part of my job as a counselor/social worker with both adults and children I used writing as a tool for exploring feelings and developing self-awareness.

A poem of mine appeared in Wayne Dyer's *Pulling Your Own Strings*. I have won awards for my poetry at literary events in colleges and other community agencies. Guest honorees Marge Piercy and Tillie Olsen presented two of them.

My high school English teacher in my senior year signed my yearbook, "I longed to spank you, but then I remembered your thoughtful comments on life and I felt I had better not spank a philosopher."

Bar-Talking

Long ago—one time, many times
we sat talking
into the dark smoky
air of our
life dreams,
you the sculptor

I the dancer-poet.

You told me you would
never bring children
into this messy world
and that we would go
to Mexico.
We never did
and I saw your children
today.
Their eyes sparkle
with all the twinkle
leftover from our
forgotten dreams.

Butterflies

We are butterflies
all of us
pinned to the velvet
of our existence.
Lacking arms
and feet for running
we depend on our
wings for escape.
Lacking futures
we depend on our captors
for comfort.
Lacking confidence
we fall back on our colors.

Wishing to feel real
we allow our beauty to
be captured, pinned
in our own smooth places,

cherished forever
in a tiny box.
The dusting of our
wings rub off to
mix with air.

Anxious to break free
we tear our wings.
With our ragged edges
we take flight.

Motorcycle Mama

You are the only woman
I know who rides her own motorcycle.
Black and sleek, like a seal
in leather pants and jacket
you arrived at work one day
your long curly hair pulled back.

I myself only held on
to the back of a man.

Alone you rode your cycle.

Alone you waited for your lover's return
Alone you waited for your son
to heal from his motorcycle accident.
Alone you watched as they cut
first one
then the second
of your only
remaining breast.
Now your hair is short
growing back

your long dark ringlets fell out.

Your son only walks with a limp
Your lover returned.
You have survived floods and ashes
chemicals and blood.
Even a child's fondling.

But I heard today
you were fixing up your cycle.

Plants

for my Mother

Plants give life to new plants,
mothers give life too.
May is the month of mothers.
I had a mother, now she
dances with sunshine,
but she is not near
my light,
not in my shadow.
Her plants are.
I talk to them when
I need her.
I water them when I
need nurturing.
They need soil now
they wobble in the
breathless house
hoping for no strong winds,
They are like her.
They have grown strong without her,
They are like me.

The Garden

My garden is dying
shriveling before the first frost.

You remember
the garden
the one
we dug
with our bare hands
in the softness of spring.

The garden isn't like that now
I wanted you to know
all sweet round bulbs
full of beginnings
of expectation.
Now it is overgrown
way too unruly
and out of control
not like neat rows
the way we planted it.
We all learn
each day
with every season
that nothing lasts
nothing lasts....

Once you said you loved the rain
and tonight
while we lay in our separate beds
the rain poured down
awakening me
to your imagined touch.

The Mountain

Driving up into the mountains
We never knew we could reach
such heights
Clouds floating
with rainbows on our edges
shimmering

Traveling down the mountain
was treacherous
The road was officially closed
Winding turns and drops
should have been a warning
moving into such dangerous territory
There was no turning back

Recovering from being
Pushed off a mountaintop
is not simple
You said you went crazy
You needed more space
You wanted to see how strong
I was

Climbing a man
is like climbing a mountain
When it's all puff & dragon
it's hard to find footing
difficult to make a connection
& falling is frightening
the suddenness forces your heart
out of your chest
& you're dangling out there
on the end of a rope

with nothing to hold onto

Building a woman
who will open like a gate
swinging and easy
to those who offer their hand
on the hard climbs
and close like a mountain
to the warning of harm
is what I am learning
Digging in with my hands and feet
I chisel away at the old
for the steep climb
toward myself

Words Of The Goddess

Stars
reached out
plucked them from
their lives
and put each
in the hands
of the goddess
There a spell
was woven.

Separations will be
the test of this love.
Heaven will protect them
Passion will sustain them
Years will not divide them.

Look into the mirror
and see your sister self

she softly moans like you
she is light where you are dark
she is the dream you dreamt
and the balance you need.

Be you well with each other
trust and truth
must be your path
care and restraint
will be the test.

Blessed be
the union
the love
the stars shine on it
the goddess protects it
Blessed be.

The Hospice

In 2005, shortly after moving to Florida, I received a phone call
from my father, who lived about an hour away. He said, "When I
woke up I couldn't walk." I told him that my friend and I would
meet him at his house as soon as we could get there. When we
arrived we decided that he needed to go to the hospital. We called
for an ambulance to take him to the hospital and we met him there.
First a nurse, then a doctor, consulted with us. It was decided that
he should be admitted so they could do some tests. After ten days
of endless tests and some bouts with hospital psychosis, it was
decided that he needed hospice care due to a recurrence of prostate
cancer and other terminal issues. I started doing research and I
found a hospice in the Port St. Lucie area near my new home.
My father was transported from the hospital to the hospice in
an ambulance. When he arrived at hospice, he was disoriented
from the hour-long ride, which he thought was on a train. He was

brought into a beautifully decorated room. It had its own bathroom and a screened porch. We later found out that all of the rooms were decorated by local organizations or individuals. There were eight bedrooms in each of two hospice houses, all with original art work. My friend gently told my father that he was in hospice. He looked around the room and said, "Somebody must have ponied up some money for this place!"

She said, "No, it's free, Sol!"

He responded by exclaiming, "Wow, It's a little slice of heaven!"

At this point he was sitting up in bed watching television. When he was in the hospital, he had experienced sundowners, hospital psychosis, and hallucinations. At times his arms had to be tied down. In hospice he was lucid and recognized a beautiful woman on the television. "Look it's Cindy Crawford!"

I asked him if he would like something to eat.

"Yes," he answered. "I'd like some chocolate ice cream!"

I got him some in the shared kitchen.

We decided to leave. It had been a long day for us all. We told him we would be back the next morning. We walked past the porch of my father's room and saw him eating the chocolate ice cream and watching television. I felt at peace that I had made the right decision about where he should be.

My father never spoke or ate again. He had worked in hospitals most of his life and I knew he did not want to die in one. I think he was peaceful knowing that he wouldn't. He lived a few more days. We were driving to come and see him early one morning and saw a vivid double rainbow. When my friend and I arrived, hospice staff told us he had passed minutes earlier.

Jim Rawlinson

Bio

Undergraduate at Western Michigan University.

Graduate with a Fellowship in Physiology at The University of Michigan.

Head of Pulmonary Therapy and Diagnostics at Wayne County General Hospital.

Editor of the Michigan Pulmonary Medicine newsletter.

Owner of three successful businesses.

The Bridge

Vicksburg—a magical town in a magical place. But the most wonderful thing about Vicksburg is that when you go to sleep at night and wake up the next morning, it is still there. It is in a different state than you, the reader, may be familiar with. It is not located in Mississippi, but in southwest Michigan. It carries the weight of its legacy heavily. Change comes only when necessary. It has survived for over fifty years with one stoplight. Then, the town government thought that it just would not do to only have one stoplight. They considered every choice and found two additional intersections where they could put one more for each. The stoplights probably were not necessary, but someone thought they should bring the town up to snuff.

Restaurants? Well, you won't find any with a Michelin rating. It is not likely that someone would be willing to pay $50 for a bowl of lobster bisque. Or $270 for a bottle of Caymus wine. But you could get a good meal at one of the few restaurants of the town and you will meet wonderful people full of life there. Someone who is pompous or full of hubris would be quietly discounted with a smile.

Vicksburg is a small farming community with little to distinguish it other than that it is the finest place on earth in which a child can be raised. From the center of town one is never more than a few blocks from the town's limits. It surrounds a small lake, Sunset Lake, which has the shape of a figure eight.

In the middle of the 8 there is a railroad bridge. The bridge allows the railroad to connect Chicago with Detroit. Having replaced another, it is in its second generation. The heavy pilings from the first bridge, however, still exist. They can be seen below the water a little ways from the current bridge. Walking across the bridge shortens the trip for those wanting to walk from one side of town to the other. Still, it attracts little pedestrian traffic.

When on the bridge, one has to be aware of oncoming trains. Surprisingly, one can be a bit inattentive and not realize that a train is coming. If that would happen, one then would have to scramble to get to the end of the bridge. That wouldn't be a problem as the bridge is not long.

For a boy growing up in Vicksburg, as I did, it was a Huckleberry Finn way to live. Get up early in the morning, grab your cane pole, go to the bridge, and fish. In a couple of hours one can get plenty of fish for the evening meal for the family.

Even for a boy the rule was, "You catch it. You clean it." I was good enough to gut the fish, cut its head off, remove the fins, then get most of the scales off. Mom finished the job to her satisfaction. One never had better fresh perch, sunfish, or bluegills than those from Sunset Lake. The best place on the whole planet to catch fish was the railroad bridge. Throw out your line, wait for the fish to examine your bait, then hook it, and bring it in. Put the fish in your pail with its brothers and sisters, and take them home. Over the many years every experience I have had eating perch at a restaurant has been a disappointment compared to the feast of fish back then. I have given up trying. I no longer eat perch at any restaurant.

One has to prepare ahead to fish. In the evening after dark I went out with a flashlight searching for night crawlers. Night crawlers are large worms used for fishing. They live in the strata beneath the grass in our lawns. Night crawlers have a way of coming part way out of their holes after dark. With a practiced eye I knew how to find the worms. I would crawl along the ground while shining my flashlight ahead of me. Then I would spot a worm that had come out of his hole. I had to be quick upon seeing it. Night crawlers are very fast when they know they have been detected and move quickly back into their holes. The problem is that they only come halfway out of their holes. Once I got hold of one I had to carefully and slowly pull him out. If I pulled him too hard or too fast, he would break in half. After catching the worm I then placed him in a can and put the top of the can on. Now I had my worm. After repeating the routine several times, I then had enough worms for fishing the next day. Catching the worms was as much fun for a young boy the night before as catching fish the next day.

I was born in 1940. I was five years old when World War II ended and ten years old when the "Police Action" started in Korea in 1950. My agemates and I had war in our veins. We all had veterans in our families. Our toys were tanks, toy soldiers, and military-configured planes. The B51 Bomber was our favorite. We played at war. We formed our own armies and picked out our battle sites. My cousin and I took our toy soldiers and moved them about on the ground in a pretend battle. Then we took tiny firecrackers and blew up the enemy.

Then, there were real-life battles on the bridge. The north-siders would go against the south-siders as adversaries. We had our trusty non-lethal Daisy Red Ryder BB guns for our weapons. The rule was that we were never to shoot our opponents above the waist. A plink in the leg was no problem. It only stung a little.

We ganged up on either side of the bridge and tried to take the bridge. We coordinated our moves as best we could. But it's not easy to coordinate ten- to twelve-year-old kids. "Okay, Rob, you and Dan to the right and, Squeaky, you and I will come in from the left. Remember, don't shoot until you see the whites of their eyes." Then, Rob went on his own, Squeaky went on his own, and so did Dan and I. We crawled on the ground to gain the best location for shooting at our enemy. To get a better look at them we stood up long enough to catch sight of where they were. That brought the expected response and our adversaries released a fusillade hitting our "scout." Naturally, he denied that he had been hit. "You missed me, you dirty Krauts!"

"You're full of it, you pieces of [garbage]!" was the response. We got braver and braver, and they did as well. We crawled along the tracks from our side of the bridge, and they from theirs. We plunked them with our BB guns, and they plunked us back. Nobody got hurt because the little BBs had lost their punch by the time they reached us. We shouted at them, "You missed but I got you."

The "enemy" shouted back, "We got *you*, you rotten Nazis!"

"No you didn't."

"Yes we did!"

It went back and forth with no resolution, nor was any needed. Then Squeaky shouted, "You got me, you dirty Nazi!"

He then fell to the ground mortally wounded. Of course, when he wanted to, he miraculously recovered and rejoined the battle. He didn't want to be a non-combatant. The war ended when it was time to go home to have lunch. Then in the afternoon the battle started anew. The only injuries were scratches from crawling on the railroad bed. And there were, of course, torn pants.

After we had had enough of war, we gathered on the bridge with our trusty BB guns for target practice. We threw bottles out as far as we could and used our BB guns to sink the "German battleships." Each of us claimed that he was the one who caused the ship to flounder. After the bottles had been hit enough, they then cracked and sunk. It is hard to imagine how much broken glass is at the bottom of the lake at that site. Likely a whole lot. It's too deep at that location for anyone to be crawling on the bottom of the lake to get cuts from the glass there.

Most of us came from families that were not financially comfortable. We wore clothes with holes in them. Often they were hand-me-downs from older brothers or neighbors. My wool pants came from Bob, who was a couple of years older than I. They were scratchy and I hated them. I had to put Vaseline on my legs to keep them from getting too irritated.

We had canvas shoes we called "sneakers." When the soles wore down enough, they got holes. We put cardboard inside them. Puddles, wet grass, or even ankle-deep water filled our canvas shoes and our feet got quite wet. No problem. Wet shoes, dry shoes—it didn't matter. In time the sole of the sneaker separated from the front of the shoe. In order to walk, I had to flip the top part of the shoe forward so it would cover the sole and I could take a step. It would be: Take a step, flip the bad shoe, and step. Then take another step. Step, flip, step. In those days I didn't typically tell my parents that one of the shoes was bad. I didn't think about it. I mostly lived with the situation until it just became too much of a nuisance. Then I went to my mother and she chastised me for being too hard on my shoes. "Jim, we aren't made of money. You have to be more careful."

"Yes, Mother."

My parents had survived the Depression, and they knew what hardship was. Mother would take me to Arno to have my shoe repaired. Mother bartered something for the repair. Bartering was a way of life in Vicksburg and my mother was a champion at it. "Now, Arno, you know the shoe should have lasted longer than this. I want you to fix it for a longer haul."

Arno used to say, "Now you know that when I fix shoes, they are better than new. Jim will outgrow the shoes before they wear out." The problem with that kind of negotiation was that the seller never knew if he could have received more and the buyer never knew if more could have been given. That was always the case with bartering. We walked away and my mother exclaimed, "It's highway robbery what Arno expects. I should never have gone there."

The real truth about that was that Arno had the only shoe repair shop in town. And he lived on a "shoestring," so to speak, in a very modest apartment. He never owned a car, and he walked to his back-alley shop.

My socks got holes in them, and my mother taught me how to "darn" them. To darn the sock there was a tool called a "darning egg" that would be placed in the sock to hold it so the hole could be sewn over. I actually got pretty good at it. I used to darn my socks over and over again.

The Williams twins were a matched pair. They had the most profane vocabulary in town. It's hard to say whether Richard was more profane than Robert or Robert more profane than Richard. They walked down the middle of the street shouting foul language at each other that could be heard a block away. They became legends. Walking down the middle of the street as they did wasn't much of a problem in Vicksburg in the 1950s because only an occasional car passed through.

It was common for us when we wanted to go swimming to go to our beloved bridge to dive off. It was a natural place for us to congregate. Many times there would be ten or more of us on the bridge. It wasn't necessary for us to have swimsuits. We would just take off our clothes except for our skivvies and dive off the bridge. We could swim for a distance, clamber up the bank, and go back to dive in once again. We knew we had to avoid the old pilings. Hitting one would be deadly.

As in any youthful group there was mischievous behavior. Dunking took pride of place among other forms of horseplay. The older and bigger boys grabbed the younger and smaller ones and held them down while removing their skivvies. They then waved them in the air triumphantly. They played keep-away with them.

After that they threw the skivvies in the water making the boys swim after them.

The day came for the most interesting happening of all. Robert and Richard Williams, the twins, were at the bridge along with the usual group of pre-teens. But, on this day, a train with its line of boxcars had stopped on the bridge. It presented a new challenge. "Okay, guys," someone shouted from the gallery, "who is brave enough to climb on top of the boxcar in the middle of the bridge and dive off from up there?"
One spirited guy, of course, always accepted such a challenge. David Jones this time climbed the ladder on the side of one of the cars that was visible to the group. "Come on you guys," he shouted. "Don't be chickens. Get up here with me, and we'll all dive off." Finally, to show he was everything he claimed to be, he jumped from the top, putting his arms around his knees as he descended, and hit the water with a terrific splash. A plume of water rose up. He sunk below the surface. We waited for him to come up, half-wondering if he had met his end. Then, after rising to the surface, he shouted, "Come on, you sissies. Climb up and jump off. It's no big deal."
"We all hesitated. We were not made of David's stuff. Then, Richard said to Robert, "Come on. I will do it if you will. We can show these sissies we're not afraid."
Robert said, "I don't know if I can get up the ladder."
Richard, who seemed to have the braver attitude, said, "Come on, I'll show you."
He then slowly approached the ladder. Robert followed. Richard, beginning his climb, said, "See, it isn't that hard."
Robert having no alternative, followed Richard. He clambered onto the ladder and climbed up. When Richard reached the top, he crawled along the top of the boxcar on his hands and knees. Robert finished his climb, crawled along the top, and joined Richard.
The rest of us waited anxiously for them to get into position. We expected to see them stand up, move to the edge of the boxcar, and

do their dives. However, they remained still on all fours on the top. We shouted encouragement, "Come on, boys. You can do it. Go for it." After some more time we shouted, "What are you waiting for? You can't stay up there in your skivvies!"

Then Robert stood up. Without hesitation he went to the edge of the boxcar, held his nose with his fingers, and went flying through the air. He appeared to turn awkwardly and then he splashed into the water. We scanned the surface for what seemed like a very long time. Then he came bobbing to the surface. He looked at us and then smiled. He swam to the bank and then made his way up it and over to us. He had his victory.

We all looked at Richard expecting him to jump as had Robert. He was on all fours, not moving. We could only see the upper part of him as our view of the top was mostly blocked. We moved to a mound next to the roadbed from which we could see him better. Still we could only see his head, shoulders, and butt. He seemed to be paralyzed. Robert shouted, "Come on, Richard. You can do it. Come on, buddy."

David said, "Maybe I should climb up and try to get him either to jump or simply climb down?"

But he stayed with us watching. What we saw was a glazed look on Richard's face. No encouragement from us was effective.

Then there was an ominous sound. There was the clacking of the boxcars' couplings, called "knuckles," that connected one car to another. We knew that the train was about to move backwards in the opposite direction from which the train would have to move. This meant that the train was positioning itself to get the extra impetus to move forward toward the west. Then there was the expected sound of the couplings being forced again. One by one, like dominoes falling, the clack of the couplings progressed from one boxcar to the next. The train slowly began to move. First inch-by-inch, then foot-by-foot, the train gathered speed.

We shouted, "Richard, you have to come down. You have to come down fast before the train gets moving and you can't get off!"

Still, Richard, dressed only in his skivvies, stayed glued to the top of the boxcar. We all watched helpless and hopeless as the train moved toward the first crossing, then passed Weather's ramshackle house. Richard had not moved. We watched as the train began to round a curve. The boxcar with Richard on it disappeared from view. I wondered if I would ever see Richard again. Then the whole train disappeared from view.

Then Steve said, "We have to go to the station to let them know what has happened. Maybe there's a way to save Richard."

We quickly put on our clothes and with shoelaces flying all of us raced hell-bent for the station. We gave it our all. Some of the less able dropped out quickly because they were not up to the mile run. David and I were the first two to arrive. It didn't matter, for we couldn't find Henry the stationmaster. We shouted as loud as we could. Soon others in our group arrived. Finally, Henry came around a parked boxcar. Dressed in his uniform of worn blue overalls with a dirty blue work shirt, he asked, "What's all the fuss about?"

We described as quickly as possible what the problem was. But, our description created confusion. With about eight of us trying to talk at the same time it was impossible for Henry to understand what we were saying. Finally he shouted to *me*, indicating that he wanted me to speak. "*You*, tell me what happened. The rest of you, keep quiet!"

I explained what the matter was in a way that a twelve-year-old would, including unnecessary extraneous details. After Henry's filtering out some of my pointless information he finally understood what had happened. He went into rolls of laughter. After he stopped laughing he said he would solve the problem. He walked to the depot with our gang following him into the small building. We crowded in shoulder-to-shoulder to see what he was going to do. I expected him to go to a device to send a Morse code message. I was disappointed when he simply picked up a telephone and made a call to a station ahead on the route the train would take.

Apparently, the recipient of the message found it equally hilarious and it took longer than I had expected for the call to be completed. Henry told us that the train would be stopped at a town about forty miles down the line so that Richard could be taken off the boxcar. Henry then asked Robert for a way to reach his family, and Robert gave him his home phone number. He explained carefully what had happened and what was being done. He gave the phone number of the station where Richard would be.

The story reached us later, told by Richard himself. He related how the train slowly gained speed and how he held on tight. He said that his hands got tired from hanging on. He said he held on for dear life. Still, he held on. The train gained speed, and the wind whipped around him. He got very cold. He knew he was going west. He could see the familiar countryside pass by. Soon the countryside was no longer familiar. He could hear the horn from the locomotive. The locomotive was far enough ahead that he could not see it. And the caboose was far enough behind that he could not see that either.

When Richard was brought down from the roof of the boxcar, he was taken to the local depot. It was a bigger depot than Vicksburg's. He was directed to the office of the stationmaster, where he sat as people bustled around him. He had to answer the inquiries both of the workers and of officious supervisors. Some of the others who questioned him were probably friends of the stationmaster or locals who for one reason or another happened to be in the station at the time. He was told that his mother was driving to pick him up. He dreaded the meeting and what would transpire. She arrived an hour later. Her next-door neighbor was kind enough to give her the long ride to that station.

Robert and I stayed at the depot in Vicksburg to learn what transpired. The stationmaster made a call to the station where Richard was and learned that Richard was safe. A later call confirmed that Mrs. Williams had picked up Richard and that he was on his way back to Vicksburg.

Naturally, the whole town of Vicksburg, all 2,000 folks, learned about the adventure very quickly. Our summer proceeded and the Williams twins continued to be an integral part of our fun on the bridge, such as it was.

Richard much later was able to enjoy the story of "Richard on the Boxcar's Roof." It never lost its appeal. He eventually became a successful attorney with many high-level clients, and one can imagine that he had many occasions as a lawyer to tell the story again and again.

The bridge had a legacy. Late in the 19th century and early in the 20th it was the collecting spot for ice that went west to Chicago and east to Detroit. Trains parked on the bridge to collect the largess of ice, which became available to cool the drinks of "La Cosa Nostra," "The Outfit," "The Purple Gang," and the needs of the general population for their "ice coolers." The lake also provided water for the hungry steam engines. When cold water in the train's refrigerators replaced lake ice and diesel replaced steam, the little town of Vicksburg became merely a pass-through for the trains, which ceased to be a source of revenue. But the railroad continued to maintain sentimental importance.

The Roeper family was new to Vicksburg. There were two boys, Billy and Danny, about the age of those of us who congregated at the bridge. At first they more or less stayed on the periphery. They slowly learned how to get involved. But they were new to us, and we to them. The pecking order was yet to be established. Billy was older than Danny, but he was the more reserved of the two.

Naturally, we tested them by calling them names to see how they would cope with our attempts to humiliate them. It was their "rite of passage." First we called Billy "Billy Boy Blue," hoping to elicit a negative response. Then we called Danny "Danny With The Big Fanny." That didn't register either. We let them join in the play, as they wanted. They had to learn how the games were played. They had to learn whose challenges they could duck and whose they could not. They quickly learned that David, the strongest among us, would be a bad target for them to pick on. And picking on the smaller among us would result in a response from the rest of us.

We had started a new game. We had an old tennis ball that we would throw some distance from the bridge. Then two or three of us would dive off the bridge in a race to get to the ball first. The winner would swim to the bank and bring the prize back to the bridge so that it could be thrown again. Dunking and pulling at each other were part of the game. The spectators on the bridge shouted all kinds of utterances at the participants. We never had a favorite unless someone had won too many times. Then we began to root for the underdogs.

After a few rounds someone shouted, "Come on, Billy, go against Ronny."

The stage was set. Neither Billy nor Danny had participated before. They had stayed in the background and shouted encouragement. They stood on the edge of the bridge waiting for the throw. David gave a good heave and the ball traveled some distance away. Ronny knew exactly where to dive to avoid the submerged pilings. But, Billy dove directly onto one of them headfirst. We peered intently to see what had happened to Billy. We expected him to rise quickly to the surface of the water, but we saw him go limp in the water without any movement of his arms or his legs.

Danny shouted, "Come on, Billy. Come on. Get up." He shouted over and over. He began to cry. "What should we do? he lamented. One of the guys said, "Someone has to go in and bring him back up."

Danny walked around while looking into the water. Not taking our eyes of Billy's limp figure, we expected him to start moving. He was face down with his arms and legs fully extended. There wasn't any movement. Then Danny ran to the edge and jumped. He had no form and looked awkward in the air. Incredibly, he hit the same piling Billy had hit, and the same result occurred. Danny went limp in the water. Two bodies faces down in the water looked so very much alike. It was overwhelmingly spooky for the rest of us.

"Come on, guys," David said. "We've got to go into the water and bring them up."

We rushed down the bank and jumped into the water. Looking back, it is not clear to me how we brought them out of the water and up the bank. We didn't know what to do. We laid them on the ground on their backs. They were not breathing.

David said, "I'm going to the gas station to get help."

The gas station was down the tracks about half a mile away. About 15 minutes later David returned with a man from the station.

Looking at the boys, the man from the station decided he had to do something. He took Billy's arms and waved them up and down as a bird waves its wings. A man who came over to see what was going on said, "That won't do any good. We have to roll him back and forth on a barrel. I'll get a barrel with my pickup."

A long time passed, over 20 minutes. The man returned with the barrel in his pickup and said, "We have to go to the station. We'll roll the boys on the barrel there."

With two boys the man carried first Billy, then Danny, to the station. It took another 20 minutes for that. At this point it had been over an hour since the boys had dived into the water. Now we had the boys at the station. The man with the barrel put Billy face and stomach down on the barrel. He took Billy's feet and pushed him back and forth. It was a heroic but ineffective effort. This was resuscitation in 1952. After some time the man realized it was of no use. He stopped rolling Billy back and forth. He took Billy's body and placed it on the ground next to Danny's. Both were face up. Lying there dressed only in their skivvies, they were pale from head to toe.

Our group stood dazed over Billy and Danny. Their bodies lay in disarray. We had all seen dead animals before. But it was the first time I had ever seen a dead person. The dead bodies seemed very strange, I wanted them to breathe. I wondered if they were sleeping and would wake up. As a twelve-year-old, I could not comprehend the reality, the finality of death. From religious services and all I had heard I thought that their souls had somehow left their bodies and had drifted off like birds flying to Heaven where they would be part of the never-ending life at the side of G-d. Only after many years passed did I recognize that questions about death might not have rational answers.

The boys and I never went back to the bridge to play. We got permission to swim at the Lintons' and at other lakeside swimming spots. But, thoughts of playing at the bridge bore too heavily on us. I found other places to fish. There was a small dam that contained the water from the lake. Below the dam there was a great place to fish. This location remained my secret. Not wanting it to get overfished, I never revealed it to others.

A few weeks after Billy and Danny drowned the Roeper family moved from Vicksburg. The family was little-known to the community. They undoubtedly took away with them agonizing emotions about Vicksburg, as we all had of them.

Anne Rockwerk

Bio

Born in New York, NY, on August 17, 1918.
Attended PS2 Elementary School and Walton High School, the
Bronx, New York, NY.
Attended Middlesex Community College in New Brunswick, NJ,
for one year.
Widowed after two marriages.
Lives now in the 55+ community of Kings Point, Delray
Beach, FL.
Anne's vocation is writing.
Her *The Life of an Amazing Woman: Memoirs of 100 Years* is the
source of the selections that are reprinted here.

[Editor's note, October 2020. Anne, of course, celebrated her
102nd birthday two months ago. We are very excited for her. Her
optimism, good cheer, and plain common sense have been an
inspiration for us all.]

The Great Depression

I was twelve years old. My uncle, who was out of work for some
time, and his family were on relief, which is what welfare was
called back then. In order to earn some extra cash, he rented a push
cart. For those of you who do not know what a push cart is, it is
a wooden flat top placed on two large wheels, with two wooden
handles protruding in back with which you pushed the cart. In
front, there was a metal rod on each side on which the cart rested
when it was stopped. My uncle would buy a load of cantaloupe
melons from a local green merchant. I would go with him the five
or six blocks to an open market in a nearby neighborhood. We sold
the melons for ten cents apiece for the small ones and twenty-five
cents for the larger ones. I never knew exactly how much money he
had at the end of the day but he always gave me one dollar for my
help.

There were many more ways people made money in those days. The cries heard from a man in our backyard, "Cash clothes," meaning he would take any discarded clothing, towels, and bedding. People would ask him to come up to their apartments and he would pay around a quarter or fifty cents for a large bundle of discards. You might then hear a violin playing, at which time we would look out to see a man performing some familiar Jewish tune. My mother would wrap two pennies in a piece of newspaper and give it to me to throw out the window for him.

These were very stressful years for many thousands of people. My family did not have it too hard. My father, who was a pattern maker in the garment industry, managed to find work. I remember a time when he was unemployed. He read an ad in the newspaper for a pattern maker/cutter in a sweater factory located in Brooklyn. We lived in the Bronx. Brooklyn was an hour-long subway ride away. And besides that, Pop did not have any experience in knitted fabrics, as opposed to silks or cotton. He made the trip to Brooklyn to apply for that position. The boss would not hire him because of his lack of experience in the knit-goods trade. Pop gave the man a deal he could not refuse. He offered to work for him for two weeks free of charge and, if he didn't qualify, he would leave. The deal was accepted. Needless to say, his work was more than satisfactory and he worked there for about two years. He finally found employment again in Manhattan, which was a much shorter and less expensive commute from the Bronx.

The Depression did not really end until the United States was forced into World War II by the bombing of Pearl Harbor on December 7, 1941.

Friendships

Friendships in my life seem to have come in series, much like watching a movie which, at intervals, blacks out for a second and comes back with a new scene. I do not remember many of the

names but there were happy times in each phase. During each
phase I became very close with one or two people.

The first group of friends I remember was from the tenement
building in which we lived when I was a child. The ages of the
children were from about seven to nine. We used to play "theater,"
dressing up in grown-up clothes, making up dialogue as we went,
mixed with much laughter and changing of words and sentences.
We had so much fun that I would often lose my voice from so
much laughing and yelling.

My next group of friends came together in my late teens through
a friend who lived in my building. Mitzie was fun to be with and
she had such an infectious laugh that we all laughed even harder
with her. Our group grew to six lively girls. I remember that Mitzie
had an older sister who was married. Her mother was so proud
of having a son-in-law that she could not stop talking about "her
Betty" and Eddie. "My Betty," she used to say, "did this and that";
and she would go on and on about "my Betty."

Our group would get together every Saturday at someone's house
and scheme about going somewhere to meet boys. Sylvia was
one of ten sisters. Going to her house was like being in a clothing
store. There were dresses hanging over every doorway and in
the bedrooms around overflowing closets. Her parents were very
pleasant. Momma was short and stocky, always smiling, always
asking if we wanted something to eat. She obviously spent a great
deal of time in the kitchen cooking for such a large family. Two of
Sylvia's sisters were already married when we met, so there were
eight girls living at home. We would go out together to the clubs
local boys rigged up in the basements of some private homes with
a Victrola, which today would be called a record player, playing
popular tunes of the times for dancing. Today this music is called
the "standards."

We were all finally married within two years. Sylvia and George
married one week before I did. They came back from their
honeymoon for my wedding and the four of us went on a week-
long honeymoon together. We remained in touch with each other

for about ten years. After World War II ended, most young couples started moving out of the city due to a shortage of apartments and the desire to own a home. A few of our group moved to Long Island where new inexpensive building was going on, such as the Levitt homes. My husband and I moved to New Jersey, where most of my family had already been living. For twenty years, however, there was little contact among the group other than occasional telephone calls.

Upon retiring to Florida, we met up with Mitzie and Eddie, who have since died. About three years ago, we met Sylvia and George in Kings Point, Delray Beach, Florida. I am sorry to say that Sylvia passed away about a year ago but George is still around.

When my husband and I moved into an adult community in New Jersey, Clearbrook in Monroe Township, we met a new group of people, some of whom became very good friends of ours. After more than twenty years of involvement in organizations together, learning line dancing and folk dancing, and many, many social events, I am sad to say that only three of my close friends from that time are still around. Two are in assisted-living facilities. One, who is my very closest friend, resides in a facility close by and I visit with her several times a week, and once in a while we go out to lunch or dinner. Her daughter lives on Long Island, New York, and her son lives in San Francisco, California. They call her daily and visit often. She has four grandchildren and four great-grandchildren.

My new friends since I moved to Florida full time are more like acquaintances. It is very hard to make close friendships at this phase of life. I am blessed with having a gentleman friend. Both his family and mine have accepted us and life is now still full of activity.

My First Date

I grew up in the era when good girls never spoke about sex—and most of us did not even know about it. I sure didn't. I chose to go

to an all-girls' high school in the Bronx because I had no interest
in boys. When I was seventeen, my friend introduced me to a
neighborhood boy. We went to an ice cream parlor for a soda and
talked about school mostly. We were both seniors in high school.
When we walked home, he started to talk about sex. I showed my
annoyance and ignorance of it. He could not believe I was so naive.
He had a book he said he would like me to read. We stopped by his
apartment building and he went up to bring the book down. I took
the book and we made a date for the next evening to go to a local
movie.

This book was some sort of a textbook. It sure was a learning
experience for me. I could not believe most of it or understand it.
When he came to pick me up the next evening, I threw the book
at him, and said, "This stuff is all made up, I don't believe it"
and refused to go out with him. I had no one to discuss this with.
However, in the next few months I started listening to some of the
girls at school discussing their dates. That got me thinking.

At that stage of my life, I was only interested in dancing. There
were small boys' clubs in the neighborhood where some friends
and I would go to dance on Friday and Saturday nights. These
were held in people's basements and two-family homes. The room
was furnished with a couch, a couple of club chairs, and of course
a Victrola. These records were 78s, which are totally nonexistent
now, and probably most of the younger generation have never heard
of them. They were the music of Frank Sinatra, Harry James's
band, and many others. Today, this music is called "standards."
We danced the fox trot, the waltz, and a dance that was all the rage
at that time, the lindy hop, which evolved into the jitterbug. My
favorite music for that dance was "Alexander's Ragtime Band."
These clubs usually had another room behind a closed door where,
every now and then, a couple who were dancing would disappear.
One night, one of my new acquaintances who introduced me to
these clubs came out of that room and, probably in order to save
face, said she was going to marry this guy someday. She was a
very pretty, tall, young woman and the guy she was with was quite

a bit shorter than she was. The guys were always trying to get us girls into that room.

I used to go to these clubs with a friend who lived in the same building as me and we met a few more nice girls there. Through them, my knowledge of sex increased and I was able at least to pretend to be a sophisticated teenager. I still was not dating much but, through this wonderful group of girls   there were six of us—I double-dated with some boys from these clubs. After the club closed, which was around eleven p.m., we would go to an ice cream parlor. The conversations were always about sex, mostly the boys bragging of conquests.

On the way home from wherever we went dancing, my friend and I would pass a building where a couple of guys were always sitting on the steps. As we passed, they would always make some remarks to get our attention. We would stop and talk with them. We talked about work and I mentioned I just started working, actually my first job, as a bookkeeper in a suspender-manufacturing place. One of the guys, who was quite obese, was trying to get me to go out with him. I resisted, but one night he asked if I could get him some suspenders from my place. When I purchased them, I called him to come over to my house to get them. He came the next day to pick them up. In order to get him to stop trying to date me, I introduced him to my sister. I guess they really liked each other. They started dating and he eventually became my brother-in-law Dave.

Getting back to my first real date. My future brother-in-law introduced me to his friend who used to sit with him on the steps of their building. When I told my sister that Dave introduced me to his friend, Hy, she tried to discourage me from dating him because, to use her words, he was "fast." That was a challenge to me. Hy had a best friend, Vinny, an Italian boy. They were inseparable. Hy asked if I had a girlfriend for him so we could double date. I introduced Vinny to my friend Rose. The four of us would date every weekend for the next two months through New Year's Eve. Vinny had a car and we drove through Times Square on New Year's Eve. It was so crowded with people celebrating that it took

us an hour to drive through the whole area. It was freezing cold.
We had the car windows down so we could be part of the crowd
celebrating.

On January 1st, Rose told me she would have to break up with
Vinnie because he was Italian. I expected Hy would break up with
me because he and Vinnie were such close friends. They both
worked for the Singer Sewing Machine Company. By this time Hy
and I were having some good feelings for each other. Instead of
breaking up with me, he asked me to go steady. We married three
years later, July 6, 1940. He had only been my second date.

A Weekend in Palisades Park

The year was 1939. I met a guy whose name was Hy. Three years
later, he became my husband. We had many experiences during
those three years getting acquainted and eventually falling in love.
One weekend we were visiting my girlfriend. Her married sister
was there, and the conversation turned to vacations. This was
during the Depression and none of us had much money to spend
on vacations. Betty, my friend's sister, told of a plan she and her
husband were considering. They were going to Palisades Park,
where they would pitch a tent for a weekend.

Palisades Park was located in New Jersey across the Hudson River
from the Upper West Side of Manhattan. We lived in the Bronx at
that time, so it was about a two-hour ride north across the Tappan
Zee Bridge. There were picnic areas and camping grounds. It was
on a hill overlooking the Hudson River. My friend Hy looked at
me and said, "That sounds like fun" and asked if I would like to go
with Betty and her husband. Mind you, we were not even engaged
at that time. However, that sounded like a nice adventure and I
agreed. My friend said, "Are you sure your parents will allow you
to go?" I replied, "My parents trust me and I'm sure they will not
object." I think I wrote about my parents earlier, that they never
questioned me about where I went or with whom or what time to

be home. This was never unusual to me. I just never thought of misbehaving or staying out late or getting intimate with boys. The following Friday after work we packed some clothes and food and a "pup tent" and drove to my friend's to pick them up with their supplies. Did I mention that we were asked to come because my boyfriend had a '29 Model-T Ford and they needed transportation? In case you do not know what a "pup tent" is, I will describe it. It is a square of heavy canvas, two poles which attach to the center of the cloth, and four small pieces of wood which are hammered into the ground at the four corners and tied with rope, which is attached to the canvas square. This is set up on the grass. There was just enough room inside for two people but all four of us slept in it together.

We arrived at the campsite around seven p.m. and started to put the tent up. It was already starting to get dark and, as this was December, it was quite cold. Before we had the tent secured, we heard thunder and rain came pouring down. In our rush to get set up we failed to completely tighten the ties in the corners as we grabbed the sheets, pillows, and blankets so we could get under cover. I'm not quite sure if we were asleep yet, but the ground started to get wet and one side of the tent leaned down on us. We wrapped ourselves up in the blankets and fell asleep. The next morning, we crawled out of the tent to a beautiful, sunny day.

We were wet and cold. We got some clothes out of the car and got dressed, then pulled all the wet, muddy sheets, blankets, and pillows out of the tent, rinsed them out in the small stream that ran along the edge of the field we were in, and hung them on some low tree branches to dry. We piled into the car to find a coffee shop for breakfast.

By noon, everything was dry. We fixed the tent in place, gathered some wood, and made a fire. We roasted some hot dogs and set up our picnic on a blanket with paper plates, plastic forks and knives, and the mustard, sauerkraut, and rolls we brought from home. Then we took a long walk through the park, climbed some trees, and played some games we brought with us. Later, we drove into town

for dinner. The weather stayed nice the rest of the weekend. On
Sunday morning, we packed up the car and headed home.

Wishes

When I heard the topic was "Wishes," I thought I had nothing to
say on this subject. I never wished for any material things. We were
never poor in the sense of not knowing where our next meal was
coming from, but never financially able to afford material luxuries
such as toys when I was little, or jewelry, or luxurious vacations as
an adult and throughout my marriage. As a teenager I dreamed of
marrying someone who would make us rich. Obviously, this never
happened. As I write this story, you will see that I was and am
rich in many other ways. In the end "Life Is Good," to quote my
granddaughter Hannah, the light of my life.
I married the love of my life and had three healthy children. That
was my first wish to come true. I enjoyed their growing up years.
I have yet to hear from them what they think about that. From the
time of their teenage years they were the cause of many bumps
in the road, giving me many years of hoping and wishing things
would someday be better.
I am addressing each of my children directly as though I am
speaking to them:
Roberta, my youngest. Even though you had been a little difficult
as a child, "hyper" and stubborn and needing discipline, you grew
up and gave your father and me much joy in your choice of a
career, to become a lawyer. Your choice to get married before law
school was a little troublesome as you know. Your divorce after
four and a half years was difficult for all of us. But we supported
you and our love for you never faltered. When you married David,
my wish for you was fulfilled and giving me a grandchild was
the most wonderful gift. I am proud of your and David's success.
Thank you for everything.
Sandy, you were such a beautiful child and, as long as you had
your blanket and thumb to suck, you were happy. You were also

very sensitive and compassionate. I'm sure you don't remember the incident when I had to discipline your little sister and you said, "Mommy, don't hit her, she will scream." I kissed you and I hugged you for being so compassionate. However, I admit that being the middle child and quiet, you sometimes fell through the cracks and you obviously thought I didn't love you at times. I loved you then, even through your troublesome teens and into young adulthood, when you fell into the lifestyle of many young people of the sixties. I was most proud of you when you came home from wherever to go back to college. Even though you continued living on the edge, I still had hope that you would someday become whole. That miracle happened when you met your beautiful wife Debbie and fell in love. With her help you turned the corner and became the wonderful person you are to this day, happily married for twenty-five years. Thank you for becoming who you are. Debbie, thank you for being who you are. I love you very much. Your thoughtfulness and understanding have added much joy to my life. Allen, my first born. You were an only child for almost seven years until your little brother was born. I can't begin to tell you how much your father and I loved you. It was so overwhelming at times that I became anxious when I thought I would not be able to have another child. You were a wonderful big brother to your brother and sister. I was very proud of you when you graduated from college. You were the first one of my entire family to go to college. At your graduation I noticed that you had joined the sixties generation and I knew your lifestyle would be a difficult time in our life. You married and had two beautiful children but things started to go wrong, and the results were disastrous for you, me, and your children. Your financial situation went down the drain. Your divorce was an even worse disaster. You paid a very high personal price. I need not tell you that my love for you never faltered, which is why I helped financially and personally all those horrible years. You suffered with a great deal of depression and self-pity. About a month ago, I saw a big change in you. You are calm, you discuss things optimistically with me. You have now told me that you decided to turn your life around and I am so proud of you. A few months ago, you received a call from Melissa on her eighteenth birthday and you are now having a wonderful relationship with her. I'm sure before long Jarett will also be in touch with you. You were a wonderful father to them and they do remember that.

As you can see, although there were many smaller bumps in the road, most of my life I kept wishing I would someday see my children happy and healthy. At this point, my cup runneth over. The only thing I keep wishing for is our good health. I never became rich, but I have something better.

The following was added on July 15, 2010 when I remembered more wonderfulness I received from my children.

Life is what it is. At age ninety, I am becoming more accepting of things as they are. There were times when the children didn't speak to each other for reasons long forgotten. I kept wishing they would someday overcome all their differences and they would be family. Now, I accept them as they are and have stopped pushing on them to fulfill this wish. All three have different personalities. I used to think they have genes of three generations back or that I must have made many mistakes in their upbringing. After all, as we all know, children are born without a book of instructions. I was not yet the person I am today. My self-esteem was still at a very low point and I was always unsure of the right way to deal with children's needs, desires, and discipline.

I recall an incident when I did a very scary thing. My husband and I went on a business trip to New York. On Sunday, after the meetings were over, we wanted the two younger children to join us so we could take them to a show and dinner. Hy called his employee, Seymour, with whom the children were staying, to put them on the bus to the New York Port Authority. Sandy was nine at the time and Roberta was seven. My husband asked Seymour to give Sandy a note to give to a cabdriver, asking to take the children to an address on the East Side. We would wait for them. What could I have been thinking? The children arrived safely and

Sandy proudly said he did not have to give the cabdriver the note. He knew what to tell him. Imagine having such confidence today when children are abducted right in front of their homes. I still have nightmares about this.

I never forgot when Allen decided to buy a house in Florida and bought one for us so we could live next door to him. He was always there for us and visited us often. He was a happy bachelor until age forty-two, when he fell in love and married Amy, who was 28. They moved into the house Allen bought and we decided to sell our house and stay in our small apartment in Kings Point. Hy became very ill that winter. We went home to New Jersey. He had surgery and died nine months later.

Roberta's engagement to David was a very momentous happening. I was on a month-long visit to Israel. I received a call from Roberta with the happy news of her engagement. She introduced me to David over the phone and the first thing he said was, "I love your daughter, do you mind if I call you MOM?" That was music to my ears. I nearly cried. Neither Allen's wife nor Sandy and his wife called me "MOM." I didn't love them less because I know that many in-law children have a hard time with this. I had a difficult time with it when I was first married and it took me a long time to come to terms with it.

Someone Who Changed My Life

My life has been changing since the birth of my first son in 1944. It then dawned on me that my life would never be the same. I, too, felt reborn. Up to that time, I was in a naive state and in some kind of a tunnel. I guess it was the same as teenagers of today. Lives revolve around them and they are totally oblivious of the real world around them.

When I met my husband-to-be at the age of seventeen, I thought my future was all settled. I would be married, he would work, and I would set up housekeeping and live happily ever after. Surprise! Surprise! The Depression was still thriving and Hy, my husband-to-be, was out of work while I was working for twelve dollars a week. Where and how would "living happily ever after" happen? As our engagement was dragging out to three years, I found myself starting to think that life is going to take work to make it happen. First, I knew we would have to be married so we could live together and together start working on our future.

This was my first step into the adult world. I observed how my husband was an outgoing person and could start a conversation with anyone, be they a person standing next to us on the street or at a party. It took me many years to learn to be more like him. The hardest thing was finding out that totally depending on my husband for decisions was not going to work. My life took on a hit-and-miss character while I was trying to develop a new personality. I started to observe how other couples lived and how they conducted themselves with each other. I talked with some of our close friends and discovered different lifestyles depending on their finances and family dynamics. Two of the wives were able to follow the standard style of the times. They became homemakers and their husbands worked. The other two, myself included, needed to work in order to put food on the table and pay the rent.

I was on the road to growing up, learning to accept my role in life. By observing and asking questions and for recipes, I learned to cook, how to furnish the house, and clean. After years of ups and downs, giving birth to two more children, and our family business ending up in bankruptcy, I evolved into the person I am today. However, my insecurities continued to raise their "ugly head" from time to time, until about two years ago when I started to write my memoirs. I am now very confident of who I am and am proud of my accomplishments at age ninety-one.

The Story of My First-Born Child

I shall never forget the day he was born, June 22, 1944. I was so pleased to have given birth to this boy, mainly because I knew that my husband would be so happy, even after many hours of horrible pain that was so unexpected. If only someone had told me. In those years, no one ever spoke about sex, conception, pregnancies, and especially about the birth process. However, as my mom used to say in Yiddish, *"Viber hubbin a katz in kop"* (women have a cat in their heads), they forget very easily and continue to have children. My first sight of this beautiful little child brought to my mind that "My life will never be the same." Love just poured out of me and brought tears of joy to my eyes. This beautiful baby is now a handsome grown man of seventy-four.

He was an only child until seven when his little brother was born and, twenty months later, another little brother was born and twenty months after that he had a little sister. He was a very happy child, made friends easily, and did well in school. His little brothers adored him and looked up to him.

When he was ten months old, we moved from the Bronx to New Jersey. My parents, my brother and his wife, and my sister and her husband had moved to New Jersey the year before and my dream was always to someday move away from New York. We had a two-bedroom apartment above some stores in the town of New Brunswick, the home of Rutgers University.

In 1946, with the influx of returning servicemen after the end of World War II, the university needed housing and asked for help from the residents of the town. We rented our second bedroom out to two young men who were freshmen. Allen was two years old and he loved having them around. They played classical music when they were home and Allen used to sit on the floor outside their room to listen.

The following year, we had an opportunity to buy a small house in Highland Park, New Jersey. This town was just across the Raritan River from New Brunswick. We were a little short of funds because we had just bought a business and had borrowed money to finance the purchase. These two young men wanted to live with us when they returned for their second year with two more friends. We explained to them that we could buy this three-bedroom house and would be able to accommodate them, but we did not have the one thousand dollar down payment. These four wonderful boys offered to pay their whole year's rent in advance. That enabled us to purchase this fifty-year-old house and take on a twenty-year mortgage of eight thousand dollars. The boys came back for the next two years, at the end of which we all celebrated their graduation with their parents.

Nephew Robbie Living with Us

My sister Sarah, who was ten years older than me, had two sons with a span of nine years between them. Unfortunately the younger one, Robbie, was not planned for; and my brother-in-law resented his birth and gave my sister a hard time. She literally had to put the baby in his crib when her husband came home from work and, as a result, Robbie was a very unhappy child who could do nothing to please his father. Not surprisingly, he became a problem child and my sister had a very hard time with him.

When I was pregnant with my first child, Robbie was three years old. I used to take him to my house for a day or two a week to give my sister some relief. I loved this little boy and kept him amused all day. I would fill up the sink with water and put in some metal cups and toys for him to play with while standing on a stool by the sink. He would take a nap for me and I would read stories to him until it was time for him to go home, which was after I fed him dinner so he would not have to have dinner with his family. He was very independent. Whenever I was fixing him a sandwich, he would yell out, "I how," meaning he knew how. I would let him help me and I would clean up the mess after him. When Robbie was with me, he was one happy little boy and we had a special bond. After my first son was born, Robbie was a frequent visitor at our house and he and Allen became friends.

Over the years, I would run interference for him when things got very bad at his home. During Robbie's first year in high school, he got into a terrible confrontation with his father and they were coming to physical blows. Sarah called me to come over and, when

I got to her house, her husband was throwing Robbie out. My sister and I ran after him and I invited Robbie to come live with my family. My sister came home with me and stayed overnight. She and I talked well into the night about her options. Although her husband never physically abused her, she had a tough relationship with him. I assured her that Robbie could stay with us and she would be welcome in our home if she should decide to leave her husband. She felt she could not do that, no matter what, and she went home.

Robbie shared a room with Allen, who was not yet in high school. There were quite a few adjustments to be made. The boys argued many times but my husband and our two younger children were very tolerant and things worked out great.

Upon his graduation from high school, Robbie decided to join the army. During his three years of service, he spent some time in Germany and, after his tour of duty, he was honorably discharged and came home to us with a German wife. She was quite a bit older than him and it was obviously a marriage for her convenience to come to the States. After a year, they were divorced. Robbie found some work, rented an apartment, and became independent.

Not long after moving out of our home, he met this beautiful Jewish girl from a very nice family, became engaged, her family made this wonderful wedding, and we assumed he was settled. However, not having any skills, he was not making enough money so they lived in her parents' two-family house. They occupied the apartment upstairs and their first boy was born within the first year. Her parents helped out but it was not a comfortable situation. One day, when Hy and I were visiting, we were discussing their financial situation. Marilyn, his wife, suggested he go to school to become a court stenographer. He agreed and we said we would help pay the tuition. Robbie being Robbie, this still unsettled child complained about how difficult it was, but Marilyn and my husband and I kept encouraging him until he received his certificate. He was never able to pass the exam to be able to work in court, however he started working for lawyers recording depositions and eventually went into business for himself.

They had a second boy fifteen months after the first but Robbie still did not seem happy about his marriage. He did not come home several nights a week. He frequented bars. Three years into the marriage, when the children were two and fifteen months old, he came home one night and announced he was not happy, he had met someone else, and he was leaving. Marilyn was devastated and called us. We called him and met with him but to no avail. The woman he had met had a year-and-a-half-old baby girl. He indeed left Marilyn, married the other woman, and adopted the little girl. He started paying child support and was obligated, as part of the divorce agreement, to pay his children's medical bills. He was usually late with the payments and other bills but he would always catch up. Still, Marilyn had to go to work and her parents took care of the children.

Robbie was a little upset with me because I chose to remain friends with Marilyn. His new marriage lasted about five years, during which time another little girl was born. When he left this second marriage, he moved to Florida and was single for about two years, during which time he met still another woman, also a very nice person. They spent a weekend with us when we were vacationing in Florida. She persuaded Robbie to become a Christian but I never figured out what sect. All I knew was that they read the Old Testament. To make this long story short, he became a new person. He would try to convert us but he knew that I was a secular person and would never embrace any religion. He started visiting his father, with whom he had not spoken for many years, and tried to convert him. His father was pleased with his visits, but he was a very religious Jew and was not to be converted, though he listened to his son's explanations and they had many discussions about interpretations of the Bible. Of course, his father never converted but they bonded and were friends until his father died.

Robbie married this young woman and they had a very good marriage. He went to church with her family regularly and he settled down with his wife and two new children, a boy and a girl. He became the wonderful person I always knew he was.

His wife died of cancer when the children were about ten and twelve. They are now out of college and the boy is in his late twenties, pursuing a career in photography for movies, and living in California. He will be getting married in May and I am planning to attend the wedding. The girl is about twenty-five, works at Disney World, and is trying to become a singer.

He is now married to another wonderful woman and we are very close. He calls me his surrogate mother. He has four grandchildren and is close with all of his six children. I expect to see them all at his son's wedding.

Our First Television Set

The year was 1950. The month was November. I had just given birth to my second son. It was a very difficult pregnancy and a difficult breech birth. This was six and half years after my first son was born. I am ashamed to admit that I was a little disappointed that he was a boy. However, he was so cute. He weighed over eight pounds and was blond with brown eyes. He was the best-behaved child as long as he had his thumb and favorite blanket. Unfortunately for him and for us, he was colicky and for the first almost-three months he cried incessantly. After many visits to the doctor and experimenting with maybe a hundred formulas, we finally found the right soy milk that agreed with him. I must say that his dislike for milk is lasting his entire lifetime. This "baby" is now 58 years old. I'm afraid I digressed a little.

In December, we decided to buy a television set. With a child and another baby, there was not much time for us to go out. We bought a Stromberg Carlson, which was the top of the line, with a little twelve-and-a-half-inch screen set into a beautiful piece of furniture. I forget the first program we watched but I was holding the baby in my lap when my husband turned the set on. It was amazing to see this black and white movie-like picture come on. I looked down at the baby and he stopped fretting and was staring wide-eyed at the screen. There weren't any shows in the daytime then. So, every evening after Sandy (his given name was Sanford) was bathed and dressed for the night, I fed him his bottle in front of the TV and then propped him up on the couch where he stared at the TV, very content, until he fell asleep. I don't remember when we got addicted to it, but my seven-year-old enjoyed the comedy shows and, of course, every Tuesday night was "Milton Berle Night."

This magical instrument eventually became as much a part of our lives as the radio and telephone. I had the radio on from early morning as I do with the television today. I still like listening to the radio and it is always on in my car. However, even though I have a few radios in my home, as they come attached to clocks, I just don't seem to get good reception in my apartment. Sometimes, I come home from a shopping trip in the middle of watching a very interesting program on TV, rush upstairs, turn on the radio, and, lo and behold, I cannot find the station or get good reception.

The TV is now my main source of news and entertainment. I even gave up reading the newspaper as it was too time consuming.

David Spindell

Bio

David M. Spindell graduated from Thomas Jefferson High
School in Brooklyn and graduated from the New York Institute
of Technology. David became a New York City master electrical
contractor, and owned and operated Call Electric Company,
which employed over 100 Local #3 electricians. The New York
Contractors' Electrical Association recognized Call Electric
Company as being a well-run electrical contracting company
in New York City. David also owned and operated a plumbing
company, a pawn shop, a bagel shop, and a jewelry store. Recently,
he started the Entrepreneur Help Group, which teaches people how
to start successful businesses on a shoestring.

My Big Escape: When I Was Six Years Old

I proudly declare I was born and raised in Brooklyn, New York.
My father used to discipline me by hitting me with a belt. It
hurt more than words can say and he didn't stop until I bled. So,
growing up, I understood that if I committed something naughty
and I got caught, there would be hell to pay!
Every now and again I would be down the block from our home,
behaving dreadfully, and when I speak of being bad, I mean
committing some sort of childhood-mischief acts of disobedience
and debauchery.
Nine out of ten times it was either stealing something or hurting
someone in a fist fight, and some of the things I did were just
plain kids' stuff. Either way, I ended up in Dutch for walking on a
crooked crutch.
My mother Sophie would catch me doing whatever and blow her
top. She would scream at the top of her lungs, "Wait 'til your father
gets home. You will be sorry." Those were the exact words that
caused a wall of worry, because I knew what that meant.

That meant getting beaten bloody with a belt. Not a soft swat on the rump, but a whipping that today would bring criminal charges of child abuse against my father (Manny).

I think back on this one particular day when I let the air out of Sherry Blatt's bicycle tires. She was a little girl who I detested. In retrospect it was more like a love-hate relationship.

What I remember most vividly is that my mother said "Wait 'til your father gets home." I did not wait for her to say anything else, so I ran away. I ran to the first corner, then walked 30 city blocks until it got dark. You have to remember, I was very young– only eight years old.

I got lost and didn't know where I was or how I would get home. I was in an African American area and I was very scared. So, in desperation, I went into a Black-owned convenience store. I do not recall the name,

When the owner saw a White eight-year-old child walk into his store, he knew I was not near my home and most likely lost. I told him, "I ran away from home because my father was going to hit me with a belt."

He asked if I knew my phone number. I gave it to him and he phoned my mother and got directions to my house. I did not want to go back home because I was so frightened of what my father would do to me.

But the nice man assured me that my father would not punish me with the belt. He promised he would speak to my father and that was the only reason I climbed into his old four-door Dodge automobile.

When I got home my mother hugged and kissed me and thanked the nice man. She then sent me upstairs to my father, who kissed me and then gave me a beating. He showed me no mercy. It was the worst thrashing of my life.

While I cried a river of tears in my bedroom, I was gnashing my teeth. I was furious at my father, my mother, and that Black man who promised I wouldn't get a thumping. Many years later, I came to realize that the Black man could not control what my father did and that telling me I wouldn't receive a whipping was the only way I'd go back home willingly.

The Invisible Rope

Back in the day of Trojans, Camels, and slicked-back pomade hair we had far too much time on our hands, and we were always up to some sort of insane antics. I mean we knew how to have a grand time of mischief and rhyme.

My friend Benny, a small blonde-haired boy, and I enjoyed playing an amusing prank at night. We would stand on opposite sides of a busy boulevard pretending we were having a tug of war with an invisible rope that we were pulling back and forth across the street. The drivers of the automobiles thought it was a real rope that they couldn't see because it was dark. The motor vehicles used to SCREECH to a grinding halt. Spotting the sheer terror in the drivers' eyes, we would laugh our asses off on each and every occasion.

We did our imaginary rope routine one time too many, for one evening the car we made stop to a hell of halt was a police cruiser. Two patrolmen with crewcuts leaped out of the squad car, lined us up alongside a building, and smacked us on our legs with their Billy Willy Clubs, looking to take away our invisible rope, a rope they never found because it had never existed.

Then one of them, an enormous chubby flatfoot, grabbed at my waist as if he had found the rope. He held the invisible rope in front of us and proclaimed, "I finally found that goddamn rope boys. That's the end of all your fun and games."

He and his partner swiftly walked away, climbed into their squad car, and drove away. Not believing what just happened, we laughed with unbridled glee.

My Father and The Robber

I was born in Brooklyn, New York, and had a very street-smart father; but I was a mamma's boy. My father was a mutineer who barely spoke more than a few words because he was a loner. He drank, gambled, came home from work, and sat at the kitchen table playing solitaire for hours.

The first time I ever had a heart-to-heart with him took place when my parents moved to Florida and my father asked me to help him drive the car down. It was then he shared with me his entire life story.

The best story I heard was when he was managing a pool parlor named "Beaches" on Livonia and Georgia Avenue right across Fortunoff Department Store in Brownsville, Brooklyn.

Three masked men came in with guns drawn, lined up all the patrons against the nearest wall, and took all their money, jewelry, and valuables.

My father looked into the eyes of one of the hoodlums and recognized him. The ghastly goon realized he had been discovered. The next day there was a telephone call for my father in the pool room.

The caller said, "Manny, you know who this is." My father said, "Yes, I know who you are. You are a rat bastard. You took $350 of my hard-earned money."

The armed robber said, "Don't worry. I will drop by tomorrow and give you back your money, as long as you keep your mouth shut." The next day the thief stopped by the pool hall and gave my father the $350. As we drove my father revealed, "I never had more than $20 in my pocket in my life."

The punch line to the story is that my father robbed the robber!

My First Fishing Trip

When I was in my mid-twenties, I became an avid fisherman going almost every weekend or anytime I could to a stream, lake, or the open seas.

This is the main reason I could justify purchasing one the most expensive fishing poles ever made, a Penn Torque Spinning Fishing Rod. Even back in the 1970s they ran more than $300! They obviously were for the well-to-do fishermen enthusiasts..

Nevertheless, my inexpensive old bamboo pole is the one I cherish most of all. My father, when I was ten, bought it with his hard-earned dollars from being an electrician and a jack-of-all-trades.

It was a shiny new fishing pole, which I took with me on my first fishing adventure at Canarsie Pier in Brooklyn.

The first thing we did was buy a bucket of minnows for bait. We put the line in the water and waited for the first bite. But it was too close to the pier. So I reeled in the line due to the fact I was having a difficult time casting the line without tangling it.

An elderly and unkempt veteran angler came over and showed me how to keep my finger on the line to prevent it from tangling. He took hold of the fishing rod demonstrating how to properly cast out my line.

He put his finger on the line and cast it far out into the water. It sunk straight to the bottom. There was nothing left. I tumbled down on the wood pier crying and carrying on uncontrollably.

My father came over to console me, "Don't worry, David. I will go and get you a brand new fishing pole." He patted me on the back, peered straight into my eyes, and then rushed off in the direction of the bait and tackle shop.

While my father was off getting a new pole, all the fishermen on the pier rushed over and cast their fishing lines in attempts to snag mine. After much effort, and tries, they snagged it!

When I reeled in the line in, I realized it had not been properly tied to the reel. All I got back was a dead killy (fishing bait). I was bitterly disappointed.

The fishermen then cast their lines way out from the pier. I took my old hook with the dead killy and placed it on the pier as I whimpered.

A couple of minutes later my father returned with a cheap bamboo fishing pole. He baited the hook with a new killy and promised I'd catch a big fish. I swung the strand in front of the pier and it drifted into the blue water. I closed my eyes and said a silent prayer.

No more than two minutes later I felt a mighty tug on the line. With the assistance of my father I pulled in a five-pound fluke. Let me tell you, it was a real beauty!

My father was delighted by my amazing catch. He hugged and kissed me and showed the fish to all the fishermen on the pier. They applauded and patted me on the back. It was a magnificent feeling.

When we arrived home, my mother cooked up the five-pound fluke and we sat down at the kitchen table for a splendid meal. My father was brimming with immense pride, bragging to my mother, two sisters, and anyone who would listen for the next few weeks.

This shall forever and a day remain a merry memory, shared between a father and son. A sentiment I shall forever treasure! For I always yearned to please my father, a man I admired and respected.

Certainly, my father was a complex man. He could be quite brutal when it came to discipline because he did not believe in sparing the rod. On the other hand, he could be incredibly generous, warmhearted, and loving.

I still have that old cherished bamboo fishing pole and from time to time I take it out and show it to my grandchildren. I grin from ear to ear for it provides so many splendid memories.

The Dating Game

After my wife Shelly passed away, I was lonely. A friend of mine, Gary Tuchman, was a typewriter salesman turned computer geek virtually overnight because the absurd printed word in the communication world was quickly turning from ice to fire.

He told me about a computer dating service, on which he said he had found his wife. So out of desperation I decided to utilize it for a series of mystery dates, hoping to rise above my loneliness and find another lady love.

The name of the dating service was "A Match Made In Heaven," located in the heart of Manhattan. Gary promised this was the perfect place where I could meet a lot of women and read about them before I met them.

I was not looking for just a roll in the hay. On the contrary, I was looking for a soulmate. Anyway, he assured me that Jane Austin Billings could hook me up with the woman of my dreams and I was so downhearted and desperate I believed him.

I went to the dating agency office and met my matchmaker Jane. She told me that I was a good-looking rich man with a great personality and that there was an abundance of available loving women out there just waiting and hoping for a man like me.

Over the course of time I realized that was not the case. For true devotion is very difficult to find, and a true-blue partner is one who will be by your side when times get tough; and the stormy seas get mighty rough.

And we all know, even when the sun is shining and the sky is a crystal blue, the weather can change on a dime. Then the sky turns black and the whirlwinds blow all your pretty dreams away. That's when you need a good woman to see you through the darkness.

That is what I was searching for, a true enduring love who would not turn her back on me if I became ill or suffered a major business setback, and then file for divorce as a matter of course. That is what I had with Shelly and was searching for again.

Anyway, I joined the dating service. I completed the questionnaire and revealed the most intimate details of my life on their dating message boards. I made it clear to anyone who could read what I was looking for. Jane then put twenty pictures of beautiful women on her desk and helped me pick out the six most appealing ones.

I was picking a lady from a glossy photograph as if that was the secret to finding my turtle dove.

We then sent out requests for the lovely ladies to get in touch with me. I received no response for two weeks. I said to myself, *This is not going to be easy. I might not be attractive to another woman.* I then sent out three more requests. I was just about to give up when I received a call from "Jungle Jane." She asked, "Why aren't you hitting your response button? You have twelve requests of women dying to meet you."

Up to now I have never shared with anyone what a technology moron I was for not knowing a response button existed. The fact is, I didn't know much about the computer age, and even 'til this very day I'm woefully dancing in the dark.

I felt compelled—and, yes, even obligated—to go out on a series of dates, for I was looking high and low above and below for a soul mate, a passionate partner. Someone I could depend upon to help me with all the tasks my first wife had undertaken way beyond the bedroom. So I decided to date the ladies who replied, and that's when the dates from hell began.

#1 was "Sideways Savage Ravage Sue," a lawyer who took over her father's prestigious Manhattan law firm which employed a hundred attorneys. I will not share with you the details of her legal beagle practices, since the witch is still alive and I don't wish to be tied up in civil court for the rest of my strife life. We went for a nice dinner and back to my boat to have coffee.

She stripped down raw naked and jumped on top of me as if I was a human trampoline, and she proceeded to wreak sexual havoc on me. It felt much like a sexual assault and not at all like passionate love-making. I wanted to call a cop and report a crime. I was so petrified that I contemplated jumping off my boat.

Do not get me wrong. I love women and I always look forward to a romp in the hay; but having sex with this vampire felt like she was committing a federal offense against me. I guess I wasn't ready to have a raunchy relationship and possible murderous marriage with a sexual predator!

#2 was "Layaway Lola," a beautiful blonde lady. We dated for six weeks. When I found a box of bugs and drugs in her pocketbook and a picture of her online being arrested for DUI, I said goodbye. You see I wasn't looking for someone who was just gorgeous. I wanted someone that was not riddled with addiction, affliction, and a criminal blast of a frigid felony past.

#3 was a commandant named "Enemy Emma." Ordering me around like I was her prisoner, she made HITLER look like a good date. It was a date from Auschwitz! I thought at any moment she was going to call me a dirty Jew and force me to recite *Mein Kampf* from cover to cover.
I believe I know a great deal about relationships from my experience over the years. I have the emotional scars to prove it. One thing I know for sure is that if a woman is an asshole on the first few dates, then her subsequent behavior will be a walking, talking holocaust.
I got away from that German shepherd, and I never phoned her or ever answered any of her messages. I was not about to live a life of being a robot or living in the chains of an authoritarian female dictator!

#4 "No Ma'am Ah Lam." She was a stunning Oriental gal, half my age. To impress her, I took her on an exclusive Tank Tour of China. As the plane took off, Ah Lam rushed off toward the lavatory.
The flight attendant stopped her and told her she would have to go back to her seat until the seatbelt sign was turned off.
I tried to inform Ah Lam the flight attendant was only doing her job. When the sign was turned off there was a mad dash to go to the bathroom and of course she was last in line.

When she finally got back to her seat, she was so infuriated she didn't speak to me for an hour. Looking back on it that wasn't such a bad thing.

On the way to get our luggage, she turned to me, putting her finger in my face and shrieked, "Don't you ever take anyone's side against me again." I never did take anyone's side against her again. I just stopped dating her.

I went through all my dates, and I completely gave up on finding a lovely lady through a dating mating service. Let's be honest, you can't find true and lasting love from a picture or a pretty face. Anyone with a brain understands that romance and marriage are built on trust and "being kindred spirits" and that that, indeed, is easier said than done.

I sold my house and gave my business to my sons. I moved my most cherished possessions and went to live on my boat in the summer. In the winter I took my boat to the southern end of the Sunshine State.

In Florida I met my new love at the dock. Her name was Amber, a beautiful, smart, successful lady. She earned all of our income, and I did all the household chores. We lived high on the hog for a while, as our days were blue skies and balmy temperatures.

A Strange Long Fishing Trip

I went on a long wet wonderful tuna-fishing trip. We loaded up my 48-foot Viking Sport Fisherman Cruiser chock-full of live bait, expensive deep sea fishing gear, fabulous food, ice cold cola, and big boy drinks (alcohol). We then journeyed 150 miles off shore to a spot called "The Canyon." This was a legendary spot where the big fish swam and the expert fishermen roamed to snag and drag in the big game. We were looking to land a whale or at least a deep-water grand prize.

My friend Jumping Jimmy (Gabby), who was captaining the boat, screamed out, "There's a little boat ahead sinking and a group of men are in the water. They are hollering and waving for help!"
I did not believe him; in fact I thought he was out of his cotton-pickin' behind mind. I thought he had way too much pooch hooch to drink so he could not think straight. I shook my dead head and quipped, "No way is it a little boat. We are over a hundred miles offshore."
I took the wheel of the watercraft and I navigated the fishing vessel to help the Amen Men (men praying to be rescued), who were indeed in dire need.
In actuality, the craft was not a little boat, nor barely afloat. The bow portion of a colossal yacht was sticking out of the water so the craft appeared to be teeny tiny. When we got closer, we saw five men in a raft screaming for us to help them. I backed up my vessel to the raft.
They all jumped into my vessel one by one clearly scared out of their wits, soaking wet, and dehydrated. They were ecstatic to be saved and thanked us over and over again. I called the Coast Guard. They first sent a helicopter, and a big Coast Guard boat came cruising by under a sun-splashed sky in minutes.
When the helicopter flew over my boat, they asked me my boat name and for a list of my crew. They also asked me for the names of the sunken boat's captain and his crew. I turned to the haggard captain of the sunken boat and asked him for his information.
He shook his head, telling me "No, I'm not saying one damn thing without my lawyer present." I had to think of a response fast, so as not to anger the authorities or get the men I just rescued in legal trouble.

So I told the Coast Guard that I didn't know their names because they were so traumatized. But between you and me, that was a bold-faced lie. I believe they had been up to no good; and without asking any questions that was understood, for a long look often tells you the entire gory story. However, I did exchange names and addresses with the sinking boat's captain and crew. The Coast Guard sent a dinghy from their big cutter transport ship, and the men refused to climb aboard.

So when we arrived at the dock, the Feds were waiting, and took into custody the five men, who suddenly forgot how to speak English. Can you imagine that? They began speaking in Russian, I believe, or some other European language. I jumped back into the boat. Not deterred by this unexpected situation, we headed once again back out to sea.

We indeed went fishing, and caught a *ton of tuna*. This was the most productive fishing trip ever, and one I shall always treasure with immense pleasure.

I guess the fishing gods looked down upon us that day and that was a blessing. Here's the ultimate kicker to the glory story. It occurred about a month later.

I still had a freezer-full of frozen fish, lobster, and clams that I had occasion to share with my new rescued friends. We got together and sat around a dining table and they told us what they really had been doing out at sea.

And that is another story. You can rest assured it had something to do with drugs not hugs. They were ever so thankful we rescued them. As mentioned, they had clammed up, saying next to nothing to the Coast Guard or the F.B.I.

To the best of my knowledge, the men we rescued far out at sea and then sat down and broke bread with never got in trouble for that misadventure. Nevertheless, I heard through the grapevine a little while later that they got tagged and grabbed (arrested) for other illegal activity. And so it goes.

My Sweetest Job Ever

I was an electrical contractor, owning Call Electric Company. Without divulging names and revealing too much, I built a multi-million dollar business by making powerful friends.

I did this by getting to know CEOs and major owners of real
estate empires including builders and proprietors of luxury office
buildings and lavish high-rise apartments. In addition, I made
friendships with influential bankers and top union leaders in New
York City.

In the business world just being great at your craft, which in my
case was electrical, wasn't enough. Success in Brooklyn and New
York City is who you know and who likes and trusts you. Many
times I would become acquainted with very influential movers and
shakers by inviting them on deep sea fishing trips and entertaining
them at sporting events like front row box seats at Madison
Square Garden to watch the *New York Knicks* when they had their
championship teams.

So this explains how I started doing work for Loews Movie Theater
on Long Island, New York. They were dividing a big theater into
two smaller theaters. They realized that they could make plenty of
money by splitting up the large theaters into small ones and show
five times as many films. There would be, for example, seven to ten
films shown at the same location, which meant packed theaters and
more customers, and it was a highly profitable venture that was fast
becoming the standard in the movie house business.

This was a common occurrence in the mid- and late-1970s and the
1980s, which swept not only the East Coast but across the country,
at breakneck speed, which in turn made a lot of coinage for those
in professions like mine. In addition, thousands of family-owned
theaters were being bought out by large media groups, both foreign
and domestically owned, all while the movie business consolidated.
This was due to deregulation and a very pro-business agenda
championed by the Reagan administration.

Back to the story. When I finished my work at the movie theater,
I made a hefty lefty profit. Six months later they added another
theater. And I made even more money, because there was much
more wiring and rewiring to do. Then another movie company,
RKO Cinemas, gobbled them up. The giant conglomerate began
buying Ma and Pa movie theaters in huge chunks, making sure

they could corner the market in order to resell them to investors and corporate cartels.

Then along came Cineplex Odeon. They acquired the entertainment first-run movie house from RKO and hired me and my company to rip out all the theaters and convert them into Super 10 Theater Complexes. It was like having Hanukkah and Christmas every day of the year. As they transformed the movie house with additional screens and upgraded amenities at the movie complexes—which included dining rooms, pinball and video gaming machines—my business soared! You talk about a corporate takeover daisy chain!

When I put in my first change orders (construction alterations) for new lights over the candy counter for $10,000, they paid me $13,000. And then when I put in a change order for $16,000 for added electrical work on a dining facility, they paid me $20,000.The final draw came when they hired me to put in a new automation system. My change order was for $75,000. My final take on that was $125,000.

I called up the general manager, a cool as a rule dude name Doug Bruno. Doug was an affable, free-spirited gentleman with a heart of gold. Well over six-feet tall, he was Senior Site Construction Managerial Director, a fancy title that meant he was the boss. Doug was an incredibly benevolent man to the outside venders, including those in the trades like me. And most of us respected and admired the big spicy Italian guy.

Over the years, out of his good nature, he threw me a heap of work that made me a pretty penny; and here's the kicker—he never asked for anything in return other than that my company and I do a great job, which we did. By doing a great job, I mean making sure we pulled all the proper permits and did the work to the specifications of the city codes and the architect's wishes and demands.

The Italian Stallion always seemed to have dangling from his lips a real thick rocket-red toothpick. Doug was my boss on this job and the one who called all the hot shots. But he was very easy to work for, because he just cared about the performance, and he never had an enormous ego. That was a mighty rare thing in my business, which was chock full of whack jobs! Because in nine out of ten jobs I landed I found myself dealing with impossible people who went out of their way, every single work day, to put up roadblocks and lay down landmines.

I rushed up to Doug and chattered, "We have to have a sit down and straighten things out because this change order quagmire is about to blow up in our faces. Listen pal, I'm getting paid way over the amount I am supposed to receive."

Doug, in his usual casual tongue in cheek, retorted, "Relax my friend, do not get your bowels in an uproar." He then yanked at his belt buckle and flashed a wry grin.

At that meeting, I told him, "Doug, I like making a lot of money, but I don't want to go to jail." After all, what was going on in the series of overcharges was unethical, and by the way, probably illegal.

He said to me: "Don't worry about it, Davie Crocket! RKO is paying for all this work that Cineplex Odeon is doing; and I am signing off on these work orders. RKO has the money to burn." He sat across from me, looking both ways, his voice full of unholy folly, "You see, buddy boy, I hate the goddamn company, and I want you to milk the cow until it no longer boos and moos!"

I didn't ask why he hated the company, because it was none of my business, for often the best question is silence. I leaned back in my chair and winked my right eye at him. He patted me on the back with a hardy but friendly slap. I nodded my head one single time to indicate that I understood what he was saying. Then I snapped, "No problem, God Bless America!"

And that was it. All the while, the funny money train came rolling in over and over again. I never brought up the topic again; and well after the job was over no one ever challenged the overcharges. So all was fine and divine.

Sydell Stern

Bio

Sydell Stern was born in Brooklyn, New York, and grew up in the Coney Island area. She met her husband at Brooklyn College. They moved to Los Angeles after they were married. There she taught elementary school and he attended UCLA. Upon completion of his Ph.D. they moved to Winnipeg, Manitoba, where Sydell worked in the Winnipeg School System with Special Needs children. 36 years later she moved to Montreal to be near her children and grandchildren. Sydell began writing professionally 14 years ago. She writes a column for *The Jewish Press*, published in New York City, called "The Person Behind the Chair and Beyond," in an attempt to heighten awareness about the lives of the spouses of the chronically ill. A memoir *Behind Prison Walls* has been published by Makor Press.

[Editor's note. In the three sections below, I have italicized and included within quotation marks only the words with the root "*krechtz*," considering them foreign words. I have italicized, but not included within quotation marks, a number of other Hebrew/Yiddish words, considering them loan words in English. A fairly new principle in editing being the primary need to accommodate readers' comfort, I have felt that a multiplicity of words in quotation marks would defeat that purpose.]

The Gallant Grandchild

It was the first night of Chanukah and I was invited to my kids for lighting the Menorah and supper. I had already bought presents for my daughter, son-in-law, and the five grandkids. Now all I had to do was transport them to my car and then to their house. As I made three trips from my condo to my car in the icy pouring rain, I regretted having been so practical. I had bought each of the grandchildren wooden toys. Heavy, bulky, handmade wooden toys. Finally I got the gifts into the car and went back upstairs for the food I said I'd bring and loaded that into the trunk on top of the toys.

Three blocks later I was there. But now the rain was coming down in buckets. I was not going to make three or four trips from my car to their house in the rain. Let these kids earn their gifts. I called my daughter and asked that the three oldest children come out to help me bring the packages into the house.

There is no problem getting eager helpers when it's the first night of Chanukah because it's the first night of gift-giving. And my grandkids know that grandma gives the biggest gifts on the first night.

Almost immediately, with the new umbrellas I had bought each of them the previous week, the big three ran to my car oblivious of the downpour and were more than eager and excited to help old granny with her things. Suddenly the fourth appeared. "Me too! Me too!" he yelled while swinging his umbrella in every direction except over his head.

With strict warnings that no one was to peek inside the packages I gave each of them a shopping bag and off they went, disappearing as quickly as they had emerged. Sheltering myself from the rain with the hatch of my SUV I reached in for the last bag reluctantly, knowing that as soon as I closed the hatch I'd get drenched. Resigned, I grabbed the parcel and closed the hood ready to make a mad dash to shelter. Much to my surprise, standing next to the car was Shaya, the five-year-old, looking much like Mary Poppins ready to take off. He stood there calmly with his tiny umbrella raised as high as he could.

"There is nothing else to take." I said. "*I* have the last package. You can go back inside."

His big eyes confused, he said, "No, *Bubby*, I came back for you so you won't get wet. I will hold my umbrella as high as I can so you can come under it."

I crouched low to get next to him and under the umbrella that barely came up to my shoulder. But the smile he gave me when I did, kept me dry inside and I felt warmer than I had all day as he escorted me to his house.

The "*Krechtz*"

Why it is that noise helps us move? The older we get the more sounds emanate from our mouths as we stand up, climb stairs, and, in general, move from one place to another. The older we are, the more noise we seem to need in order to be mobile.

This is something I have observed in others and always wondered about. Not being a "*krechtzer*" as yet, I have never been able to examine the relationship between mobility and noise first hand. That is, until last week. Climbing the steps to my daughter's entrance way, I walked into the house to hear my four-year-old granddaughter declare with glee, "*Bubby*'s here! Yea! *Bubby*'s here! I can hear the noise she makes when she comes into our house."

Okay, so maybe I am deaf as well. They do say you never hear yourself. Maybe that is why no one has ever explained the connection between "*krechtzing*" and mobility. Everyone is sure it is the senior next to them who is making the noise. Not them. But now, confronted with the truth from a four-year-old, I have to admit it. I am a "*krechtzer*," too.

What can I say? It helps me get up those stairs. In all honesty I don't think I could do it silently. I know I wouldn't get past the first step without the help of at least a little "*krechtz*."

But whoever thought "*krechtzing*" could be outsourced. A good entrepreneur could make a fortune. I know just the one to do it. He didn't have monetary gain in mind when he came up with the idea. He just wanted to help his *Bubby*, who was in denial about her "*krechtzing*." He came up to me, this loving six-year-old, as I was getting up from their *Shabbos* table to go home. Looking at me with those big caring eyes, he told me he was going to help me up. He then proceeded to close his eyes and, standing next to me, gave the longest, loudest "*krechtz*" as I began to stand. "See how I'm helping you!" He said. Wasn't it easier for you to get up when I made the noise instead of you?"

Lesson learned. I have been a closet "*krechtzer*" and haven't even heard myself. Maybe I need to get my hearing checked as well. I guess it's time to accept what everyone around me seems to know. I am aging quicker than I think. This old-age stuff isn't for sissies. But, as long as I'm on the right side of the grass I will embrace "*krechtzing*" or whatever else it takes to keep me mobile.

Oy vey, vey, vey, vey. It's time to move on to another topic.

Zaidy and Not-*Bubby*

Most of us who are past a certain age remember Abbot and Costello, the comedians who are most famous for "Who's on First." For anyone too young to remember this sketch, I recommend you look it up on Google. It is considered a classic of comedy.

My grandson, at the age of four, already viewed things very philosophically. He often would have long talks with his handicapped *Saba* (grandpa) about the items of equipment he needed to use and their function. Very interested in how each piece of apparatus helped his Saba, he digested the information with an attitude that might mimic an experienced ninety year old. With a sage nod, he'd listen to the explanation and accepted life as it was without challenge.

This grandchild had no knowledge of the team of Abbot and Costello. Yet his experience with his teacher, related below, mimicked the sketch perfectly, if unintentionally. His great-grandparents were visiting and his unique way of looking at situations made his interchange a classic. I think his teacher is still confused about it after all these years.

The great-grandparents arrived for a long overdue visit. They had not been able to make the long trip for many years due to several reasons beyond anyone's control. And so, they had never seen any of their great-grandchildren and now there were many of them. They came with presents and good humor and played with the children. The children developed a close relationship with them immediately. But there was one problem. *Bubby* was *Zaidy's* (great-grandfather's) second wife. Being sensitive to the situation, she was very careful about not being called *"Bubby."* She felt that title belonged to the other great-grandmother and she didn't want to usurp it. She just told the family and the grandchildren to call her by her first name and mostly everyone did.

My four-year-old grandson didn't like this set up. It was illogical to his way of thinking and philosophical bent. And so he decided it made much more sense to call his new great-grandmother, "Not-*Bubby*" instead of using her first name. And so he insisted on calling them *"Zaidy"* and "Not-*Bubby."*

After a weekend of fun with the visiting great-grandparents, the children went off to school Monday morning. And so it was when my daughter came to pick up my little philosopher from school, he announced to his teacher that he was very excited about the visit of *"Zaidy"* and "Not-*Bubby."*

"Don't you like your *Bubby*?" asked the teacher. "Aren't you excited to see her too?"

"Oh yes!" He said. "I love *Zaidy* and Not-*Bubby*. *Zaidy* and Not-*Bubby* are so much fun to play with."

The teacher tried again. She told him how he needed to give his *Bubby* respect and surely she loved him very much. He readily agreed. After all he wanted the conversation to end so he could go and play with *Zaidy* and Not-*Bubby*. The more he told the teacher how he wanted to go see *Zaidy* and Not-*Bubby*, the more the teacher tried to influence him to have a relationship with his *Bubby*. This made my grandson more confused and he began to loudly protest how much he loved his *Zaidy* and Not-*Bubby* and wanted to go home to play with them.

The conversation between this child and his teacher quickly escalated. It was very much starting to sound like Abbot and Costello's "Who's On First," with the teacher feeling she was not getting this kid to see her point and the child just wanting to go home and play with his beloved *Zaidy* and Not-*Bubby*. Finally, the teacher gave up, having finally gotten her confused student to agree to give his *Bubby* another chance. Another chance at what he didn't know, but he had figured out that agreeing to do this was the only way to finally go home and play with his great-grandparents.

Feeling great that she had gotten through to her student, and very concerned about what was causing the vehement negative feelings toward his great-grandmother, the teacher handed her charge over to his mother. My daughter having overheard the entire conversation between student and teacher couldn't successfully hide the amusement that was evident on her face.

"Let's go play with *Zaidy* and Not-*Bubby*!" My daughter said loud enough for the teacher to hear, unable to not be part of this self-perpetuating routine of misinformation. The teacher's hostile stare was priceless. I can't wait to hear what happens when other relatives come. Relatives with family members that a grandchild or great-grandchild *really* doesn't like.

Helene Suzann

Bio

Helene Suzann is a facilitator of achieving optimum health and well-being.

She has promoted her practice–which began in the early 1970s in New York, Pennsylvania, and Texas–throughout the United States, Canada, and the British West Indies.

An artist with a unique technique, she has sold many of her paintings.

She is a Reiki Master Teacher, Yoga instructor, and Hypnotherapist. Reiki is a laying-on-of-hands healing technique; Yoga is an Eastern philosophy, engaging the body and mind connection; and Hypnotherapy cleanses the subconscious mind.

A writer as well, Helene published *Thank you God, I'm Havin a Ball,* which is available on Amazon. *Divorce and Enlightenment* is in the works.

Ode to Arlene Joy

Arlene Joy was my favorite sister and my only sister through marriage.
We were married only one year and five months, when we got the heartbreaking call that changed our lives forever.
Arlene was an amazing 20-year-old precious girl. She was born before her time. She was going to Boston University and was home for the summer. She got a great summer job working for Mayor Lindsay in New York City. We were all so proud of her. She was such an intelligent, loving, and wonderful beautiful person. Whenever we came over for Friday night for Shabbat, she would fly down the stairs when she heard us come in and shout out where's my beautiful sister-in-law!

She would give me the biggest hug. She always made me feel so
welcome. Arlene was so funny! I'll never forget when we went
to Woolworth's together because she needed a shower cap. I was
looking around for some things myself. She came running over to
ask me with a shower cap on like a beret how do I look? She made
a crazy expression. I laughed so hard she joined in and people
were watching us crack up and they started laughing too. It was an
incredible moment. Arlene was a free spirit.

It was 7:30 a.m. when the phone rang on August 28, 1965. It was
my in-laws' neighbor Honey. When I heard her voice I was ready to
ask her why she was calling so early. I never got to say a word. She
immediately asked to speak to Robert. I said he's sleeping we were
sleeping. Then she raised her voice and said let me speak to Robert!
I woke him up and told him who it was and he took the phone. I
realized something terrible had happened when I saw the look on
his face. He said okay I'll be right there.

He started to sit up and started yelling my sister's dead she's dead!
My sister Arlene is dead I have to go.

I said I'm going with you I'll drive you and I started crying as I got
up and got ready to go. I couldn't believe this was happening. I was
hoping I could drive in this condition. We lived in Queens and they
lived in Brooklyn. It would take us at least 40 minutes to get there.
My husband was running around in circles and didn't know where
his clothes were. I had to direct him and help him. He was a basket
case.

We finally got ready after I made some coffee and toast. He said
I can't eat. I said I'll take it with us because I knew I needed
something and we could eat it on the way.

As we were driving I really had to concentrate because I was so
terrified to see them. I didn't know what to expect. I was never in a
situation like this before. I kept my cool trying really hard.

We finally arrived and Robert jumped out of the car before I even
turned off the ignition. There was a neighbor waiting by the front
door on the porch.

She nodded at me and said this is really bad your Mother-in-law is a mess. I did not need to hear this when I was so nervous and scared.

As I went in I walked over to the couch where my Mother-in-law Miriam was lying down. I bent down to touch her and she was crying and said I just want my daughter I just want Arlene. She kept saying that over and over again.

When I stood up I didn't know where to go or what to do. There were some neighbors sitting and walking around. Robert was with his father and Sam kept saying Dear God over and over again and crying. Robert was so distraught and tried to be strong for his parents.

People were bringing in food. Uncle Irving came in to drive us up to the Catskill Mountains where Arlene had died in a car accident. It was raining and all of us were going because someone had to identify the body.

Editor's discussion. I had hoped to publish the preceding piece together with the following treatment as a whole; but the combination was considered too long, and probably pedantic, and it was not accepted as presented. Since length is not a criterion in this anthology and since the sequel piece is particularly relevant here in showcasing the work and value of the Club, I am appending it to Helene's "Ode to Arlene Joy."

Introducing Helene Suzann

I have been considering for many months that the Kings Point Creative Writing Club (KPCWC) is Kings Point's "best-kept secret." Though I am prone at times to hyperbole, I assert that our 20-or-so writers and poets are among the best of our craft in the entire state We have developed into a high-powered critique group, and our critiquing is top-notch. As an alumnus of the Philadelphia Writing Project affiliate of the National Writing Project, I know what I'm talking about! I don't mean to boast about my background; I just wish to establish my credibility.

Something remarkable happened in the KPCWC group members'
critiquing last November! It pertained to Helene Suzann's piece
on the tragic death of her sister-in-law many decades ago. Sharp
polarization about the punctuation and paragraphing of the
piece emerged in the group, which I characterized—with self-
deprecating irony—as a conflict between the "punctuation police"
and the "free-thinking heretics." Ironically, I am the most fanatical
adherent of the former group, and yet I saw merit in the orientation
of the latter one.

The controversy is two-fold. On the one hand, enclosing quotations,
however short, with opening and closing quotations marks and
starting a new paragraph with every change of speaker. Or laying
out a relatively long, but tight, paragraph with no quotation marks
at all and little other punctuation, which nonetheless would not
burden the reader.

Intuiting that the differences of approach in the group reflected
genuine literary depth, because proponents of one approach were
tolerant of the alternate one, I conceptualized a sample of a passage
treated in the two respective ways. Two members weighed in
privately in emails that I would be invading the writer's privacy in
publishing such a passage. I consulted with Helene and explained
to her what I had in mind. Having no objections, she gave me her
permission to write the piece. Here is its essence with respective
comparative analysis.

From the Version of the "Punctuation Police"

I said, "I'm going with you. I'll drive you." I started crying as I got
up and got ready to go. I couldn't believe this was happening. I was
hoping I could drive in this condition. We lived in Queens, and they
lived in Brooklyn. It would take us at least 40 minutes to get there.
My husband was running around in circles and didn't know where his
clothes were. I had to direct him and help him. He was a basket case.

We finally got ready after I made some coffee and toast. He said, "I can't eat."

I said, "I'll take it with us," because I knew I needed food and we could eat it on the way. As we were driving, I really had to concentrate because I was terrified about meeting my in-laws. I didn't know what to expect. I had never been in a situation like this before. I had to try really hard to keep my cool. We finally arrived and Robert jumped out of the car before I had even turned off the ignition.

From the Version of the "Free-Thinking Heretics"

I said I'm going with you I'll drive you. I started crying as I got up and got ready to go. I couldn't believe this was happening. I was hoping I could drive in this condition. We lived in Queens, and they lived in Brooklyn. It would take us at least 40 minutes to get there. My husband was running around in circles and didn't know where his clothes were. I had to direct him and help him. He was a basket case.

We finally got ready after I made some coffee and toast. He said I can't eat. I said I'll take it with us because I knew I needed food and we could eat it on the way. As we were driving, I really had to concentrate because I was terrified about meeting my in-laws. I didn't know what to expect. I had never been in a situation like this before. I had to try really hard to keep my cool. We finally arrived and Robert jumped out of the car before I had even turned off the ignition.

The punctuation system of the first version helps the reader keep straight who the speaker is; that of the second conveys more "mimetically"—that is, representing the flow better—the emotionality of the situation. Helene's original, in fact, was closer to the latter; and the "punctuation police," including me, took notice and gave her due praise.

Stella White

Bio

I was born and raised in Miami, Florida, along with nine siblings: eight brothers and one sister. Mary had Down Syndrome and passed in 1997 from natural causes.

My college major was in the Fine Arts, with a focus on painting, photography, and mixed media. I've studied both here in the states and abroad at universities and studios with instructors who guided my creative path. I enjoy teaching people of all ages, especially the art of collage. My experience includes gallery administration and event planning, and chairing membership and other committees in several art associations nationwide. I still volunteer at community events, having recently become involved with All Peoples Day, an organization created to invite people of all ages, races, and cultures to communicate with one another. (www.allpeoplesday.com)

My "real" job was as a real estate appraiser, both residential and commercial. I worked for local private and commercial bank appraisal companies. The national commercial appraisal company I worked at in their Miami office offered travel throughout the Southeast United States. I have wonderful memories of the many people I was fortunate to meet.

I may be the only one who misses the Miami-based Eastern Airlines, or one of the very few who do. On one return trip home from Nashville, Tennessee, I raced to the gate, hoping to make the last flight to Miami, only to see the door closing. I stood at the window, looking at the pilot as he pulled away. He saw me standing there, in my suit, briefcase in hand, large carry-on on my shoulder, so very sorry to have missed the flight. He pulled the plane back to the gate and I was boarded. He later said as I departed, "Don't pull that one on me again," and winked.

I have always found writing short stories a favorite pastime. I've kept a diary of the antics of my three sons. It's a volume of interest to their girlfriends, who, when they ask me, "What was he like as a child?" I get out the book and read a story or two. It embarrasses my sons, but their friends love to hear the tales.

Not My Bear, I Swear
(a sketch of the author/poet)

Not my Bear, I Swear

I was in the kitchen preparing dinner, watching my sons play in the backyard. Kevin

came running towards the house. I went outside to meet him. He said, "Mom, there's a baby bear in the tree!"

It was actually a black kitten, newborn, abandoned as animals do when they determine their offspring are not fit for survival. It's a human trait as well. We think we're the highest in the evolution chain, but that's not always the case. Enough psychology.

I took the kitten to a neighbor. She had a cat that had just birthed a litter. We presented the "baby bear" to it and it was reluctant to nurse it. The momma cat hissed at it. Perhaps it was the one she abandoned in our backyard? My neighbor's daughter worked at a local vet's office and took the kitten with her to the office the next day. I never heard about the kitten's fate; but it prompted me to write a story of meeting a black bear. It's all true. I swear.

Black Bear got into my car, took my granola bar
Left the car door open, and the wrapper on the pavement
Left the bottle of water where I had placed it
And left paw prints on the car seat
While at a friend's house we heard a commotion from the dogs
Barking wildly and scratching at the plate-glass window
We looked out to see my car rocking side to side
A mama bear and cubs had broken into my car
We saw them running away with the fruit platter I had left in the
back seat
I thought *there goes my breakfast. Was that my bear?*
A neighbor reported that a black bear got into her car
Locked itself in, then honked the horn until she came to let him out
Was most likely my bear
A friend told me that she pulled into the driveway
Took her children and most of the groceries inside
She returned to the car to gather the rest
And found a black bear in the rear seat eating the groceries
Was most likely my bear
He was at the door one night as I was about to open it

I used my air-horn and he ran away
Next day I was sitting at the dining room table
Sorting through closet items: sewing box, scrap folder, first-aid kit
I had left the back doors open to allow the house to air out
The blind old dog, Sparky, was, as usual, sleeping on the sofa
He had a funny name
I looked up from the table and saw a black bear
Sniffing at the door
His head was just over the threshold
About to enter my house
I got up from my chair and yelled "NO!"
That bear jumped over the wooden gate and ran up the hill
In my backyard
I think of my bear
The one I saw in my dreams as a child
Chasing me home after I woke him from a nap
The one I saw in my mother's car, sitting in the driver's seat
At my front door eating pizza
Eating my lunch at the picnic table
Chasing my dog at the park
Sitting on grandma's lap, reading a book,
I saw a baby bear in a tree
But now the bear's fine, all mine
I swear it's my bear

For My Sister

My sister Mary was an avid pianist. She would approach the
piano, open the bench, and extract several of the music books.
Mary would sit and place the books on the piano, opening them
to various pages, perusing all, then begin to touch the keys and
pedals. This was a signal to my multitude of brothers (four older
and four younger) to become aware of "other things to do." In
other words, they quickly scrambled and ran the heck away from

the house, calling out as they ran, "Gotta go!" "Late for work!" "Gonna walk the dog!" or "Mowing the lawn!"

My mother and I were busy in the kitchen preparing dinner. We would side-glance each other and ask God for patience. Mary's fingers would begin by tapping one key ever so gently and repeatedly, and ultimately with vigor! She stepped on the pedals randomly to shorten or extend the notes. She then caressed all of the keys, lovingly, passionately, loudly. Her recital was, quite frankly, horrible. The funniest part to me was when she stopped to turn the pages and again carefully consider them, and resume. Short, soft, then emotional outbursts of notes and chaotic chords. Even the dog wanted to be let out of the house.

Mary did not know how to read music or apply it to the piano, or actually how to read at all. But she had a passion for the piano. And that is what we experienced. That is what we heard.

Mary had Down Syndrome. She was placed in a home for the mentally retarded at the age of four. We saw her on weekends and holidays. Every Friday afternoon several of us hopped into the station wagon and drove to The Haven School, about 25 miles south of our house. We met the administration, signed the release form, and then greeted Mary and her housemates Kathy Kline and Janie Clementi, two of her best friends. Miss Lyons was the infamous housemother. According to Mary, Miss Lyons "don't give me no coffee, no dessert." This upset Mom. On Sunday, after our noon family supper, we drove Mary back to The Haven School.

My sister-in-law recalls, "I remember Mary's busyness as she went about her weekend at home. It always seemed to me your Dad had just a little bit more love for her. I think because she caused him little trouble and loved unconditionally. In my heart, I always felt it must have been tough for Mary's folks to make the decision to put her in The Haven School. I heard many stories of why, including

her escape from the family fortress and swimming naked in
the neighbor's pool; her outbursts that led to holding a brother–
John Paul, I think–against the hot radiator, and several other
mischievous antics.

"I did experience the wrath of Mary when we visited one weekend.
It centered around not understanding what she was saying. Of
course it was an adjustment all the way around for me to enter
this large Miami home and then meet Mary Ora. [Her birth name,
Mary Aurora, is in honor of her grandmothers Mary and Aurore.]
One of my usual experiences while visiting would be Mary
standing in the upstairs hallway and talking to me. When I didn't
understand her, or mistakenly smiled and said yes, when NO was
the desired response, she GOONGed me. 'Goong, Goong, Goong!'
she would say in a disgusted tone and then she would stomp
away?"

Since the 1970's, it has always stayed in my head that around
dinner time Mary would repeat over and over when she would
see Mom and ask "green beans." Mom would reply, "Yes Mary,
we're having green beans." At the dinner table, it became a loving
gaze as she looked at her plate and a soothing *greeeeen bean*
acknowledgement was heard.

I will never forget going to visit Mary at the school. She kept
pulling us up from the picnic table with the request to "go party
in your car and go to Burger King." Dad was excited at one point
when Janie walked by and announced, "I remember you!" He
jumped up and told Janie, "I remember you, too!" Then the next
person walked by and Janie announced again, "I remember you!"
And who's to say, maybe she did remember every person she ever
laid eyes on.

In the American Indian culture children with Down Syndrome,
or other mental challenges, are considered to be closest to God

because they are far more genuine, honest, and pure. Ironically, to this day, I can't help but think of Mary every time I eat green beans.

Mom and I went to the Miami Public Library downtown on Biscayne Boulevard once a month to pick up a reel-to-reel movie. We'd bring it to The Haven School where the children and the staff gathered in the cafeteria to watch the movie. The film was laced through a projector and viewed on a large pull-down white screen. The children and staff were always excited. The one I recall, because Mom was so appalled at it, was an animated story about a young black boy in Africa. He was naked. Mom did not know how to stop the projector quickly enough, so she nonchalantly let it roll to the end. The children and staff were happy to watch any movie, no matter the subject.

I do not recall where Mary slept in our three-bedroom house on 29th Road. I remember sharing a bedroom with three brothers, all of us sleeping on two sets of bunk beds. When a fourth brother joined us, a crib was placed in the room. At our new house on 4th Avenue, I had a room to myself. I shared a bathroom with two other siblings; but my room was all mine until Mary or relatives came to visit. I slept at a neighbor's house or on the blue vinyl sofa in our living room more often than in my own bed (perhaps exaggerating the memory).

Mary arrived on Friday afternoons and proceeded to take command of my bedroom. She would lock the door from the inside and commence her routine of redecorating. I would knock repeatedly until she yelled "Dalla, go away!" Apparently she knew the art of "Feng Shui," the Chinese practice of harmonizing one's environment, because when I was finally able to reclaim my domain, I would find everything was rearranged. Often items were missing, like my school uniform and other clothing, homework due on Monday, and any item that was shiny. My brothers noticed that several of their items were missing as well. I felt frustrated and unnerved that I had to spend Sunday evenings recapturing my belongings and restoring *my own harmony.*

Mary became referred to by us as "The Bag Lady." She would have several bags ready for departure to The Haven School. Whoever rode in the station wagon was responsible for retrieving the items needing transport back home. This was very unsettling for Mary. Taking her bags apart in her presence unnerved her. She always became enraged and defensive. In her mind, I supposed, she took these items fair and square and they were rightfully hers to keep.

I know from past experience that she would re-gift items to her best friends Kathy and Janie. I noticed familiar items on their dresser tops during visits. There was no possible way to reclaim items given to these two friends. I cannot imagine, even to this day, what the consequences would have been from taking anything back. War, at the very least, would have erupted. Mary's outbursts of anger scared people. Learning her triggers was a part of knowing her as a person.

My siblings and I were told that she would not live a normal, long life, and that people with Down Syndrome typically live 20 to 30 years of age. But she was a part of our lives that enabled us to learn tolerance and compassion and to thrive and grow towards, and along with, her and others.

On a few occasions, Mom and I would take her to the new Dadeland Mall on Kendall Drive. It was on our way to and from The Haven School, which was in West Kendall. We would have lunch and of course order coffee and cake for dessert. This always pleased Mom.

Mary would approach people in the mall as we walked, stop them, and say: "Happy Birthday" or "Merry Christmas" and offer a hug.

Most responded with kindness and acceptance, but a few chose to back away from her advances. Children, even my own, were apprehensive about her forthright exhibit of friendliness. She did not know her own strength. Her hugs were like a gladiator's, bear-hugs that included lifting one up off the ground. But she meant well.

As my brothers and I got older and obtained driver's licenses, we would be assigned the pick-up and drop-off duty of Mary. This included a bribe. A quarter bought Mary a soda from the Coke machine. Any promise of food resulted in total compliance. An extra quarter would buy Kathy or Janie one, too. "Calm the Beast with a Coke," I would think. Offer a piece of candy or a visit to Burger King and she'd follow us anywhere. This window of opportunity, luring her into the car inattentive to anything else, was when we could retrieve our items, leaving a bag or two for her to bring back in with her.

My brother Bill recalls, "One of my memories of Mary was one when we were all sitting at the dinner table, and for whatever reason Mary said very plainly to Dad, 'Oh, go to hell, Joe.' It was very funny; but given Dad's temperament, I'm fairly certain no one really wanted to laugh or even dared to. But when I (and I suppose others at the table) looked at Dad, I saw that he had a big smile on his face. I think everyone felt comfortable laughing at this point; and so it brought a very lighthearted moment to the table."

Mom said a lot of things under her breath in reaction to his unkind words. It could have been our dear Miss Mary Brown, our maternal grandmother, who was the initiator of such words. Mary heard it from one of them. Like she heard from Miss Lyons, "No cake, no dessert."

I remember visiting Mary at Mercy Hospital in Miami, Florida just before she passed. It was in 1997. I walked in and said, "Let's open the windows," and pulled the drapes open. She got up out of the bed and looked out at the view of Biscayne Bay. "Ah, America!" she said.

I recently woke up with a thought, *My mother asked me and my siblings to write our memoirs of Mary after she passed.* But I have not until now. Another thought, *I did not include my sister Mary in my wedding party, or even think for her to attend. I do not know what my parents' reaction would have been had I suggested it. I imagine that Mary would have been thrilled to be in attendance, even walking down the aisle with the other girls, laughing and giggling the whole time. She would have loved the cake.*

This story has been on the back burner, until I recently started a charity for Special Olympics in her memory. She couldn't bat a baseball or run; but she could beat the shit out of you. A dear friend said to me upon my telling her of Mary's passing: "She went straight up. No turns."

Lillian

My friend JR and I were running errands on a Saturday. His girlfriend Debbie called while we were in the car and invited him to dinner later that night. He said he really didn't want to go because Debbie lives with her elderly mother; and she does not leave her alone to go out unless the caretaker is available. Her regular "Mom-sitter" was not available, so I volunteered.

JR told me: "Oh, no, Stella. You'll have a terrible time. Her mother tells the same jokes and stories every time I go there. She does have a wry sense of humor, though. I would rather go see Randi Fishenfeld tonight" (If you don't know this musician, then google her. She is a master violinist who performs many musical genres). He said that Debbie had never been to one of Randi's concerts.

I told him it was no big deal for me to stay with "Mom," that it would be a *"mitzvah"* (a good deed). He called me about an hour after dropping me off at my apartment to ask if I really meant it, that I would stay with Mom. He said that Debbie was delighted she could go out after dinner. She had prepared plenty of stuffed peppers and was happy I would be joining them. During dinner Mom told one of her jokes:

"The postman was retiring, and the close-knit neighbors got together to discuss what ideas they had to make his retirement special and show their appreciation. One of the women, Rose, went home to tell her husband about the meeting. Rose showed up at the door the next day, dressed in very sexy see-through negligee, took the postman's hand, led him upstairs and commenced to have sex with him.... She then made him breakfast. He found wrapped around the coffee mug handle a one dollar bill. He asked Rose what the dollar bill was for. She said, 'I told my husband of a neighbor's idea for a retirement gift and he said 'fuck him, give him a dollar.' Breakfast was my idea."

I said to Lillian, "Only a man would partake in a situation like this and ask questions later...." We had hit it off.

Well, dinner ended, JR and Debbie took off, and I sat down with Lillian in the living room. She looked at me and asked, "What's your name again?" I said "Stella." "Oh, I should remember that name because I had a good friend Stella in New York. And why are you here and not going out with them?"

I told her that Debbie was concerned about leaving her alone and that I was happy to stay with her. She said "We've been maneuvered!" She seemed genuinely concerned. She told me that Debbie often leaves her alone. I felt a little uneasy.

She did ask if I knew of the arrangement and I said yes. "Well, I've been maneuvered.... Hey, do you have a car?" I told her, "No." She said "Well, if I wanted you to leave you'd have to wait outside on the bench. Oh, I couldn't do that to you. You seem like a nice person."

She then began to conjure up a plan to get back at Debbie's obvious subterfuge. She suggested that if I had a car, we could go out to the movies, and when Debbie and JR got back we wouldn't be here, and we wouldn't have left a note! "Oh, but you don't have a car. Oh, we, no I, have been maneuvered, because you already knew about this!"

I picked up an art book from the coffee table and, while perusing it, told her that I have a background in Fine Arts. Lillian disclosed that her passion was Language Arts. She described her life as a first-grade teacher during her years in New York, and as a student of French, Italian and Portuguese. She said that she remembers fondly her trips abroad.

We talked about living in South Florida. I was born in Miami and remember the coconut trees on every block and the not-so-tall skyline. Lillian told me that she is one of the original residents of Century Village in Deerfield Beach, and that her husband of 30 years passed almost 20 years ago. She said that he was not an ideal mate, that he was "a no good scoundrel". After he passed she met a man, Ike, who became her constant companion. She said they had truly been in love.

I told her the story of my mother's third wedding. I was her Matron of Honor. In the middle of my story she blurted out "Oh, I've been maneuvered!" Lillian had been staring into space during my story but was suddenly back on track in her plotting to get back at Debbie. She seemed quite determined to come up with a plan. So much for my mother's wedding story.

She then told me of Ike's passing. They were in Miami for a day visit to the museums, window shopping, and lunch. At the end of their day, they sat together on a bench where their bus was to pick them up. Quietly enjoying the warm sun, he rested his head on her lap and died. "He came and went! But not at the same time." She looked at me with a sparkle in her eyes and a sly grin.

Her intent on getting even was once again her focus. We really had no rehearsed plan, just the frequent ideas that popped into our heads. We agreed we'd improvise when JR and Debbie returned.

Lillian then got up to visit the restroom. A minute later, JR and Debbie entered the apartment and I greeted them. The next moment Lillian re-entered the living room, took Debbie's arm, and said to her: "Where have you been? You left me all alone! And who is this person here? What, I don't even know what's going on, and who are YOU?" she said to Debbie.

Debbie said, "I'm Ira Lipshitz and this is my friend Roger," motioning towards JR. Lillian looked at me and I said, "I'm Jane." "Oh, you must be in the wrong apartment," she said to me. "And who are these people again?" I said, "The Lipshitzs." She then said, "Oh, that's a common name. I know a Lipshitz from New York. Maybe they're related. I wish they'd get out of here." She gave me a wink.

She sat back into her place on the sofa and I stood up to say good-bye. I gave Lillian a hug, then gave Debbie a hug and whispered, "She's jerking your chain." Debbie said quietly, "I know."

On the way home I told JR details of the evening's events. He said, "I thought you all were going crazy." I paused, looked at him and said: "You know, maybe she was jerking my chain, too. Hey, I've been maneuvered!"

Forrest Tucker

I typed his memoirs per request of his then-wife Jewel Centers. It was in the late 1990s when my husband represented Forrest Tucker in Federal Court. The "Over the Hill Gang" case was the talk of the court personnel in Miami, Florida.

His memoirs were both typed and hand-written. Jewel had obtained them from Tucker's files and told me that her husband desired that his story be published and eventually become a movie. His story is that of a career criminal. Charming his way into a bank vault was his forte that led from his life of crime to a life of time.

I recently saw the movie *The Old Man and The Gun*, directed by and starring Robert Redford. With my pre-disposed memory, "Stupid title!" was my first reaction. The movie, for me, had no passion, tension, or intrigue about the person I read and wrote about.

At the time of Mr. Tucker's trial, my husband told me, "He never used a gun," which was his best defense. He used a plastic water-gun," was the second remark. "He never shot or killed anyone," furthered the list of creative defenses, including "He's an old man and never meant any harm." Forrest was sentenced to serve life in prison, where he eventually died.

I recall the many stories of his escapes from prison, especially Alcatraz. Tucker and his cohorts managed to build a dinghy in shop class. They fashioned it to match the boats from the Golden Gate Yacht Club, painting it blue and white. They named it the "Rub-a-Dub." They were seen by guards wrestling with the boat, which was stuck in the rocky edge of Alcatraz Island. Tucker and mates called out to the guards that their boat went adrift. Initially they were waived on, but they were soon captured and returned to Alcatraz.

My favorite, though, was his first escape. Forrest had been an orphan, a street urchin. He was caught by the police after stealing a piece of fruit from a vendor and sent to a juvenile detention home. His recollection of this story I felt was a scene from *Oliver Twist*.

I remember that his notes described his arrest, the chaos at the detention center, and one day in recess. My version of the opening scene imagined for the silver-screen is a close up of a young boy, baseball glove in hand, eagerly awaiting a play in the outfield. We hear noise from the crowd cheering and the crack of the bat hitting the ball in the background. The young boy in the outfield runs backward, eyeing the ball, misses it, chases it and continues running, running into the woods. Pan out, we see the baseball game is part of an exercise at a detention center. Guards are shocked. Dogs are released to hunt. Forrest's life of crime had truly begun.

Fricassee

I traveled to Puerto Rico with my husband on a business trip. He met there with a client accused of drug-smuggling. Charlie, my "wasband" (ex-husband), is a criminal defense attorney. His client Manuel provided a room for us at the Dupont Plaza on San Juan Beach. The hotel had a casino, restaurant, and beautiful ocean views.

I was five months pregnant with my first child and happy to have a weekend off from my hectic job as a real estate appraiser for a national firm.

Manuel picked us up from the hotel in the morning and drove us through the "Old Town," narrating the history of San Juan during the tour. We then headed towards El Junque, the National Rain Forest of Puerto Rico. The winding road took us through the lush beautiful landscape, but the increasing elevation and back-seat riding started to make me car sick. I asked that we turn back. Charlie didn't like the idea but Manuel said: "*Oye, amigo*, the woman must be happy with the baby." He set his lawyer straight and turned the car around.

Nausea aside, we drove back to Manuel's house and the two men talked outside while I walked over to the chain-link fenced yard that contained a lone baby goat. I coaxed it over and petted it, scratching its head and neck, and spoke to it gently and lovingly, using nonsensical words.

I heard Manuel tell Charlie that we were invited to come back in the evening for dinner and that the family would all be gathered for "*un barbeque, una fiesta, fricassee!*"

I looked at him and said, "'*Fricassee*' what?"

He answered, "The goat!"

Frantically, I fumbled with the gate latch, and opened the gate, and yelled at the goat, "*Corre, corre, por su vida!*" (run, run for your life). Manuel caught the goat and corralled it back in. He said: "*Aye, no*, he is dinner!"

I thought I was going to faint and, of course, started crying. Charlie cried because he knew that he would not be having *fricassee* that night. Or ever, as far as I was concerned.

A year later, the Dupont Hotel was set on fire on New Year's Eve, reportedly by disgruntled employees. It started on the ground floor in the casino and then engulfed the restaurant and several floors.

Guests were escorted to the roof via the stairwell and several were rescued by helicopter, but many others perished.

The room we had occupied was on the seventh floor. We had visited the casino, eaten at the restaurant, and taken the elevator to the seventh floor. As I read the newspaper article, I imagined the panic and wondered if we would have survived.

A month before a later Thanksgiving event, as I shopped for food for the big dinner, I recalled that my babysitter, Estela, mentioned she did not have the money to make *fricassee* for "sansgibing." I bought a second turkey, tomatoes, garlic, potatoes, and herbs. I put the items in a separate box and drove it to her house, my two children in tow. I pulled up to her house to find her standing outside, alone, inside her chain-linked fence, looking skyward. She exclaimed joyfully, "I was just praying to God for someone to bring me a turkey!"

My Next-Door Neighbor

I was never a lover of Salvador Dali's art. Surrealism is an art genre that was included in the required Art History courses I attended in college. I felt the selected images disturbing, yet intriguing to view. They represented dreams and metaphors not quite understood by me at the time.

Two of his pieces viewed in class did, however, make an impression on me. One is *"Persistence of Memory,"* a piece that depicts melting clocks in a landscape of desert and ocean side. The image is rather contradictory. The other is a photograph of him standing poised and well-dressed in a suit, undisturbed by the flying cats and splashes of water passing by in front of him. I imagined him and his assistant in the studio tossing water at the poor cats several times in order to capture the perfect photo. This led me to ponder what it would have been like to be his next-door neighbor. Those images piqued my curiosity and have persisted in my memory—"memory," as defined as that which takes us into the exploration of the subconscious.

I recently moved to a new place in Florida. My new neighbor is a man who feeds stray cats. There must be a dozen cats that live in and out of his apartment. I have seen them, and him, wander in and out of his home. Maybe they are not stray cats after all. The new kittens are adorable and they and the adult cats are acknowledged and greeted by the many people who walk past my and my neighbors' apartments on their way to and from our building. I am aware of the daily gathering of friends and neighbors, as they make a commotion during every visit. Sometimes these gatherings are brief visits early in the day, and sometimes they involve long-winded discussions often late at night. I find this acceptable and disturbing, as well. My feelings toward them and my neighbor are contradictory, as they are about Dali's art.

My neighbor plays music every day at a high volume. His taste in music is pleasing, though, and I often find myself singing along with it. The music, like the daily gatherings outside, is heard at various times throughout the day and night. Ironically, last Sunday he played Cat Stevens' greatest hits. That record played repeatedly for over four hours. I would complain if he played Rap music. I find that genre displeasing and obnoxious. My sons are aware of this disdain and play it on their sound systems while driving me in their cars. I have told them this must be payback for my dressing them in my favorite pattern, plaid, when they were babies.

I was concerned one morning when I heard the music skip, as if the CD or record player was broken. I decided to get dressed and walk over to check in on him. A neighborly thing to do. Perhaps he was injured or dead? He had adjusted the music disruption by the time I arrived at his door. I went back to my apartment without meeting him. I had not actually met him. I had, though, seen him outside and had often heard him growl and commune with his cats. I had even filmed him during such an episode.

The cats are shy. I'm not quite sure if I like that there are so many of them. They look up at me when I leave from and return to my apartment; and then they quickly dart into the landscape to hide. I was hoping they would not find out that it was I who tossed leftovers into the garden. I think to myself, *Why throw food into the garbage when I know the cats will enjoy finding it?*

One morning, as I was leaving, I saw on the pavement outside of my apartment a dead lizard. I have heard and read that cats will do such things for people as their way of saying "Thank you." I found it repulsive and left it for my neighbor "Cat Man" or someone else kind enough to dispose of it. Upon my return I was relieved to find the "love offering" had been removed.

I awoke at 5:30 a.m. one morning to the sound of bongo-drumming and low moaning. "*Was he ok?*" I thought. The music was not a nuisance and the time of day, no surprise. It occurred to me "*Now I know what it's like to live next door to Salvador Dali.*"

I came home from grocery shopping one afternoon, saw my neighbor outside, and said hello. I opened the front door to my apartment and one of the kittens, an adorable black and white critter, was friendly and followed me into my home. It proceeded to wander around, sniffing at the floor and even playing with one of my floor plants. My neighbor walked over, too. I invited him to come in to retrieve his cat. I told him that I am allergic to cats. He told me "I am, too." He took a seat at my dining room table and asked for a drink of water. I obliged, noticing that he was crippled by a hunched back, had a very distinguished limp, and was cross-eyed. He was not easy to look at. But I felt that he was a person with a kind soul. Perhaps he was misunderstood by me and others.

We introduced ourselves. His name is Mike. He told me his story
in the few minutes during his visit. His mother died two years ago
and left him and his sister $200,000 and the apartment he resides
in. His sister passed recently, and his brother-in-law manages the
estate, gives him a monthly allowance, and he is crippled from a
motorcycle accident. He commented that my apartment is so clean
and smells good. He said, "I am a hoarder. There's no room for
anything." I replied that I look forward to tossing or giving away
items I no longer want or need.

Mike continued with his story. He said that neighbors are mean
and complain about the cats. He said that the particular one still
exploring my home sleeps with him and purrs all night. He told
me that he has a raven that lives under his bed. A neighbor has
confirmed this. The raven wakes up early in the morning and
makes a groaning noise. I thought, *And it plays the bongos, too*!
I asked if the bird was in a cage and if the cats try to attack it. He
said, "No, it flies around his apartment, eats and then goes back
under his bed." He said he found the bird as a baby, injured on the
ground, and he took it home to nurture it. This seems like a good
example of NOT placing an animal back into the wild. It has no
natural defenses.

Mike told me that recently the police came to his home, that he was
high on a substance, one I do not recall the name of, and that he
was taken away via an ambulance against his will. I recall that visit
by the police late one night and heard some of the discussion. I had
not seen any ambulance that night.

I began to wonder how to get him to leave, so I suggested to him
that I had a number of phone calls to return. He got on the floor and
crawled towards the kitten and picked it up, purring along with it.
I took a video of that. Mike brought the kitten close to me to hear
it purring. I thought, *No one will believe me, even when I tell them*

that I cannot make such events up. That the truth is much more interesting and entertaining.

Before Mike left, he asked me, "Do you want to keep him? What would you name him?

"What could I say but 'Sal'?

Ron Ziffer

Bio

Ron Ziffer was born and raised in Kew Gardens, New York.

He holds degrees from Brooklyn College and Hunter College of the City University of New York.

Playing semi-pro baseball in the 1970s, he was a first baseman and outfielder for Joe DiMaggio's Restaurant team in the Queens Nassau Baseball Alliance.

He taught Debating and Parliamentary Procedure in the 1980s in the Brooklyn College School of General Studies.

He has had a successful career in sales and sales management, has taught classes in sales, has written articles and books reflecting his experience, and has received multiple awards in these areas.

Ron and his wife of 22 years Nereida, accompanied by their beloved dog Mabel, currently maintain residences in New York and Florida.

My First Year in AA

It was the fall of 1986, a great time to be a New Yorker. The Mets had just won the World Series in miraculous fashion. The Giants and Jets were both steamrolling into the playoffs with a real possibility of meeting in the Superbowl. The yuppies were buying suspenders faster than the mills could produce them. People were buying co-ops and condos in anticipation of flipping them at exponential pricing. Crockadile Dundee was the folk hero. And I was attending my first AA meeting!
On a rather warm Saturday evening in early December I reluctantly and quite cautiously entered a smoke-filled church basement in Richmond Hill, Queens, the neighboring town to

Kew Gardens. The only woman in the room was the one who was speaking. The guys sitting in the room looked like they were either ex-cons or had just hopped out of an OTB (Off-Track Betting) parlor. I found a seat close to the door in anticipation of making a quick and inconspicuous getaway. As I settled in and absorbed my surroundings, I began to feel a lot better.. I was hearing some things that were really making sense. They call that "identification." I stayed till the end of the meeting and made connections. That was the unofficial beginning of my AA journey. After the meeting was over, a few of the guys came up to me and offered hugs and handshakes. I found it somewhat odd, but strangely endearing. Why were these guys befriending a total stranger? A man named George walked me to my car and offered his phone number. It was my first point of contact and it felt really good.

I went home after the meeting feeling very uplifted. I was a bit concerned that my story did seem somewhat mellow compared to the stories I had heard in that room.

After all, my alcoholic saga was not one filled with violence, larceny, promiscuity, or womanizing. I drank alone in a room with loud music and long cigars. I touched no one and no one touched me. I was God's lonely man, and I believed it to be my fate. As much as the imprint of that meeting was very powerful, the seeds of denial remained and I was to drink for another three months. I was still in control of the timing and geography of my drinking, so I was not convinced I was an alcoholic (or so I thought).

A brief synopsis of the events leading up to my first meeting is in order. I was 37 years old when I first attended AA. For some reason, I told everybody I was 36. Like one year really mattered! I was living with my terminally ill mother, who was deteriorating very rapidly, and I had just suffered the loss of an older brother, who was killed in a car accident in Florida. I was in emotional free fall and using booze as my escape hatch. I restricted my drinking to after seven p.m. and pretty much held myself to that. I was in that purgatory place where I wanted to stop drinking without admitting to being an alcoholic. I was extremely conflicted, but somehow open to change. I was having trouble fighting my way out of the abyss of my uniqueness. I needed to try something and AA seemed quite convenient.

Once I got hold of an AA schedule I saw that there was a meeting one block from my house. It met twice a week. I attended meetings, on and off, through January and February, but more for recreation than recovery. It was a nice place to have coffee and cake and meet new people. I was noticing, however, that my denial was progressively chipping away, and I was beginning to see AA as a way of life and not just a social outlet.

On March 2, 1987 my denial came to a screeching halt. I woke up in a White Castle parking lot in Bayside at 6:30 in the morning with a splitting headache and nausea. Somehow, I drove the six miles back to Kew Gardens and got right into bed. My mom, who was bed ridden, never knew I had been gone. She repeatedly called out my name. I yelled out across the hall that I wasn't feeling well. Fortunately, she accepted it at face value and backed off. Two aspirin and a half bottle of Pepto somehow got me up and about. I called George and arranged to meet him at a meeting. It was on that day that I became a bona fide AA member. George and I went to an afternoon meeting in Ozone Park, had ice cream sundaes in Jahns, and mapped out my immediate future in AA. The journey had begun for real. It was now official.

I started attending AA meetings every night of the week. I was amazed to find that there were ten meetings in my immediate area, with half in walking distance. If sobriety was in the cards for me, I certainly had no excuses to avoid it. I was told to go to 90 meetings in 90 days and to get a sponsor. That was, and still is, the protocol and formula for the newcomer's success. I had no trouble following whatever was necessary. I had no place else to go and nothing else to do. I accepted that I was in for the long haul and that AA was to be at the center for everything that was to be down the road in my life.

Literature is a big part of the AA process. All newcomers are encouraged to read *Living Sober,* a light-reading book which conveys abundant reassurance to the self-doubting alcoholic. In those days the book cost a buck and a quarter, which was 25 cents more than the buck we threw in the basket. Now the book is five bucks and people are still throwing a buck—perhaps more now—in the basket. Go figure! Certain things happen in AA which always seem to baffle me. I guess that's part of the reason I decided to write this piece. As my thoughts begin to unfold, I am sure some of the information disseminated will draw reactions of controversy from readers. My opinions reflect my own personal experiences, spanning over twenty years in the program. I have remained fully sober and clean for that entire length of time. I do not preach AA gospel! I do, however, have strong insights that I choose not to water down in the interest of maintaining superficial diplomacy. I do love AA! A good many people who have challenged my beliefs have come and gone. I am still here. Enough said!

When I hit 30 days of continuous sobriety, my mother and I agreed that it was okay for me to take a part-time job. I was starting to feel really good about myself and needed to become more productive within the limitations of my situation. I began working as a four-hour-a-day telemarketer, setting appointments for a graphic design firm. It was a posh office and I was receiving a high hourly rate. I didn't feel like the typical phone jockey that people make fun of and hate. It was somewhat prestigious! I also started getting to meetings in Manhattan and meeting different AA members.

A daytime meeting I started attending was called Fog Lifters. The crowd looked like wealthy overachievers, who probably made more in a day than I was making in a week. I was intimidated but somewhat encouraged by it. Perhaps this was what was in store for me. Everything looked positive! They called it a "pink cloud." A rather attractive woman walked up to me after the meeting. Let's call her Janet. She complimented my sharing in the meeting and suggested we go out for coffee sometime. I was not used to being validated, but I do speak well and sound somewhat more intelligent than I may actually be. Though I am not so well-read, I do have a good command of the language.

I agreed to meet Janet for coffee. We were the same age, yet she had been sober for 14 years. She had a high-level-position in a prestigious advertising firm and was about to be transferred to the West Coast. Any notion of a possible relationship was squashed, but I was very impressed with her path of recovery. She was a true power of example. I was amazed by how easy I was able to connect with a woman. A woman this attractive and accomplished would never have sought me out in any other circumstances. Was this to be the forerunner of things to come?

Janet left town, but my confidence was renewed. Somewhere around 40 days of sobriety, I knew that AA was going to provide new avenues for relationships, meaningful or otherwise. Get my drift! They say no relationships the first year, but that's part of the AA rhetoric that generally never makes it past the "exit" signs. You can probably fill a dozen sperm banks with the amount of semen discharged in early sobriety. I had been celibate and isolated for about three years prior to AA, so I was slower getting off the ground than most, but I still had my share of opportunities. The wheels of the AA soap opera were constantly spinning. In the rooms people talked program, maintaining the facade of recovery. Outside the rooms people generally followed their own social agendas. After all, we grew up in the fifties, sixties, and seventies when codependency was the norm. This quest for intimate emotional and physical relationships was not exclusive to the mentally stable. AA was a closed community with a good deal of mutual commonality. It was like a salesman getting strongly qualified leads.

I made 90 days right around Memorial Day weekend. When I shared this in meetings, I got a tremendous round of applause. It was like Mickey Mantle having his name announced by Bob Shepherd. Man, did it feel good! It was a tremendous milestone for me amidst all the chaos, tragedy, and misfortune that beset my life. At that moment I truly believed that all the wrongs in my life would be righted by AA and this new sober path. It was quite a rush!

I started getting more involved in AA service. I took on commitments in virtually every meeting that I attended. I was brimming with optimism. The next six months were truly a honeymoon with AA and the association. The love and support seemed genuine.

On Thanksgiving Day Mom passed away. I was sad but relieved. Her quality-of-life issues had diminished to the point where her death was merciful. The expression of support from AA members was noticeable, but could have been better. I wasn't really upset. A new AA chapter had begun. The ten or so people who showed up were good enough for me. I was now the single guy, living alone, and examining my social possibilities more closely. I was closing in on a full year of sobriety and feeling a lot better about my identity. Some of the women were showing interest in me, and my confidence was growing. I knew it was just a matter of time before I would be able to socialize in a meaningful way.

ADDENDA of the
KINGS POINT WRITERS CLUB
SUPPLEMENTARY (KPWCS)

Allan Korn

Bio

Allan J. Korn was born in New York City and resided in The Bronx and Queens until 1971 when he moved to New Jersey. He earned a B.A. in Economics with Honors and an M.B.A. He is a member of the Delta Mu Delta National Honor Society of Business Administration. Achieving several sales accolades, he was the recipient of Dupont's Business Achievement Award in 1991. Married to Ellen Pennock Korn, he is the father of two and the grandfather of five.

A newly fulfilled writer, he thanks the Kings Point Writers Club Supplementary for welcoming him into the group.

An Exceptional Heart Surgeon

The unexpected events of 2020 provided an opportunity for me to examine some of the more memorable events of my life and career. My professional life began in 1966, a time when society was not as litigious or politically correct as today. It was an era when individual initiative was rewarded, risk taking was welcomed, and education respected.

I was hired to be a sales representative by a major pharmaceutical company, impressed with my interest in retail pharmacy acquired first-hand as a part-time employee at the ages of 14 to 23. Making deliveries on my bicycle, sweeping the floor, restocking shelves, serving customers, and learning the names and profiles of many drugs finally paid off. I was sent to Mission, Kansas, for three weeks of intense training. The program concentrated on pharmacology (far more of it than most physicians received), the proper way to pronounce medical terms and long-winded chemical names, anatomy and physiology, and sales training. The days were long, the quiz after each section intense, and I returned home feeling fully prepared and ready to share my knowledge with the doctors in my territory.

The company felt that training was not enough and sent me to St. Michaels Hospital in Newark, New Jersey, to shadow a doctor for two weeks to learn how to give physicals, discuss issues with patients, and above all respect the patient. Today this training is accomplished with a learning manual. I was finally ready, I picked up my company car and territory information, and set out to break all sales records.

After my first two days on the job my confidence kept increasing and I was shocked to find how much more I knew than my physician customers. At that time many physicians had their offices in their homes and hung their shingles on posts outside. I remember coming home and telling my mother I was going to cut down some of the shingles at night because "These docs don't know anything." Particularly upsetting to me was their lack of knowledge of drug interactions (what combination of drugs can be fatal), what drugs should be taken with food and which should not, which antibiotics have their effectiveness reduced by milk and dairy products, their not advising patients not to eat or drink after taking cough syrup, etc. I learned how to deal with their "ignorance," mastered the art of selling and proceeded to win several sales achievement awards. My sales accomplishments were met with increased company responsibilities and the opportunity to learn and develop my sales skills in critical-care medicine in the hospital.

I returned to training to learn cardiology, emergency medicine, surgical procedures, and follow-up care. Once again book learning was followed by the "real thing," time in the OR in an "apprentice like" situation to watch and ask questions. After several minor procedures I was ready for the "big time," cardiac bypass surgery scheduled to take between four and five hours. I entered the operating suite of prestigious New York Hospital at 7 a.m., was met by several staff members who would be in the OR, directed to the locker room, given scrubs and a locker for my clothes, and told to wait for assistance in scrubbing in. I met the cardiac surgeon a few times. He was a very friendly and easy- going guy and was surprised and pleased that he met me and was able to guide me through the scrub procedure. The procedure in the OR itself is a well-orchestrated play, all the actors have their places and respective props (instruments or machinery), the mood is upbeat with good music, cool temperature, and personable staff.

During the set up I was told that the doctor who invited me was the lead surgeon and was just named chief of cardiac surgery the previous week. When he entered the room immediately after the patient had been wheeled in, everyone snapped to attention waiting for the appropriate review of the procedure, such as being certain it is the correct patient, and other necessary hospital protocol. Before going to his place at the patient's side the surgeon came to me and asked me if I had a good view, gave me some boundaries and places I could stand and move around in, and told me to meet him in his office at 4:30 p.m.

Show time. The procedure began at 7:50 a.m. Surprisingly, the noise, smell, and smoke from the saw and the breaking of the chest bone and the lack of blood was not what I had expected. Once the cutting began everything was just as I had learned. I walked around and the assistants moved so I could get a better view. About 10:30 the surgeon left for five or ten minutes. When he returned, he came over to me to see if I had any questions and I was shocked to smell liquor through the surgical mask. Everything continued as planned until 11:45 when I noticed the patient's numbers on the anesthesiologist's gauges were off, and I seemed to be the only person concerned. An alarm went off about five minutes later that seemingly woke up the anesthesiologist and got some people moving to the drug carts and adjusting the gas levels. The potential crisis was avoided and the play continued as written. The curtain came down at 12:35 and the patient went to recovery and cast members returned to their lockers and offices.

On my way to my locker, a nurse stopped me and asked me if I had smelled the liquor. I said yes, and she told me the doctor is an alcoholic who knows his limitations and is the finest cardiac surgeon in NY. She said if she ever needed cardiac surgery she would use this doctor and buy the bottle.

4:30 p.m. I entered the surgeon's inner office. The door was
closed and the scotch came out. The conversation was relaxed and
informative. The doctor was the perfect host and teacher. As the
second drink was being poured, the doctor asked me about the
anesthesiologist. He knew from one of the nurses that I had seen
the problem before the others, and he proceeded to lecture me that
I was his guest and I should have told him and not worry about
looking "stupid." Our friendship continued over the years I covered
that hospital with many late afternoon drinks and a few interesting
surgeries.

Vacation

Vacation is defined as a period of suspension of work, study, or
other activity—usually for the purpose of rest, recreation, or travel
during a period of recess or holiday. Vacations are well planned,
researched, and expected to be fun. We have all anticipated and
experienced the predictable and expected joy of a vacation. What is
difficult to deal with is the unlikely misfortune that turns the plan
into a frightening, terrifying, and horrendous occurrence that will
be remembered and retold over and over again.
It was the first day of spring vacation and I am 13 years old. The
first event on the schedule of my well-planned ten-day break
from school was a long bike ride with my friend Phil. We rode for
about three hours and decided to head home for some food and
drink. The thought of lunch was burning in our heads, so a critical
decision was made to take a short cut through some driveways and
sidewalks to speed up our return. One half mile from home Phil
rode up a driveway, onto the sidewalk, around some trees, and into
an alley way. I followed, paying more attention to Phil than to the
ground conditions. In a split second I was on the ground, the wheel
of my bike spinning in a hole caused by the removal of several
bricks taken to protect the trees. At first it was like other falls. I
dusted myself off and by the time Phil returned to my side I was
ready to go. On my return to my bike I discovered I was unable to

move my right arm and it looked like there were bones protruding under the skin on the top of my hand.

Once we were home it was clear that there was some damage to my elbow and medical help was needed. My mother (who did not drive) called a friend who transported us to our local GP; his quick look told him this is a case for the hospital. Off to the hospital we went and we were met by an orthopedic surgeon who set my elbow, put on a cast, and admitted me. A hospital stay was necessary so that I would remain as still as possible and X-rays could be taken to check my progress. This was Friday and the doctor would not see my X-rays until Monday. Four days of my vacation down.

Monday morning. The orthopedist took me into a small room, asked if I had any pain, and removed the cast. He told me to look at some diagram on the wall, removed a hammer from a drawer, and hit my elbow hard enough so that I literally saw stars. Fortunately for the doctor he had explained what he had to do before I was able to reach the hammer and take a swing at him with it. The bones were not lining up properly and he needed to operate on my elbow and insert long pins to hold the bones in place. The operation was scheduled for Tuesday with a two-day hospital stay, three more days of my vacation down.

My elbow was X-rayed so many times they could have filled an album with all the different views. Everything looked good and I was told I could go home on Thursday. My roommate, an friendly older gentleman, noticed that my arm above the cast was red and purple and, rightly so, told the nurse. Her response was a quick temperature check and an emergency call to the surgeon. My dream of going home fading, I accepted the fact I had an infection that would keep me in the hospital another two or three days. Another three days of my vacation spent in a hospital bed.

Finally, the antibiotics worked and they could not find another reason to keep me hospitalized. My entire vacation lost, I was now left with pins in my right arm, the inability to fully extend my arm, and the memory of the doctor hitting me with a hammer. I believe there is a bright side to everything if you look for it. Years later the damage to my elbow earned me a "4F" draft status.

Claude

2020 was the birth of "stay at home" orders, and the endless differing opinions of the "experts" about the COVID-19 virus. Our natural fondness for social interaction has been reduced and trepidation of it reigns. What we miss most is the basic human need for companionship, the vital connection with someone or something that promotes a sense of closeness. The more good relationships we maintain the happier and healthier we tend to be. Companionship encourages mental stimulation and increases a person's sense of purpose. On daily walks, I would meet many dogs getting their exercise and providing companionship for their owners. These encounters reminded me of the unique relationship I had with my dog Claude.

My wife and I bought Claude, a chocolate brown royal standard poodle, from a breeder in New Jersey when he was six weeks old. I never had a dog. My wife did and because I had developed a liking for her family's dog I agreed to make Claude part of our family. We never had to "train" a dog before and made many "errors" which gave Claude a distinctive personality complete with some unpleasant habits our neighbors did not appreciate. Fortunately, Claude was housebroken quickly, enjoyed his walks, and loved to bark (his way of expressing himself and getting what he wanted). He was a wonderful companion. When we walked three or four blocks to get the Sunday *New York Times*, he sat patiently while I waited to pay; and he greeted other customers with his deep loud bark. One aspect of Claude's unique personality was that he appeared to be having an actual conversation with the person or persons he was communicating with by modulating his voice and moving his head.

Claude grew quickly and apparently was not conscious of his increasing size. He had many "safe" places in our apartment—the bathtub for thunder, under the kitchen table for forbidden food crumbs, and under a credenza for his peace and quiet. One day, we could not find Claude and finally found him under the credenza, stuck in place. The adventure to get him out (unhurt) took almost two hours. He was very cooperative as he allowed me to move his front paws to try to flatten his body to get him free. I eventually emptied out most of the insides of the piece of furniture and carefully tilted it enough so that Claude could rush to freedom. He was a fast learner; he never went near that piece of furniture again. He took a liking to the couch and made it his bed; he was aware of our disapproval and waited until we were not in the room before curling up on it. It took a few gentle mousetraps to teach our fast-learning dog that the couch was off-limits to him. Claude grew to be a 90-pound companion who gave of himself unselfishly and provided our family and friends many humorous and memorable incidents.

The neighbors did not enjoy Claude's conversations, especially the many long ones when we were not at home. Some were not too pleasant about it and Claude knew it. He would sit in front of the two most vocal protestors, move his head back and forth, and make an attempt to win them over.

We lived in an apartment building with a doorman, swimming pool, health club, U-shaped hallways with four apartments at each end, and 20 apartments and an elevator in the long center hallway. We heard there were some burglaries in the building but did not give them much thought. One afternoon my wife came home to find the master cylinder in the front door lock ajar. Fortunately, no one had entered our apartment. When I came home, I noticed deep gashes in the metal fire doors (which, if they have not been replaced, are still there today). The incident was reported to the proper authorities and I invited our neighbors (who did not like Claude) to see how he had saved our apartment. It took several weeks for everyone to realize there were burglaries in the long hallway, the other side of the hallway, above and below our four units, but not near our apartment. Finally, Claude received his recognition; his deep bark had provided the protection that a burglar alarm, deadbolt, and doorman could not. Claude was greeted warmly henceforth in the elevator, and the neighbors never complained about his barking again.

Clauderupes Inspirans et Amicus Recapitatus

"Clauderupes" plays on *"quadrupes"* (quadruped); *"Inspirans"* has the range of "inspiring" and "inspirational"; *"Amicus"* is both "friend of Claude" and "friend of Eddie"; and *"Recapitatus"* connotes restoration from Allan's photo on page 351 of his decapitated head in the original photo of the dog and him.

Succeeding in Teaching

I have always been a supporter of the "show me" (apprentice) style of learning. However, most of my formal education both undergraduate and graduate was filled with inactive learning. In 1988, a recommendation for my personal development, at the conclusion of my performance review, was to teach a college class. My initial reply was "What do I know about teaching?" My manager reiterated that it was just an idea for me to consider, to increase my effectiveness in communicating to large groups. After several wrestling matches with my pillow, as I thought about the possibility of teaching, I remembered the story of "The Little Engine That Could." The theme of this story is to believe in oneself and to overcome a challenging situation by thinking positively. I was ready to face the challenge of facing a college class; the hard decision had been made. I had to secure a position. Using my network of key contacts, I learned of a position for an adjunct professor in a community college. I spoke with the chairman of the business department, who explained he needed an instructor for an introductory marketing class that met once a week for two hours and fifty minutes. A formal interview was scheduled, and as they say the rest is history. I was armed with a copy of the text book; the syllabus used the previous semester; and advice to stay two to three chapters ahead of the class, not upset the students, and finish the semester. My new supervisor told me I would know in three or four weeks if I had the "makings" of a professor or not. I had two weeks to prepare my first lecture and decide how to best deal with 28 students for 170 minutes. Panic was beginning to set in. I was never able to pay attention to any lecture for even an hour, how would I do this for more than double that time. What could I do to hold the students' attention and change classroom behaviors from the dreaded "listen and take notes and not have any idea of what was said" that I hated so much? I had never taken any formal education courses so I was not saddled with a preconceived formula for classroom learning and I was free to change the paradigm. My approach (which I improved upon in every class during my college teaching career from 1988–2010) was designed to break the tradition of memorizing definitions of the textbook but to have the students grasp the concepts and to be able to put them into their own words as well as to individually develop their own key understandings.

The game plan was set. Executing it required some initial background research on my part. I had to review other basic marketing texts to gather additional wordings of definitions and concepts so I did not have to develop them myself. I practiced saying these definitions as fast as I could, then began to change words, and each time I said them the exact words were not the same but the general meaning was. Finally, the day of my first class passed and the results were pleasing. The students tried as hard as they could to write down what I was saying, but continuously got confused by my constantly changing the words. Some ignored my appeal that they listen and try to understand what we were discussing and scrambled to continue their hard-to-break habits of useless note taking. After the first 90 minutes I explained my game plan that when they leave the class they would understand what had been discussed and only a short review of their notes would provide an adequate review for the next class and any quiz or exam preparation. I showed them my reference texts and allowed them to read some of the authors' words to bolster their confidence about their being on the right wavelength. To prove that they were able to make this adjustment in classroom protocol, I asked several students to read their own definitions.

I left class with a new understanding of intrinsic rewards. Motivated by my own satisfaction, I was certain that the next class and all the ones that followed would benefit the students. I was very surprised how successful my approach was. Enrollment in my class increased to 34 the second week of class and remained at that level the whole semester.

Our First Home

My wife Ellen and I grew up apartment dwellers, and our first home as a married couple was an apartment. Shortly after our honeymoon we began discussing the pros and cons of home ownership and apartment living. Some advantages of owning a home include stable monthly payments, opportunity to build equity, and "It's cheaper than renting over time." Owning provides tax advantages, builds credit, and is a solid investment. Some cons for living in an apartment include smaller living space, less privacy, more noise, difficulty with parking etc. These discussions lasted eight months and resulted in the decision to buy a house in New Jersey.

We selected three ads from the Sunday *New York Times* to begin our search. It was 1971, before GPS, so we found our first choice with our maps in hand. This was not what we were looking for, so we began our journey to destination #2. On our way we came upon a construction site with three model homes and a trailer serving as a sales office which had many interested potential customers waiting to meet with a sales representative. We had stumbled upon a custom builder who was planning to build 60 homes on his family's farm. The sales rep explained to us he was accepting $100 deposits that would hold the lot of our choice for one week. If we decided not to move forward, our check would be returned. We climbed through trees, branches, thorns, and what a city person might have called a forest rather than a farm, selected a lot about one third of an acre in size on a hill. We left our $100 check and headed home elated about the prospect of building a house.

The following Monday I started investigating the town we were considering moving to. I spoke with the mayor, a pharmacist, and the rabbi of the Conservative synagogue; and all had basically the same comments. The town had great schools, a growing middle class population, good shopping, minimal crime, and reasonable taxes for New Jersey. My wife and I decided we were ready to buy/ build our first house.

Our plan was to combine the lower level of one of the builder's models with the upper level of a different model, and we exchanged many ideas for our future home on the trip. Our exhilaration lessened as we continued to drive around in search of the trailer/ sales office. Were we duped? "Oh well," I said. "It was only $100. I wonder how many $100 checks they collected. Should I stop the check?" Not willing to accept that we fell for some plot to collect $100 checks, I decided to continue to search for our elusive sales office. Finally, out of the corner of my eye and behind a tree, I saw a line of cars surrounding the trailer. We were relieved we had found our future home site. We met with Monroe, the builder and owner of the farm. Monroe, a mild-mannered man in his forties dressed in coveralls, liked the idea of combining the levels of the two model homes and suggested we add a spiral staircase. The basic negotiations went well and the contract was signed. The builder arranged the financing and we were home owners.

The construction site had a life of its own. Heavy equipment, sounds of saws, hammering, men talking, piles of planks of lumber stamped "Weyerhauser" in bold red letters. It was exciting when the front end loader appeared on our lot to dig the hole for the foundation and the cinder blocks of the foundation were put in place. Magically, the pile of lumber started to take shape—the lower level, garage, upper level, and attic. The framing took a few days and seemed to stop. On questioning the builder, I learned that the head carpenter had quit because he could not get the spiral staircase to fit properly. A closer look revealed that the lower level was not as planned. The French doors leading to what would eventually be a deck were not in the kitchen but in the family room. "Thanks for calling it to our attention," said Monroe, the builder. "No problem, we will fix it." Everything continued to be cordial and potential major mishaps were avoided until the framing, siding, and roof were completed.

The nickel and diming started. "You can have a light switch there, but it will cost $50." "A third light switch to control the outside lights from the bedroom, $75." "Storm windows and screens as shown on the models, $500." "Stained moldings, $150." The list was too numerous to continue and the resulting discussions over the additional costs were no longer handled by Monroe. Phillip—a man in his fifties wearing an expensive suit, monogrammed shirt, and tie—was the new negotiator to handle the business side. Phillip's personality was the opposite of Monroe's. He was arrogant, overconfident, and condescending; and he aggravated everyone. I visited the office twice and found two of my future neighbors in tears because of him..

The "little things" I thought were essential parts of a home and standard equipment suddenly became options with high price tags. It was time for a sit down with Philip to put an end to the almost daily request for more money for "extras" that should have been included in the original price. I wracked my brain to think of a bargaining edge that Philip might consider of value to him. Philip and I met and we agreed to come up with a final list of extras and their costs. I was fairly certain that many of the "extras" had already been installed so I decided to call Philip's bluff and tell him he could remove the storm windows and some of the lght switches. His reply was to offer them at 50% off. Realizing I had the winning hand and that Philip could not risk my telling others, I came up with a counteroffer. I offered him 10% of the total cost for extras and I said I would allow him to show our house to any future buyers who would want to consider our combination of the two models. He accepted the deal. Philip and I remained cordial with a mutual respect that lasted until all the homes were sold and the office was closed.

Allan Korn and Eddie Levenson

Who Says We're Not What We Say We Are?

by Allan Korn and Eddie Levenson

[Allan's turn first.] I am a salesperson at heart who has mastered the art and skill of convincing customers to part with their money. In my verbal communication I utilize proven outer- and inner-directed techniques. I learned quickly that the most common mistake of a salesperson is talking too much. True conviction is conveyed not with more words but fewer. Lincoln's Gettysburg Address, for example, contains 267 words; the Ten Commandments, 163. Saying less but communicating more, while employing strategic silence, has been my key to success.

How could I change from using sparse words verbally to becoming a multi-written-words author? I stared at my blank computer screen for what seemed to be an eternity and decided to write about a real event. I showed the draft to my wife Ellen, a retired English teacher. Her critique was scathing. "Your punctuation is atrocious. You mix up tenses. Other errors of yours are unspeakable. You have no dialogue. The piece is a total mess. You must rewrite it."

Claude and Allan Korn

[Eddie's note. Our wives, Ellen and Reva, are "the loves of our lives." But, in the immortal words of Joe E. Brown at the conclusion of *Some Like It Hot*, "Nobody's perfect!"]
Our daughter Rachel also had something to say, "Dad, what is this? You can't say this. Just describe things. Listen to what Mom said. And don't show this to me again!"
[Eddie's second note. Not even daughters.]*

Nothing, however, was said about the content. I decided that writing is telling a story as best as one can for the reader's enjoyment. I'll leave the editing of grammar and punctuation to the experts. Repeating to myself "I am a writer! I am a writer!" I steeled myself to ignore my wife's and daughter's severe criticisms. It is my own opinion of my writing that is the one that counts. Feeling this way, I produced each of the four last pieces of mine in this anthology more fluently than the respective preceding one; and each, I felt, was progressively more interesting to me.
Writing has become enjoyable and rewarding. I've become expansive in my written self-expression. I have become a writer!

---

* Note to the two "Eddie notes" above. I mean this note to be a *volta* (an ironic turn in the manner of the concluding couplet of a Shakespearean sonnet). Yes, humor is important, but it can be oversought and overdone; and Allan and I may well be guilty of that. Somewhat, at least. In making wife Ellen and daughter Rachel "exaggerated comic foils," we, in a way, exemplified the foolishness excoriated so repeatedly in the Book of Ecclesiastes that "Vanity of vanities, all is vanity"; for Ellen and Rachel had, of course, benevolent intentions and constructive purpose.
I myself have experienced my own personal *volta* during this past year because, in the midst of a number of difficult challenges, I have returned to my religious roots. That corresponds with the conclusion of the Book of Ecclesiastes (12:13), a *volta* as well, "At the end of the matter everything has been heard, fear God and observe God's commandments."
Readers may recognize that I quoted Ecclesiastes' disparagement of "the making of many books" at the beginning of this book. Perhaps the author had frivolous books in mind, not serious ones, and would have been impressed by the great wisdom and depth of all 20 writers in this anthology, the editor of which I have been so enormously proud to be.

[Second, Eddie's turn.] Whereas my new friend and colleague Allan has mastered the art and skill of precision and concision, I, though paying lip service to those ideals, sin greatly on the side of excessive verbosity and don't really expect that I will ever be cured of that. I'm fortunate not to be in sales. What I, however, wish for more than anything in the world, I often think, is for my sense of humor to be praised, or at least acknowledged. I crave compliments when I say something funny and don't ever seem to get as many for doing so as I would like.

[Editor's note on Eddie's plea. Actually it's the expression of the simple hope that the play on the words "Editor's" and "Eddie" introducing this note got more than a groan. Because it was "personal."]

My insecurity about ambivalence re my humor stemmed from the "barely grudging acceptance" it received on the part of my father, William Julius Levenson of blessed memory—or so he pretended—when I was growing up. He was the champion wit in the family, not I. After ironic *double entendres* of mine Dad used to narrow his eyes, shrug his shoulders, and look over at my brother Rob, who was doing the same. Both, then, simultaneously used to utter the words, in mock disassociation, "Edward's humor." I titled my first multi-genres collection, which included a "Humor" section, *"Edward's Humor" and More* as if to appeal retrospectively to my Dad Heavenward, "See, Dad, some people down here do think I'm funny."

This anthology has taken a year to come to fruition. I have put together a different kind of collection–forthcoming shortly, God willing–in a fraction of that time. It is *Edward's Xlibris Best*, and it has a "Humor" section, as did my first book. When readers would have a glimpse at that section in particular, I pray they would not forget to laugh.

Of my four children, my youngest, Ben, it has seemed, gets the most embarrassed by my funny stories. Maybe, I should admit, it's because I regale total strangers with them on our way out of restaurants when he is in a hurry and since he has heard the same stories a number of times previously.

Sensing Ben needed an infusion of cash for his recent June vacation in North Carolina, I mailed him a check and gave him a heads-up about it on Facebook Messenger, "Ben, Santa Claus will be coming down the chimney early this year with something for you."

Pausing about seven seconds, I messaged again, "Ben, if the house where you're staying doesn't have a chimney, I hope the owner has Homeowner's Insurance."

Pausing another seven seconds, I added my signature question, "Ben, WHO SAYS I'M NOT FUNNY?"

This time Ben replied with unprecedented praise, "Hahaha! *Abba* (Dad, in Hebrew). That was *really* very funny!"

Moved almost to tears, I needed a few extra seconds to compose myself and I messaged my response, "Ben, you've just made me the happiest *Abba* in the world!"

Lightning Source UK Ltd.
Milton Keynes UK
UKHW011841081220
374864UK00008B/481/J